ON PAUL RICOEUR

Paul Ricoeur is one of the giants of contemporary continental philosophy and one of the most enduring and wide-ranging thinkers in the twentieth century, publishing major works ranging from existentialism and phenomenology to psychoanalysis, politics, religion and the theory of language.

Richard Kearney offers a critical engagement with the work of Ricoeur, beginning with a general introduction to his hermeneutic philosophy. Part One explores some of the main themes in Ricoeur's thought under six headings: Phenomenology and Hermeneutics; Language and Imagination; Myth and Tradition; Ideology and Utopia; Good and Evil; Poetics and Ethics. Part Two comprises five dialogical exchanges which Kearney has conducted with Ricoeur over the last three decades (1977–2003), charting and explaining his intellectual itinerary. This book is aimed at a broad student readership as well as the general intelligent reader interested in knowing more about one of the most enduring major figures in contemporary continental philosophy.

Transcending Boundaries in Philosophy and Theology

Series Editors:
Martin Warner, University of Warwick, UK
Keith Vanhoozer, Trinity International University, USA

Transcending Boundaries in Philosophy and Theology is an interdisciplinary series exploring new opportunities in the dialogue between philosophy and theology that go beyond more traditional 'faith and reason' debates and take account of the contemporary reshaping of intellectual boundaries. For much of the modern era, the relation of philosophy and theology has been conceived in terms of antagonism or subordination but recent intellectual developments hold out considerable potential for a renewed dialogue in which philosophy and theology have common cause for revisioning their respective identities, reconceiving their relationship, and combining their resources. This series explores constructively for the 21st century the resources available for engaging with those forms of enquiry, experience and sensibility that theology has historically sought to address. Drawing together new writing and research from leading international scholars in the field, this high profile research series will offer an important contribution to contemporary research across the interdisciplinary perspectives relating theology and philosophy.

Also in this series:

Divine Knowledge
A Kierkegaardian Perspective on Christian Education
David Willows

Kierkegaard, Language and the Reality of God
Steven Shakespeare

Impossible God
Derrida's Theology
Hugh Rayment-Pickard

On Paul Ricoeur

The Owl of Minerva

RICHARD KEARNEY

Boston College, USA

ASHGATE

Published by
Ashgate Publishing Limited
Gower House
Croft Road
Aldershot
Hants GU11 3HR
England

Ashgate Publishing Company
Suite 420
101 Cherry Street
Burlington, VT, 05401–4405 USA

Ashgate website: http://www.ashgate.com

British Library Cataloguing in Publication Data
Kearney, Richard
    On Paul Ricoeur: The Owl of Minerva (Transcending Boundaries in Philosophy and
    Theology)
    1. Ricoeur, Paul.
    I. Title
    194

Library of Congress Cataloging-in-Publication Data
Kearney, Richard
    On Paul Ricoeur: The Owl of Minerva / Richard Kearney.
        p.   cm. – (Transcending Boundaries in Philosophy and Theology)
    Includes bibliographical references.
    1. Ricoeur, Paul. I. Title. II. Series
    B2430.R554K43   2004
    194–dc22

                                                                          2003024002

ISBN 0 7546 5017 0 (hbk)
ISBN 0 7546 5018 9 (pbk)

Typeset by IML Typographers, Birkenhead, Merseyside
Printed and bound in Great Britain by MPG Books Ltd, Bodmin, Cornwall

Contents

Ricoeur's Philosophical Journey

Paul Ricoeur is one of the most challenging and enduring thinkers of the twentieth century. Born in Valence, France, in 1913, he taught as professor of philosophy at the universities of Strasbourg, Paris and Chicago, and served as director for the Centre of Phenomenology and Hermeneutics in Paris in the 1970s and 1980s. He published over thirty major works, ranging from existentialism and phenomenology to psychoanalysis, politics, religion and the theory of language. But Ricoeur is much more than a brilliant intellectual negotiator between competing schools of thought. He also, and most significantly, developed his own particular brand of philosophical hermeneutics. In this introduction we offer a brief overview of some of the most salient features of Ricoeur's philosophical itinerary before going on to analyse these in six separate, detailed studies. In the second part of this volume, we explore a number of other key issues in Ricoeur's work by means of five critical exchanges conducted with the author over the last twenty-five years (1978–2003).

Taking his cue from such German hermeneutic thinkers as Dilthey, Heidegger and Gadamer, Ricoeur elaborated a complex set of enquiries into what he called the enigma of 'semantic innovation'. How does new meaning come to be, and, in doing so, reconfigure the meanings of the past? This fundamental hermeneutic question is based on the thesis that existence is itself a mode of interpretation (*hermeneia*), or, as the hermeneutic maxim goes: *Life interprets itself.* But where Heidegger concentrated directly on a fundamental ontology of interpretation, Ricoeur advances what he calls the 'long route' of multiple hermeneutic detours. This brought him into dialogue with the human sciences, where philosophy discovers its limits in what is outside of philosophy, in those border exchanges where meaning traverses the various signs and disciplines in which Being is interpreted by human understanding. Ricoeur thus challenged Heidegger's view that Being is accessible through the 'short route' of human existence (*Dasein*) which understands itself through its own possibilities; he argued instead that the meaning of Being is always mediated through an endless process of interpretations – cultural, religious, political, historical and scientific. Hence Ricoeur's basic definition of hermeneutics as the 'art of deciphering *indirect* meaning'.

Philosophy is hermeneutical to the extent that it reads hidden meanings in the text of apparent meanings. And the task of hermeneutics is to show how existence arrives at expression, and later again at reflection, through the perpetual exploration of the significations that emerge in the symbolic works of culture. More particularly, human existence only becomes a self by retrieving meanings which first reside 'outside' of itself in the social institutions and cultural monuments in which the life of the spirit is objectified.

One of the critical targets of Ricoeur's hermeneutics is the idealist doctrine that the self is transparent to itself. In two of his early works – *Freedom and Nature: The Voluntary and the Involuntary* (1950) and *The Symbolism of Evil* (1960) – Ricoeur explodes the pretensions of the *cogito* to be self-founding and self-knowing. He insists that the shortest route from self to self is through the other. Or to put it in Ricoeur's felicitous formula: 'to say self is not to say I'. Why? Because the hermeneutic self is much more than an autonomous subject. Challenging the reign of the transcendental ego, Ricoeur proposes the notion of *self-as-another* – a *soi* that passes beyond the illusory confines of the *moi* and discovers its meaning in and through the linguistic mediations of signs and symbols, stories and ideologies, metaphors and myths. In the most positive hermeneutic scenario, the self returns to itself after numerous hermeneutic detours through the language of others, to find itself enlarged and enriched by the journey. The Cartesian model of the *cogito* as 'master and possessor' of meaning is henceforth radically subverted.

We thus find Ricoeur steering a course beyond the rationalism of Descartes and Kant, on the one hand, and the phenomenology of Husserl and Heidegger, on the other. (Ricoeur actually began a translation of Husserl's *Ideas* during his captivity in a German prisoner-of-war camp in the early 1940s; it was published in 1950.) Where Husserl located meaning in the subject's intuition of the 'things themselves', Ricoeur follows the hermeneutic dictum that intuition is always a matter of interpretation. This implies that things are always given to us *indirectly* through a detour of signs; but it does not entail an embracing of existentialist irrationalism. The interpretation (*hermeneia*) of indirect or tacit meaning invites us to think *more*, not to abandon speculative thought altogether. And nowhere is this more evident than in the challenge posed by symbolic meaning. By symbols Ricoeur understands all expressions of double meaning wherein a primary meaning refers beyond itself to a second meaning which is never given immediately. This 'surplus meaning' provokes interpretation. 'The symbol gives rise to thought', as Ricoeur puts it in a much-quoted maxim.

Ricoeur's first application of his hermeneutic agenda is to be found in *The Symbolism of Evil*. Here the human experience of guilt, finitude and fallibility – as limits to our consciousness – finds expression in the encounter with the enigma of evil. And so we witness a vast hermeneutic detour via the avowals of fault inscribed in the symbols of the major Western traditions – Greek, Hebraic and Babylonian. By interpreting (a) the *primary* symbols of stain, guilt and sin, (b) the *secondary* symbols of wandering, decline, fall and blindness, and (c) the *tertiary* symbols of the servile will, Ricoeur develops a hermeneutics of double meaning.

But Ricouer's hermeneutics is by no means confined to readings of symbol and myth. In a debate with Freudian psychoanalysis in the 1960s – *Freud and Philosophy: An Essay on Interpretation* (1965) – he was to discover a 'semantics of desire' where unconscious drives challenge the primacy of reflective consciousness, exposing hermeneutics to a basic conflict of interpretations. This conflict centred on three fundamental, often competing, approaches: (1) an *archaeological* hermeneutic disclosing an unconscious origin of meaning prior to the conscious ego (Freud); (2) a *teleological* hermeneutic pointing forward to a goal of meaning beyond the conscious ego (Hegel); and (3) an *eschatological* hermeneutic testifying to a transcendent or sacred dimension of meaning before the beginning and after the end (Eliade). In each case, the putative sovereignty of consciousness found itself in question, exposed to dimensions of meaning outside of itself.

An additional challenge was posed by Ricoeur's encounter with structuralism (Saussure and Lévi-Strauss) and the sciences of language (Greimas and Benveniste). Here again the primacy of subjective will is put in question by the disclosure of hidden structures of language which operate involuntarily – behind our backs, as it were. The hermeneutic field was thus enlarged by the encounter with semiotics and structural linguistics, enabling Ricoeur to extend his model of hermeneutic phenomenology by incorporating language as an unconscious system of structures deeper than the intentional subject. It prompted a radical amplification of his project.

This semiological challenge motivated a turn in Ricoeur's philosophy towards the model of the *text*. Where the earlier hermeneutics of symbols was limited to expressions of double intentionality, the later hermeneutics of texts extended interpretation to all phenomena of a textual order, including narratives (*Time and Narrative*, 3 vols, 1983–85) and ideologies (*Lectures on Ideology and Utopia*, 1986). This opened a new dialogue with the human and social sciences encapsulated in Ricoeur's maxim: 'To explain more is to understand better' (*Expliquer plus c'est comprendre mieux*). Here the traditional bias of hermeneutic philosophy against 'explanation' (*Erklären*) and in favour of 'understanding' (*Verstehen*) – running from Schleiermacher and Dilthey through Heidegger and Gadamer – was finally redressed. Moving from 'speech' (the immediate dialogue of speaker and listener) to 'text' (mediated discourse), Ricoeur acknowledges the alterity and distantiation of meaning as essential dimensions of the hermeneutic process – dimensions which had been largely distrusted by Romantic existentialism as symptoms of scientific objectivism. In so doing, Ricoeur endorses a positive hermeneutic conversation with the sciences – a conversation which, it could be said, has been engaged in by many great philosophers in the history of thought: Plato with geometry, Aristotle with cosmology, Descartes with algebra, Kant with physics, Bergson with biology, Husserl and Whitehead with mathematics and so on. In the interpretation of texts, scientific 'explanation' and phenomenological 'understanding' converse and converge. Philosophy thus opens itself once again to a productive dialogue with its other.

But if the semiological challenge restores hermeneutics to the model of the text, it does not in any sense enclose it in some prison house of language. On the contrary, the hermeneutic dialectic advanced by Ricoeur is one which passes through the detour of the text in the name of something beyond it – what he calls the 'matter of the text'. Here we encounter the ontological horizon of world-meaning opened up by the textual workings of language.

This ultimate reference – to a world not merely represented by the text but disclosed by the text – brings us beyond epistemology to ontology. Thus the ultimate horizon of Ricoeur's work remains, from beginning to end, the horizon of being which signals to us obliquely and incompletely: a promised land but never an occupied one. We encounter here a truncated ontology – provisional, tentative, exploratory. And this limitation on the pretensions of speculative reason signals for Ricoeur a renunciation of Hegel and all other versions of systematic closure. The interpretation of being is always something begun, but never completed.

The implications of Ricoeur's privileging of the text as a model of interpretation are radical. Meaning is no longer construed as an essence to be intuited (Husserl), nor as a transcendental condition of possibility to be reflected upon (Kant). The text breaks the circuit of internal reflection and exposes us to intersubjective horizons of language and history. Meaning, as Ricoeur constantly reminds us, involves *someone saying something to someone about something*. This requires us to pay attention to the particular contexts and presuppositions of each speaker and each reader. Interpretation is described accordingly by Ricoeur as the process by which, in the interplay of question and answer, the interlocutors collectively determine the contextual values which inform their conversation. Interpretation explodes the confines of the timeless reflective subject and discloses us as language-using beings in a world with others.

The hermeneutic model of the text reveals complexities of meaning beyond the face-to-face of spoken dialogue. It goes beyond the direct reference of two interlocutors co-present to one another in an immediately identifiable situation 'here and now'. This involves a 'long' intersubjective detour through the sedimented horizons of history and tradition. In *The Conflict of Interpretations* (1969), Ricoeur demonstrates how the *short* intersubjective relation (of two speakers in conversation) is invariably intertwined with various *long* intersubjective relations, mediated by various social institutions, groups, nations and cultural traditions. The long intersubjective relations may thus be said to be sustained by a historical tradition, of which our immediate dialogue is only a part. In short, hermeneutic explication coincides with the broadest historical and cultural connections.

The mediating function of the text becomes exemplary in this respect. The extension of meaning beyond the original reference of spoken utterance is analogous to the written text where meaning survives the absence of the original author and addressee. Here the sense of the text enjoys a certain autonomy with respect to: (a) the author's original intention, (b) the auditor's original reception, and (c) the *vis-à-vis* reference of the initial situation of speech. Hermeneutic interpretation, concludes Ricoeur, produces a 'second-order reference' *in front of the text*, soliciting a series of multiple, and often conflicting, readings.

Interpretation may thus be said to engage us in a hermeneutic circle of historical intersubjectivity, precluding the idealist claim to occupy an absolute or total standpoint. To interpret meaning is, for Ricoeur, to arrive in the middle of an exchange which has already begun and in which we seek to orient ourselves in order to make some new sense of it. His hermeneutic wager is, moreover, that our self-comprehension will be enhanced rather than diminished by our traversal of the circle. The more we explain alien meanings, the better we understand our own inner meaning. Ricoeur accordingly renounces both the Husserlian pretension to a transcendental foundation and the Hegelian claim to absolute knowledge. The central thesis of hermeneutics, he insists, is that interpretation remains an ongoing process which no one vision can totalize. This entails a belonging to meaning in and through distance. Or to put it in another way, hermeneutics endeavours to render near what is far – temporally, geographically, scientifically, culturally – by reappropriating those meanings that have been 'distantiated' from our consciousness. Once again, the textual paradigm proves exemplary. By exposing myself to the textual horizons of 'other' meanings, I transcend the familiar limits of subjective consciousness and open myself to possible new worlds.

If then subjectivity continues to exist for hermeneutics, it is as that 'self-as-another' attained only *after* our intersubjective detours of interpretation. Hermeneutic selfhood is not that which initiates understanding but that which terminates it. It exists at the end, not the beginning. But this terminal act does not presume to rejoin the so-called 'original' subject (*moi*) which first intends meaning. On the contrary, it responds to the *proposal* of meaning which the matter of the text unfolds.

This retrieval of selfhood at the far end of the hermeneutic circle is the counterpart of the distantiation which establishes the second-order reference of the text beyond the first-order reference (of original author, situation and addressee). Ricoeur's notion of appropriation, therefore, far from signalling a triumphalist return of the sovereign ego, offers a way of understanding oneself in front of the text. It is a question of exchanging the *moi*, master of itself, for the *soi*, disciple of the text. For this reason, Ricoeur's hermeneutics may be said to serve as a critique of both *egology* (the view that the self is origin of itself) and *ideology* (the view that understanding is a matter of false consciousness).

Let us return to Ricoeur's central claim that the working of the text is itself a process of 'semantic innovation'. In the case of the symbol, this involves a crossing of intentionalities at the level of the *word*. In the case of metaphor, it involves a production of new meaning at the level of the *sentence*. In the case of narrative, it takes the form of an emplotment (*mise-en-intrigue*) which synthesizes heterogeneous temporal elements at the level of *language* as a whole. This last is what Ricoeur names *configuration*. And like symbol and metaphor before it, he relates it to the schematizing function of productive imagination. Emplotment, as Ricoeur writes in the first volume of *Time and Narrative* (1983), engenders a mixed intelligibility between the theme of a story (its intellectual component) and the intuitive presentation of characters, events, circumstances and reversals of fortune that make up the denouement. In this way, Ricoeur says, we can speak of a schematism of the narrative function.

This schematizing role of narrative operates a dialectic between the dual hermeneutic demands of *tradition* and *innovation*. Each supplements the other. Tradition needs innovation in order to sustain itself as a living transmission of meaning capable of being reactivated in its inaugural moments, while innovation needs tradition in order to make sense as a form of expression governed by rules. Even in its deviant or transgressive guises, it is always a matter of 'rule-governed deformation'. The *nouveau roman* and *anti-roman* presuppose the *roman*. Once again, Ricoeur reminds us that we are part of a hermeneutic circle of distantiation and belonging, of novelty and familiarity, of far and near. The possibility of deviation is inscribed in the very rapport between sedimented paradigms and actual works. Apart from the extreme case of schism, as Ricoeur notes, this is the very opposite of servile application. Rule-governed deformation is the pivot around which the various changes of paradigm through application are organized. It is this diversity of applications that confers a history on the productive imagination and that makes a narrative tradition possible.

This dialectic of innovation and tradition involves not just writing but reading. We pass accordingly from what Ricoeur calls *configuration* to *refiguration* – from the text to the reader who acts in a world. Hence the title of Ricoeur's volume *Du texte à l'action* (1986). Written narrative requires the reader for its completion. Or to put it in Ricoeur's terms, emplotment is a joint work of text and reader. It is the reader who accompanies the interplay of innovation and sedimentation, who schematizes emplotment, plays with narrative gaps, and, finally, refigures what the author configures and defigures. This re-creative labour signals, in the last analysis, a reshaping of the world of action under the sign of the plot.

Plots are not, of course, confined to texts signed by individual authors. They are also to be found at the level of what Ricoeur calls the *social imaginary* –

that body of collective stories, histories and ideologies which informs our modes of socio-political action. Social imagination, he argues, is constitutive of our lived reality. Ricoeur goes on to analyse this phenomenon under the dialectical headings of *ideology* and *utopia*. While ideology tends to promote collective images which integrate a community around a shared identity, utopian images work in the opposite direction of novelty, rupture and discontinuity. The social imagination serves *both* an ideological role of identification *and* a utopian role of disruption. The former preserves and conserves; the latter projects alternatives. Thus one of the central functions of hermeneutics identified by Ricoeur is the critical interrogation of the socio-political *imaginaire* which governs any given society and motivates its citizens. In relation to society, no less than in relation to the text, Ricoeur promotes a dialectical balance between belonging and distance. Ideology as a symbolic confirmation of the past and utopia as a symbolic opening towards the future are, he insists, complementary. Cut off from one another, they run the risk of pathological extremes: ideology imprisoning us in reactionary conservatism, utopia sacrificing us to a schizophrenic image of an abstract future without the conditions for its realization.

In this regard, Ricoeur manages to combine a Gadamerian respect for tradition with a Habermasian critique of ideology. The risk for Gadamer is innocent obedience to the authority of inherited prejudice; the risk for Habermas is obliviousness to the truth that critique is also a tradition – one which, as Ricoeur points out, reaches back to the Greek narratives of Socratic questioning and the biblical narratives of exodus and resurrection. The danger is severing our utopian horizon of expectation from the ideological horizon of past and present. One of the most urgent hermeneutic tasks today, insists Ricoeur, is to reconcile these two tasks of the social imaginary – reanimating tradition and realizing utopia.

The dialectic of critique and creation – to which we shall return in several of our studies below – is, in fact, a typical exemplification of Ricoeur's canonical play between a hermeneutics of *suspicion* and *affirmation*. Suspicion takes the form of a critique of false consciousness by the three 'masters of suspicion' – Freud, Marx and Nietzsche. By contrast, the hermeneutics of affirmation emphasizes our fundamental *desire to be*, keeping us open to an irreducible 'surplus of meaning' (*surcroît de sens*). The former, Ricoeur argues, is a necessary prelude to the latter. We can only recover our ontological *desire to be* authentically in a 'second naïveté' by first interrogating ourselves as we exist *outside of ourselves*. Authentic meaning must traverse the purgatorial fires of alienation. Hence the crucial importance of Freud's disclosure of unconscious desire, Nietzsche's genealogy of will-to-power, and Marx's critique of false consciousness. All three recognized that meaning, far from being transparent to itself, is an enigmatic process which conceals at the same time as it reveals. Ricoeur insists therefore on the need for a hermeneutics of suspicion which demystifies our illusions, permitting us to decipher the masked workings of desire, will and interest. Hermeneutic doubt reminds us again and again that consciousness (individual or social) is a relation of concealing and revealing which calls for a specific interpretation.

But critique is not the only task of hermeneutics. Once divested of illusions, we often find ourselves faced with a remainder of ontological meaning which exists beyond the self. And it is this surplus meaning which re-invites and re-ignites the affirmation of our *desire-to-be*. But the promised land of ontological affirmation is at best a hope which the interpreter, like Moses, can only glimpse before dying. That is why hermeneutic truth takes the form of a wager. It is less an acquisition than a task. Because we are finite beings, our understanding always remains within the historical limits of the hermeneutic circle. The myth of absolute reason must always be resisted in favour of a plurality of critical debates and detours. A creative conflict of interpretations is inevitable. This explains Ricoeur's characteristic willingness to open his hermeneutic phenomenology to a open debate with such interlocutors as structuralism, psychoanalysis, analytic philosophy, political theory, sociology, theology and the sciences of language. Here as elsewhere his hermeneutic maxim prevails – *the shortest route from self to self is through the other*.

The ontological surplus of meaning is, for Ricoeur, ultimately an invitation to create. This theme of creation may be said to run from Ricoeur's first hermeneutic studies on symbolism to the later studies of 'narrative identity' in *Time and Narrative* and *Oneself as Another* (1990). But such a poetics of creation cannot be removed from an ethics of just action. It is always a question of moving back and forth between text and action. That is why it is no accident that Ricoeur's hermeneutic studies of narrative identity in *Oneself as Another* lead directly to what he calls his 'little ethics' – a discussion of how cultures seek to realize the Aristotelian goal of a 'good life with and for others in just institutions'. This is a task which the Greeks identified with the conjunction of practical wisdom (*phronesis*) and creativity (*poiesis*). Ricoeur's hermeneutics represents, I believe, one of the most significant contemporary realizations of this most ancient of philosophical tasks.

That Ricoeur's final writings – in the last decade of the twentieth century and in the early years of the twenty-first – are devoted to issues of loss and pardon, memory and mourning, melancholy and forgetfulness, by no means signals an abandonment of this task. On the contrary, Ricoeur's ceaseless efforts to reconfigure our projects of creative hope in the shadow of the past – both individual and historical – is testimony to his uncompromising commitment to a conflict of perspectives. Hermeneutic enquiry is, for Ricoeur, an indispensable way of giving a future to the past.

This volume is intended as a critical engagement with the hermeneutic writings of Paul Ricoeur. It does not claim to be comprehensive or exhaustive, but rather to focus on a number of key themes in Ricoeur's intellectual odyssey which we consider emblematic of his work – namely, the dialectics between (1) phenomenology and hermeneutics; (2) imagination and language; (3) myth and tradition; (4) ideology and utopia; (5) evil and alterity; (6) narrative and history. The investigation of these selective themes comprises the first part of our current volume. It is followed, in Part Two, by a series of five exchanges which we conducted with Ricoeur over the past three decades. By letting the Master of Suspicion and Affirmation speak for himself in this manner we hope to offer the reader a special insight into some of Paul Ricoeur's deepest philosophical commitments and convictions.

On a more personal note, I would like to acknowledge the honour and pleasure it is for me to publish this particular selection of studies and dialogues. The selection is not entirely neutral, for it is assuredly informed by my own experience of working with Ricoeur as my doctoral adviser in the University of Paris in the late 1970s and by our enduring friendship ever since. Such themes as narrative imagination, poetics of possibility, the ethics of self-as-other or the ontology–eschatology debate have been topics of continued discussion between us over the years. There are few philosophers from whom I have learnt so much and even fewer whom I have had the privilege to know so well. The fact that this book is completed twenty-five years since I first met Ricoeur, and in the ninety-second year of his life, encourages me to offer it as a heartfelt tribute from a learner to a master.

The title of this work also has something of a personal connotation. Every time I visited Ricoeur over the years at his home in Chatenay-Malabry, outside Paris, I was invariably struck by the hosts of owls furnishing his offfice and library. Ricoeur is, in more ways than one, the living epitome of the Owl of Minerva – a thinker who has always preferred the long route over the short cut and has never written an essay or book until he had first experienced and questioned deeply what it was he was writing about. He, like the Owl of Widsom in Hegel's famous example, only takes flight at dusk when he has fully attended to what transpired (as both action and suffering) during the long day's journey. The fact that he has endured for almost a century – following in the footsteps of his fellow hermeneut, Gadamer (is there something in the hermeneutic water?) – additionally qualifies him, of course, for the emblematic title of a wise old owl. Someone born in 1913 who witnessed three world wars (counting the cold war), endured years of prison captivity under the Nazis, taught in dozens of universities and countries and wrote over thirty major books knows, I think, what he is talking about when he completes a book in his ninetieth year called *La Mémoire, l'histoire, l'oubli*. It is a privilege, I would suggest, for us, his readers, to learn deeply from his lived reflections.

I wish to thank my assistants at Boston College, John Manoussakis and Todd Sadowski, for the invaluable editorial assistance they offered me in the preparation of this manuscript. I am also grateful to Martin Warner and Kevin Vanhoozer, editors of the series on Transcending Boundaries in Philosophy and Theology at Ashgate, for inviting me to contribute this volume to their collection. Finally, I would like to thank the editors of the various journals or publications where several earlier versions or sections of the studies below have appeared over the years. A special acknowledgement note is appended to each study.

PART ONE

Between Phenomenology and Hermeneutics*

In this study I propose to explore in more detail how Ricoeur reworked phenomenology in a new direction. Taking a lead from Heidegger and Gadamer, he moved beyond both the 'eidetic' phenomenology of Husserl and the 'existentialist' phenomenology of Sartre and Merleau-Ponty to embrace a 'hermeneutic' phenomenology in dialogue with the human sciences. Where Sartre tended to privilege the role of negating consciousness and Merleau-Ponty that of embodied perception, Ricoeur emphasized the primacy of a signifying intentionality. This new emphasis led him to advance a general hermeneutics where phenomenology confronts its own limits – that is, where the intuition of essences ends and the interpretation of symbols begins.

As noted in our Introduction, Ricoeur's international repute as a philosopher arose not only from his influential role as exegete and teacher of phenomenology, but more importantly from the singular character of his 'hermeneutic turn'. Redefining hermeneutics as a method of deciphering doubled or multiple meaning, Ricoeur's major hermeneutic works from the 1950s to the present day have been devoted to the interpretation of the 'mediations' of meaning through symbol, myth, dream, image, text, narrative and ideology.

In some of his early phenomenological studies of the will, for example *Freedom and Nature: The Voluntary and the Involuntary* (1950), Ricoeur analysed certain limit situations where 'freedom' comes face to face with 'necessity'. Here the voluntary intentionality of our consciousness encounters involuntary or opaque experiences – such as birth, death, the unconscious, suffering, evil, or indeed transcendence. All these encounters, Ricoeur demonstrated, are irreducible to the subjective transparency of intuition (that is, Husserl's model of phenomenology). By describing how our finite and historically situated existence transgresses our subjective intentions, Ricoeur was able to affirm one of the guiding principles of his hermeneutic project: we do not *begin* with a pure reflective consciousness – this remains a task to be accomplished by means of a long detour through those significations of history and culture that reside outside our immediate consciousness. The human subject thus comes to realize that it can only interpret itself by interpreting the 'signs' of an external world not its own. The hermeneutic self is not a self-sufficient *cogito* but an

---

* A shorter version of this study first appeared in *Modern Movements in European Philosophy*, Manchester University Press, 1987.

incarnate being which discovers that it is placed in language before it possesses itself in consciousness.

Human being, for Ricoeur, is always, a *being-interpreted*. It cannot start from itself or simply invent meanings out of itself *ex nihilo*. Therefore, instead of proceeding according to the model of the Cartesian *concept* – a pure and distinct idea transparent to itself – hermeneutics is committed to the primacy of the *symbol*, where meaning emerges as oblique, mediated, enigmatic, layered and multiform. 'In contrast to philosophies concerned with starting points', Ricoeur explains, 'a meditation on symbols starts from the fullness of language and of meaning already there; it begins from within language which has already taken place and in which everything in a certain sense has already been said; it wants to be thought, not presuppositionless, but in and with all its presuppositions. Its first problem is not how to get started, but from the midst of speech to recollect itself.'[1]

Ricoeur does not for all that renounce the ideal of rationality proposed by philosophical reflection. He simply points out that such an ideal must always presuppose the revealing and concealing powers of language. The ideal of rationality remains therefore a project rather than a possession, the end of philosophy rather than its beginning. Ricoeur argues furthermore that the hermeneutic meditation of symbols answers to the particular situation of philosophy in our modern culture. It corresponds to the recognition that there is no 'first truth', no 'absolute knowledge', no transcendental vantage point of consciousness where the dispersal into multiple meaning could be definitively overcome in one final synthesis.

Ricoeur's hermeneutics thus exposes phenomenology to a radical awareness of the limits and obstacles of consciousness. It opens reflection to the world of the unconscious and the supraconscious. And this hermeneutic detour through the hidden or suppressed meanings of symbolic signification – preceding and exceeding the immediacy of intuitive consciousness – is less an option than a necessity. We find Ricoeur's hermeneutic trajectory progressing consequently as a series of reflections upon the primary sources of cultural interpretation. These include:

1   the symbols of religion and myth (*The Symbolism of Evil*, 1960; *Figuring the Sacred*, 1995; *Thinking Biblically*, 1998);
2   the dream images of the unconscious (*Freud and Philosophy: An Essay on Interpretation*, 1965);
3   the signifying structures of language (*The Conflict of Interpretations*, 1969; *The Rule of Metaphor*, 1975; *Interpretation Theory*, 1976; *Hermeneutics and the Human Sciences*, 1981);

---

[1] P. Ricoeur, 'The Hermeneutics of Symbols and Philosophical Reflection' (1962), in *The Philosophy of Paul Ricoeur: An Anthology of his Work*, ed. by Charles E. Reagan and David Stewart (Boston: Beacon Press, 1978), p. 36f.

4   the social and political imaginary (*History and Truth*, 1965; *Lectures on Ideology and Utopia*, 1986; *From Text to Action*, 1991, *The Just*, 1995);

5   the function of narrative time, identity and action (*Time and Narrative*, 3 vols, 1983–85; *Oneself as Another*, 1992);

6   the workings of remembrance and mourning (*Memory, History, Forgetting*, 2000).

All of these works share a common project – the retrieval of thought in symbolic mediation and the extension of symbolic mediation into thought. The overriding maxim of this general hermeneutics is Ricoeur's celebrated claim that the 'symbol invites thought' (*le symbole donne à penser*). As the author explains:

> This maxim that I find so appealing says two things. The symbol invites: I do not posit the meaning, the symbol gives it; but what it gives is something for thought, something to think about. First the giving, then the positing; the phrase suggests, therefore, both that all has already been said in enigma and yet that it is necessary ever to begin and re-begin everything in the dimension of thought. It is this articulation of thought ... in the realm of symbols and of thought positing and thinking that I would like to intercept and understand.[2]

The Critique of Husserlian Phenomenology

Before proceeding to analyse Ricoeur's development of his hermeneutic project in more detail, we shall take a closer look at his decisive departure from Husserl's original formulation of phenomenology.

Ricoeur considers that the extension of phenomenology into hermeneutics requires a critique of Husserl's idealist model of consciousness (as advanced in such texts as *The Cartesian Meditations* or *Ideas*). He rejects Husserl's notion of an ultimate foundation of knowledge to be achieved by an 'absolute suspension of presuppositions'. Ricoeur responds that the call for a presuppositionless starting point in the self-immediacy of consciousness labours under the illusion that there exists an order of full intuition where the contingency of meaning could be reduced to the pure immanence of a transcendental subjectivity. In what Ricoeur refers to as his 'idealist phase', Husserl maintained that such a realm of pure immanence could be reached by means of a 'transcendental reduction' which would bracket out the temporal and historical context of our experience – that context which makes all knowledge inexact in so far as it evolves through successive horizons or profiles (*Abschattungen*). By

---

[2] Ibid.

removing consciousness from the contingency of the natural world, Husserl believed that he could attain a transcendental knowledge that would be self-grounding and thus certain of itself. This realm of transcendental immanence was granted an immunity against doubt by Husserl. Why? Because Husserl believed that 'it was not given by profiles and hence involved nothing presumptive, allowing only the coincidence of reflection with what has just been experienced'.[3] Ricoeur concludes that Husserl, by proceeding in this manner, reduced phenomenology to an idealism wherein knowledge could be considered autonomous and self-positing, and therefore alone responsible for its own meanings.

Against this idealist reading of the early Husserl – and some might add the early Sartre – Ricoeur protests that phenomenology requires a surpassing of itself towards hermeneutics. Instead of issuing a refusal to history (understood in the broad sense of a transsubjective dispersal of meaning in the world), hermeneutics makes good the intention of phenomenology to return to our lived experience. And it does this by embracing history as its ultimate challenge. Here Ricoeur endorses the initiatives of Heidegger, Merleau-Ponty and also indeed of the later Husserl (for example of *The Crisis*). He confirms that the ideal of knowledge as an absolute self-justification encounters its limit in the phenomenological description of man's being-in-the-world. This description lays bare the radical finitude of consciousness, the fact that we exist in a historical horizon of language whose meanings precede our own subjective creations. As Heidegger's phenomenological ontology clearly showed, consciousness is bound by a relation of *belonging* to past sedimentations and future projects of meaning, a 'hermeneutic circle' wherein each subjectivity finds itself already included in an intersubjective world whose significations encompass it and escape it on every side. Consequently, it is not sufficient simply to describe meaning as it *appears*; we are also obliged to interpret it as it *conceals* itself. This leads us inevitably beyond a phenomenological idealism of pure reflection to a phenomenological hermeneutics of interpretation which acknowledges that meaning is never first and foremost *for me*.

'Interpretation', writes Ricoeur, 'is interpretation by language before it is interpretation of language.'[4] We belong to a language that has been shaped and formed by others before we arrive on the existential scene. And this language can only be recovered for reflection by a long process of decipherment. Hermeneutics reveals how we are always bound to an ontology of prior signification (what Ricoeur calls the 'tradition of recollection'). It attests to the priority of ontological pre-understanding (based, as in Heidegger, on a description of our being-in-a-world-with-others) over the epistemological

---

[3] Ricoeur, 'Phenomenology and Hermeneutics', 1975, in *Hermeneutics and the Human Sciences*, ed. John B. Thompson (Cambridge: Cambridge University Press, 1981), p. 101f.

[4] Ricoeur, 'What is a Text?', 1970, in *Hermeneutics and the Human Sciences*, p. 145f.

category of an autonomous subject which posits itself in some absolute present. Thus Ricoeur counters the Husserlian demand for a return to the immediacy of intuition with the claim that all understanding is of necessity mediated by meanings which are not constituted by the self alone. In his watershed essay of 1969, entitled 'Existence and Hermeneutics', Ricoeur settles his account with the master as follows:

> It remains that the early Husserl only reconstituted a new idealism, close to the neo-Kantianism he fought: the reduction of the thesis of the world is actually a reduction of the question of Being to the question of the sense of being, the sense of being, in turn, is reduced to a simple correlate of the subjective modes of intention.[5]

Ricoeur does acknowledge, however, that the later Husserl came to see the inadequacies of his early idealism, particularly in *The Crisis* (written in the mid-1930s just before his death) where he began to sketch an ontology of the intersubjective life-world. But, as Ricoeur notes, if the final writings of Husserl 'point to this ontology, it is because his effort to reduce being failed and because, consequently, the ultimate result of phenomenology escaped the initial project'.[6] It is really only in the wake of this escape that one can begin to speak of a phenomenological hermeneutics.

Philosophical Encounters

Ricoeur's critique of Husserlian idealism and his subsequent reformulation of phenomenology were influenced by a number of philosophical encounters. First, there was the lasting impact of his formative engagement with the 'concrete ontologies' of Gabriel Marcel and Karl Jaspers in the 1930s and 1940s. It was in fact these non-phenomenological existentialists who initially impressed upon Ricoeur the radicality of the confrontation between freedom and finitude. Any philosophy of reflection, Ricoeur became convinced, would have to reckon with Marcel's analysis of 'incarnate existence' and Jaspers' notion of 'limit situations' (death, war, disease, crisis and so on). This seminal conviction resulted in the publication of *Gabriel Marcel and Karl Jaspers* in 1947 and *Karl Jaspers and the Philosophy of Existence* (co-authored with Mikel Dufrenne) in the same year.

During the immediate postwar years, Ricoeur was working on his major critical commentary and translation of Husserl's *Ideas*. Not surprisingly, the combination of Husserl's reflective phenomenology with the concrete

---

[5] Ricoeur, 'Existence and Hermeneutics' in *The Conflict of Interpretations* (Evanston, IL: Northwestern University Press, 1974), p. 11f.

[6] Ibid.

ontology of Marcel and Jaspers prompted Ricoeur in the direction of an 'existential phenomenology' which approximated in several important respects to the work of Heidegger, Sartre and Merleau-Ponty. Thus in the first three parts of his 'Philosophy of the Will' – *The Voluntary and the Involuntary*, *Fallible Man* and *The Symbolism of Evil* – we find Ricoeur exposing Husserl's phenomenology of reflective consciousness to the challenge of an existential appraisal of man's limiting experiences of facticity and alienation. This exposé took the form of an existential phenomenology of such related themes as 'guilt', 'finitude', 'fallibility' and 'fault'. Consciousness could no longer be described as a sovereign choosing will transparent to itself. The transcendental *cogito* was exploded in the collision with the 'involuntary' limits of human existence. But this collision, as noted, already necessitated a transition from a pure phenomenology of consciousness to a hermeneutics of symbols. Ricoeur sees this transition not as a betrayal of phenomenology but rather as a fidelity to its original discovery that the intentional meaning of consciousness resides *outside of itself*. The analysis undertaken in *The Symbolism of Evil*, published in 1960, was to be of crucial importance here. Ricoeur writes:

> The servile condition of the evil will seemed to elude an essential analysis of phenomena. So the only practicable route was that of a detour via the symbols wherein the avowal of the fault was inscribed during the great cultures of which ours is the heir: the primary symbols of stain, guilt and sin; the secondary symbols or myths of tragic blindness, of the fall of the soul, of wandering or decline; the tertiary symbols and rationalisations of the servile will or of original sin. *The Symbolism of Evil* thus marked the turning of Husserlian phenomenology, already extended to the problematic of fallibility, towards a hermeneutics of symbols. By 'symbols' I understood ... all expressions of double meaning, wherein a primary meaning refers beyond itself to a second meaning which is never given directly.[7]

Ricoeur's itinerary of 'hermeneutic detours' was also deeply affected by his open debate with two of the major modern rivals to the phenomenological movement – psychoanalysis and structuralism. The former's emphasis on the hidden structures of the unconscious and the latter's on the hidden structures of language added further dimensions to the dramatic struggle between the voluntary and the involuntary. This meant for Ricoeur that phenomenological hermeneutics would have to renounce the idealist concept of a universal exegesis wherein the alienations of consciousness could be resolved in a totalizing subjective synthesis. It would have to accept that there are 'only disparate and opposed theories concerning the rules of interpretation'.[8] By disclosing the ways in which the unconscious structures of dream symbols

---

[7] 'A Response by Paul Ricoeur', in *Hermeneutics and the Human Sciences*, p. 32f.

[8] Ricoeur, *Freud and Philosophy: An Essay on Interpretation* (New Haven, CT: Yale University Press, 1970).

subvert the sovereignty of our immediate consciousness, psychoanalysis compelled phenomenology to advance towards an open-ended hermeneutics 'internally at variance with itself'. Ricoeur assesses the impact of Freudian psychoanalysis on his hermeneutic project as follows:

> In my earlier works, the great detour via signs had not called into question the primacy of the subject. I found in Freud not only the counter-pole to hermeneutics conceived as recollection of symbols, but also an incisive critique of the whole reflective tradition to which I continued to link myself through Kant and Husserl ... The notion of a semantics of desire ... introduced me to the theme of the *conflict of interpretations*.[9]

But the hermeneutic field was even further enlarged by the encounter with structural linguistics. This confrontation enabled Ricoeur to amplify the model of hermeneutic ontology inherited from Heidegger, by incorporating a model of language as an unconscious system of deep structures common to both the 'intentional' symbols of a phenomenology of existence and the 'disguised' symbols of psychoanalysis. Ricoeur explains this second crucial encounter thus:

> It appeared that the linguistic dimension of all symbolism had not been made the object of a distinct and systematic treatment in my earlier works, in spite of the fact that the detour via symbols had, since *The Symbolism of Evil,* taken the form of a detour of reflection on the self via an investigation of the mediating signs of this reflection. It is upon this terrain of the investigation of language that I encountered a new challenge, that of French structuralism, which eliminated any reference to a speaking subject from its analysis of signifying systems. I thus discovered a convergence between the structuralist critique originating from linguistics and the psychoanalytic critique originating from Freud, a convergence in what I called collectively the *semiological challenge*.[10]

This semiological challenge was to motivate the final phase of Ricoeur's philosophical project. It set in train a methodological overhaul which resulted in a new definition of hermeneutics based on the model of the text. Where his earlier hermeneutics had been limited to symbols as expressions of double or split intention, the new hermeneutics extended this model of interpretation to embrace all phenomena of a textual order. And these phenomena would include, for Ricoeur (as for such structuralist thinkers as Barthes and Lévi-Strauss), reference to a 'social imaginary' in the broadest cultural sense. In this manner, hermeneutics inaugurated a new dialogue with the human and social sciences.

In short, Ricoeur responded to the semiological challenge by privileging the concept of the text as the guiding thread of his investigations into the creation

---

[9] 'A Response by Paul Ricoeur', p. 14f.
[10] Ibid.

and recovery of meaning. He aimed to show how the text is the exemplary level at which (a) the 'structural explanation' of the scientific approach and (b) the 'hermeneutic understanding' of the phenomenological approach confront one another:

> It was then necessary, however, to expand the hermeneutical project ... to the dimensions of the problem posed by the passage from the structure immanent in every text to its extra-linguistic aim (*visée*) – the aim or reference which I sometimes designate by other related terms: the matter of the text, the world of the text, the being brought to language by the text.[11]

We shall return to this decisive theme in the final section of this study.

Towards a General Hermeneutics

Ricoeur's mature exposition of the hermeneutic model of the text required not only a revision of the original project of phenomenology but of the hermeneutic tradition itself.

Hermeneutics first arose within the framework of biblical exegesis. Its traditionally motivating question was: how are we to understand the divine intention of Holy Scripture given its successive reinscriptions throughout the historical generations of Jews and Christians? Within the more specific tradition of Christian theology, hermeneutic models were proposed to deal with the fact that texts could have several different layers of signification – for example historical or spiritual – which a logic of univocal meanings could not adequately account for. St Augustine's *De Doctrina Christiana* was a good case in point. The guiding impulse of such hermeneutic exercises was to overcome the distance of the different historico-cultural reinterpretations in order to restore the original meaning of the texts of Revelation, making the divine inspiration of the past contemporaneous with the exegetical reading of the present.

Ricoeur (following Schleiermacher, Dilthey and Heidegger) argues that hermeneutics is not limited to the specialist science of biblical exegesis. He insists that the phenomenon of 'polysemy' – that is, of multiple meaning – is a fundamental feature of all language, not just theological language. Hermeneutics can thus be raised to the level of a universal philosophy which acknowledges that when we use language we are already interpreting the world, not *literally* as if it possessed a single transparent meaning, but *figuratively* in terms of allegory, symbol, metaphor, myth and analogy. In this manner, philosophical hermeneutics relates the technical problem of textual exegesis to the general problem of language as a whole.

---

[11] Ibid.

The first steps towards such a general philosophy of hermeneutics were taken in the late nineteenth century by Friedrich Schleiermacher and Wilhelm Dilthey. In *The Origin of Hermeneutics* (1900), Dilthey raised the problem of how the historical and human sciences (*Geisteswissenschaften*) could acquire a method of interpretation different to the positivism of the natural sciences (*Naturwissenschaften*). How, he asked, could a specifically human science be founded in the face of the methodological hegemony of empirical objectivity? Dilthey advanced a 'psychological' model designed to explain how one's finite understanding could transpose itself beyond the 'objective' limits of empirical facts so as to empathically coincide with another human understanding, removed from it in time and space. But Ricoeur criticizes the hermeneutics of Schleiermacher and Dilthey for remaining within the limits of a Romantic epistemology which saw all forms of 'objective knowledge' as a negation of self-understanding. The ideal of a lived interiority of consciousness, secured by becoming one with the original experience of another historical consciousness, remained the touchstone of Romantic hermeneutics. As such, it succumbed to 'psychologism' and 'historicism', treating cultural artefacts as 'alienated' expressions which can only be salvaged by an 'empathic reliving' (*nacherleben*) of the original spirituality of their authors. Dilthey's *Lebensphilosophie* tended to construe hermeneutics accordingly as a form of *psychological transposition*, whereby I transcend the horizons of my present historical situation in order to relive the privileged life-experience of the author's original subjectivity. In this way, it worked to render the self 'contemporaneous' with another creative understanding, before the latter's alienation in the objectified expressions of cultural documents, artefacts or institutions.

Thus Romantic hermeneutics, no less than idealist phenomenology, tended to view the historical 'distantiation' of meaning as a threat to reflective subjectivity. Ricoeur, by contrast, sponsors a phenomenological hermeneutics which will restore priority to the historical symbolizations of understanding over the pure interiority of consciousness.

> History [he writes] precedes me and my reflection; I belong to history before I belong to myself. Dilthey could not understand that, because his revolution remained epistemological and his reflective criterion prevailed over his historical awareness … Dilthey still begins from self-consciousness; for him subjectivity remains the ultimate point of reference. The reign of *Erlebnis* (lived experience) is the reign of the primordiality which I am. In this sense, the fundamental is the *Innesein,* the interior, the awareness of self.[12]

In response to the shortcomings of Romantic hermeneutics, Ricoeur chooses to raise interpretation from the level of epistemology to that of ontology. Together

---

[12] Ricoeur, 'Hermeneutics and the Critique of Ideology', 1973, in *Hermeneutics and the Human Sciences*, p. 63f.

with Heidegger and Gadamer, Ricoeur considers interpretation not on the basis of a psychological self-consciousness, but against the historical horizon of a finite being-in-the-world. But while Heidegger takes the 'short route' to Being, where interpretation culminates, Ricoeur opts for the 'long route', which examines the various inevitable detours which interpretation undergoes through language, myth, ideology, the unconscious and so on – *before* it arrives at the ultimate limit of Being. Our final project is indeed a being-towards-death whose fundamental encounter with 'nothingness' provokes the question of Being. But between birth and death, human understanding is compelled to traverse a range of hermeneutic fields, where meaning is dispersed, hidden, withheld or deferred. Ricoeur's hermeneutic project resolves accordingly to occupy this conflictual terrain of enquiry, a terrain which he locates *between* Dilthey's epistemology of interpretation and Heidegger's ontology of understanding. In 'Hermeneutics and the Critique of Ideology', Ricoeur explains his medial position thus:

> The long route which I propose also aspires to carry reflection to the level of ontology, but it will do so by degrees, following successive investigations ... My problem will be this: what happens to an epistemology of interpretation, born of a reflection on exegesis, on the method of history, on psychoanalysis, on the phenomenology of religion etc., when it is touched, animated, as we might say inspired by an ontology of understanding?[13]

Ricoeur embraces the challenge of rival interpretations which he believes is the hallmark of our contemporary understanding. Heidegger circumvented this challenge by confining his attentions to a fundamental ontology of Being in general (*Sein überhaupt*), thereby relegating the conflict of interpretations to 'regional ontologies' concerned with this or that particular kind of being (for example the natural and social sciences, religion, psychoanalysis, linguistics and so on). Ricoeur chooses otherwise. He enters the fray and works his arduous passage towards a fundamental ontology by first debating with the various contesting models of interpretation. The phenomenon of multiple meaning – in its alienated or creative forms – becomes for him the primary hermeneutic focus. The notion of a universal field of Being – where the plurality of meanings would find an ultimate grounding – is preserved as a final possibility. But it is just that, a *possibility*. It cannot be realized in the immediate present.

The Conflict of Interpretations

The conflict of interpretations is for Ricoeur a logical consequence of the symbolic nature of language. Because signs can have more than one meaning,

---

[13] Ibid.

they often say more than they appear to say at first sight. The ostensible meaning of a word frequently conceals another meaning which surpasses it. It is this typically equivocal or multivocal character of symbolic language which calls for the deciphering activity of the interpreter. Ricoeur defines as symbolic 'any structure of signification in which a direct, primary, literal meaning designates, in addition, another meaning which is indirect, secondary and figurative and which can be apprehended only through the first'.[14] The decipherment of expressions with double or multiple meanings thus prescribes the hermeneutic field. Interpretation, as the dialectical counterpart of the symbol, is described accordingly as 'the work of thought which consists in deciphering the hidden meaning in the apparent meaning, in unfolding the levels of meaning implied in the literal meaning'.[15]

The 'hidden' meaning of symbolic expressions can be interpreted in a variety of ways. The psychoanalyst interprets it as a transposition of the repressed desires of the unconscious libido; the theologian as a cipher of divine transcendence; the poet as a projection of the creative imagination, and so on. The common feature of all these hermeneutic models is a certain architecture of multiple meaning whose function is to 'show while concealing'. However much their conclusions may contradict one another, each is concerned with the symbolic transfer of meaning from one plane to another through the linguistic agencies of metaphor, allegory, simile, metonomy and so on.

It is the business of philosophical hermeneutics, Ricoeur urges, to provide a 'criteriology' which would situate and demarcate the theoretical limits of each hermeneutic field. The critical task of such a hermeneutics is to arbitrate between the absolutist claims of the respective interpretations, demonstrating how each one operates within a specific set of theoretical presuppositions. In other words, every particular hermeneutic translates a surplus of meaning, produced by the multiple determination of symbolic expressions, according to its own 'key' frame of reference. Ricoeur cites the following example of how rival interpretations arise:

> The phenomenology of religion deciphers the religious object in rites, in myth, and in faith, but it does so on the basis of a problematic of the sacred which defines its theoretical structure. Psychoanalysis, by contrast, sees only that dimension of the symbol ... which derives from repressed desires. Consequently, it considers only the network of meanings constituted in the unconscious, beginning with the initial repression and elaborated by subsequent secondary repressions.[16]

But Ricoeur maintains that psychoanalysis cannot in itself be reproached for its exclusivity, any more than the phenomenology of religion. The methodological limits of these respective readings are their very *raison d'être*. Since

---

[14] Ricoeur, 'Existence and Hermeneutics', p. 11f.

[15] Ibid.

[16] Ricoeur, *The Conflict of Interpretations*.

psychoanalytic theory confines the rules of its decoding of dream-texts to a semantics of libidinal desire, it stands to reason that it can only discover there what it seeks. It is entirely logical that it will interpret religious symbols and rites as instances of obsessional neurosis, just as a specifically religious hermeneutics will interpret obsessional neurosis as a disguised longing for the sacred.

The task of hermeneutics is not, says Ricoeur, to resolve such conflicts of interpretation; it is to clearly establish the particular frameworks of pre-understanding – what Wittgenstein calls 'language-games' – within which our various interpretations arise, predisposing us to this or that reading of the signs. To dissolve this contest prematurely by appeal to some meta-language of univocal meaning or some absolute consciousness *à la* Hegel is to succumb to the temptation of a reductive idealism.

But Ricoeur equally resists the temptation to reduce hermeneutics to a purely linguistic analysis of meaning. This would be to treat significations as totalities closed in on themselves. Ricoeur takes his distance here from what he terms the 'ideology of an absolute text' which came into vogue with structuralism. He does not wish to deny that as soon as discourse is inscribed in a text, the author's intention ceases to coincide with the meaning of this text. He readily concedes this. The text's career, he knows, always escapes the situated horizon lived by its author. 'What the text says now matters more than what the author meant to say', writes Ricoeur, 'and every exegesis unfolds its procedures within the circumference of a meaning that has broken its moorings to the psychology of its author.'[17] But to acknowledge that the text suspends the *direct* reference to a situation commonly experienced by the interlocutors of a spoken discourse, is not the same as saying that the text has *no reference at all*. And this is where Ricoeur takes his stand against linguistic imperialism. Language, even as inscribed in an autonomous text, cannot fail to be *about* something. Nearly all texts speak in some manner or other about a world. It is, of course, true that the text suspends the original reference to the author's experience, and is thus free to enter into relation with other texts. This, after all, is what allows for the creation of literature. This is what enables us to speak of symbolic worlds – for example the Greek world or the Byzantine world – that are *represented* in texts rather than *presented* in a spoken situation. But in such instances, reference is not entirely obliterated; it is simply deferred. To suggest that we suppress the referential function altogether is, Ricoeur charges, to abandon meaning to 'an absurd game of errant signifiers'.

Instead of adopting the structuralist ideology of the absolute text, then, Ricoeur's hermeneutic proposes to retain the link with a phenomenological ontology. This allows him to show how the text (for example a Greek tragedy) can indeed free itself from its initial direct reference to both an author (for

---

[17] Ricoeur, 'The Model of the Text: Meaningful Action considered as a Text', in *Hermeneutics and the Human Sciences*, p. 197f.

example Sophocles) and to the circumstantial reality of a historical situation (for example Sophocles' ancient Greece) and still retain the notion of reference – albeit a radically revised reference to the symbolic projection of possible worlds. Ricoeur makes a fundamental distinction here between a situational reference to an actual world (*Umwelt*) and a non-situational reference to a symbolic world (*Welt*).

> In the same manner that the text frees its meaning from the tutelage of the mental intention, it frees its reference from the limits of ostensive reference. For us, the world is the ensemble of references opened up by the texts. Thus we speak about the 'world' of Greece, not to designate any more what were the situations for those who lived them, but to designate the non-situational references which outlive the effacement of the first and which henceforth are offered as possible modes of being, as symbolic dimensions of our being-in-the-world. For me, this is the referent of all literature; no longer the *Umwelt* of the ostensive references of dialogue, but the *Welt* projected by the non-ostensive references of every text that we have read, understood and loved. To understand a text is at the same time to light up our own situation, or, if you will, to interpolate among the predicates of our situation all the significations which make a *Welt* of our *Umwelt*. It is this enlarging of the *Umwelt* into the *Welt* which permits us to speak of the references opened up by the text – it would be better to say that the references *open up* the world. Here again the spirituality of discourse manifests itself through writing, which frees us from the visibility and limitation of situations by opening up a world for us, that is, new dimensions of our being-in-the-world.[18]

In this manner, Ricoeur's hermeneutic model renounces the structuralist hypostasis of language – the cult of the text as an end in itself. It remains faithful to the discovery of phenomenological ontology that the basic intention of the sign is to say something *about* something. And this, in the case of symbolic language, means to designate *possible modes of existence* which surpass the limits of any given, present situation. 'Language itself, as a signifying milieu', Ricoeur affirms, 'must be referred to existence.'[19]

But if language refers to a world, it also addresses an audience. It always says something about something *to someone*. At the same time as it instigates a new mode of reference, symbolic expression also instigates a new mode of communication. The meaning of a textual symbol is not therefore confined to its original creator but addresses an actual or potential audience that it makes possible. In short, it is an open-ended communication whose addressee is just whoever knows how to read or interpret it. In referring to possible worlds, the

---

[18] Ibid.

[19] Ricoeur, 'The Critique of Religion', 1973, in *The Philosophy of Paul Ricoeur: An Anthology of his Work,* pp. 213–23.

symbol remains open to an infinite horizon of possible interpretations. Indeed, it is precisely because there is no one true reading of a symbol or text that we find ourselves condemned to an unending conflict of interpretations.

Ricoeur assesses this condemnation in positive terms. Because my ontological self-understanding as a being-in-the-world can only be 'recovered by a detour of the decipherment of the documents of life' – that is, by means of a hermeneutic critique of the various 'signs' of existence – it always remains a *desire to be*, a project of interpretation that can never be completed in any total sense. Finding ourselves thus exposed to an inevitable plurality of interpretations, we learn that a philosophy of consciousness which holds to the hegemonic claims of the *cogito* is a philosophy of false consciousness. To reduce the *desire to be* to the immediacy of self-consciousness, removing it from the mediating detour of interpretation, is to hypostasize it. But the *desire to be* can never relinquish its role as a *being-interpreted*. Fully cognizant of the propensities of consciousness to contrive premature solutions, Ricoeur conjoins (1) the project of phenomenological hermeneutics and (2) the critique of 'false consciousness' advanced by the three Masters of Suspicion.

The three hermeneutic models of suspicion, as noted in our Introduction, were welcomed by Ricoeur as reminders that there exist levels of signification removed from the immediate grasp of consciousness. Freud dismantled the prejudices of the *ego cogitans* by disclosing how unconscious meanings can be organized and structured in a site beneath the jurisdiction of our sovereign consciousness. Nietzsche showed how our so-called timeless concepts of value and reason are in fact genealogically determined by the hidden strategies of the Will to Power. Finally, Marx's critique of ideology disclosed how the meanings of human existence were often conditioned by socio-historic forces of domination which surpass the ken of the self-possessed subject. Ricoeur holds that these Masters of Suspicion teach us that we can only hope to recover our ontological *desire to be* by first understanding ourselves as we exist outside of ourselves. All three recognize that meaning, far from being transparent to itself, is in fact an enigmatic process which conceals at the same time as it reveals. Thus Ricoeur can write that if 'we are to succeed in understanding together the theory of ideologies in Marx, the genealogies of ethics in Nietzsche, and the theory of ideas and illusions in Freud, we will see the configuration of a problem – hereafter posed before the modern mind – the problem of *false-consciousness*'.[20]

Ricoeur believes that the 'hermeneutics of suspicion' makes possible a new critique of culture. Admittedly, it remains a negative hermeneutics of 'demystification'. But precisely as such, it deals with falsehood and illusion not just in the subjective context of epistemological error, but as a dimension of our social discourse as a whole. Thus Marx conceived of false consciousness as a

[20] Ibid.

reflection of the class struggle; Nietzsche as the resentful vengeance of the weak against the strong; and Freud as a history of human desire repressed by cultural prohibition. All three were motivated by a common scruple of *hermeneutic doubt* which, observes Ricoeur, compelled them to demythologize the established cultural codes in order to decipher concealed strategies of domination, desire or will. And to the extent that it recognizes the duplicitous workings of meaning and strives to unmask the ploys of consciousness, this moment of doubt marks an essential contribution to the general project of hermeneutics:

> The problem of false-consciousness could only appear by way of a critique of culture where consciousness appears in itself as a doubtful consciousness. But ... this doubt can only work through a totally new technique which is a new method of deciphering appearances. This deciphering will enable us to grasp what we have to say about demystification: What distinguishes false-consciousness from error or falsehood, and what motivates a particular kind of critique, of denunciation, is the possibility of signifying another thing than what one believes was signified, that is, the possibility of the masked consciousness. Consciousness is not transparent to itself ... but a relation of conceal/reveal which calls for a specific reading, a *hermeneutics*. The task of hermeneutics has always been to read a text and to distinguish the true sense from the apparent sense, to search for the sense under the sense ... There is then, a proper manner of uncovering what was covered, of unveiling what was veiled, of removing the mask.[21]

Ricoeur contends, consequently, that hermeneutics cannot afford to dispense with this strategy of unmasking. It is only by smashing the idols of false consciousness that we can begin to allow the genuine symbols of our culture to speak. We cannot affirm the positive ontological content of our significations – that is, the projection of authentic possibilities of being – without demythologizing their false content. Nor can religion presume to obviate this hermeneutic discrimination. The atheistic critique championed by the Masters of Suspicion is an essential ingredient of the mature faith of modern man. We must incorporate the critique of religion as a mask of 'fear, domination or hate'. As Ricoeur concludes: 'A Marxist critique of ideology, a Nietzschean critique of resentment and a Freudian critique of infantile distress, are hereafter the views through which any kind of mediation of faith must pass.'[22]

Hermeneutics of Affirmation

Only when we have become aware of the discontinuities and estrangements of our cultural expressions, says Ricoeur, can we genuinely embark on a

---

[21] Ibid.
[22] Ricoeur, *The Conflict of Interpretations*.

hermeneutics of *affirmation*. But we now appreciate that a universal ontology of understanding is a project rather than a *fait accompli*. The proper ontology for hermeneutics is therefore an *implied* ontology. It is only in and through a conflict of rival hermeneutics that we perceive something of the Being to be interpreted. For the philosophical subject cannot begin to ask the question of the fundamental meaning of Being until it has been dispossessed of the illusion that it already possesses this meaning. And so to complement psychoanalysis, which reveals an *archaeology of the subject* where meaning emerges *before* or *behind* our subjective consciousness, Ricoeur endorses a 'philosophy of spirit' which reveals a *teleology of the subject* where the origin of meaning is also displaced, but this time *in front of consciousness*. In this manner, Ricoeur contrives to rehabilitate and conflate the respective models of Freud and Hegel within the hermeneutic project.

The archaeological and teleological arcs of hermeneutic enquiry both effect a decentring of the traditional concept of the subject. The former does so by favouring a return to the archaic meanings of the unconscious which precede it; the latter by anticipating new meanings which stretch out before it. Ricoeur argues that these two hermeneutic directions constitute human existence as a movement of interpretation beyond itself *qua* given, self-centring subject. They demonstrate how the human subject always understands its present significations in terms of 'other' signs implicit in the past and future horizons of what Ricoeur broadly calls *culture*.

> Philosophy remains hermeneutics that is, a reading of the hidden meaning inside the text of the apparent meaning. It is the task of hermeneutics to show that existence arrives at expression, at meaning, and at reflection only through the continual exegesis of all the significations that come to light in the world of culture. Existence becomes a self only by appropriating this meaning which first resides 'outside', in works, institutions and cultural monuments in which the life of the spirit is objectified.[23]

Finally, Ricoeur affirms that man's ontological *desire to be* – expressed in the archaeological recovery of lost meanings and in the teleological anticipation of proposed meanings – finds its ultimate articulation in an *eschatology of the sacred*. This third hermeneutic direction marks the most complete displacement of the Cartesian subject. The symbols of the sacred designate both the alpha of archaeology and the omega of teleology. They represent the irrecoverable origin *before* the beginning (*arche*) and the unrealizable goal *after* the end (*telos*). 'This alpha and this omega', observes Ricoeur, 'the subject would be unable to command. The sacred calls upon man and in this call manifests itself as that which commands his existence because it posits this

---

[23] Ibid.

existence absolutely, as effort and desire to be.'[24] In short, the sacred demands that consciousness divest itself of the illusion of self-sufficiency and acknowledge its ultimate dependence on a meaning that exists beyond the ego.

Precisely as something that cannot be possessed, repossessed or prepossessed, the eschatology of the sacred remains, for Ricoeur, the paramount example of the *risk* of interpretation. Contrary to the teaching of much traditional metaphysics, it does not sanction a triumphalist ontology which would break from the circle of interpretation. On the contrary, it at best solicits what Ricoeur refers to as a 'militant and truncated ontology' which consigns us ever more intensely to the internal warfare of conflicting interpretations. As such, Ricoeur's eschatology requires an absolute renunciation of the self-righteousness of certainty. Yet in spite of this renunciation, or rather because of it, the eschatology of the sacred expresses a genuine hope – hope in the ultimate possibility of a unified or reconciled discourse. In so doing, it complements critique with prophecy, suspicion with affirmation. In a rare moment of enthusiasm, Ricoeur ventures a discreet mention of a 'hermeneutics of God's coming, of the approach of his Kingdom ... representing the prophecy of consciousness'.[25] But as prophecy, the affirmation of the sacred can never be verified. We can only hope for something that is *not yet* given. The sacred, explains Ricoeur, is at most that 'promised land' of a fulfilled ontology which the interpreter, like Moses, can only glimpse before dying.[26] Because we are finite human beings, we remain within the historical limits of the hermeneutic circle. The philosophical claim to absolute knowledge is a false myth that must be perpetually demythologized. The hermeneutics of affirmation must then always be coupled with a hermeneutics of suspicion. 'It is because absolute knowledge is impossible', concludes Ricoeur, 'that the conflict of interpretations is insurmountable.'[27]

The Hermeneutic Model of the Text

Let us return, by way of concluding this first study of Ricoeur's work, to what is arguably his most original contribution to contemporary thought – his hermeneutic model of the text. Whereas Husserl approached meaning as an essence to be intuited (*Wesenschau*), Ricoeur approaches it as a text to be interpreted. He recognizes, moreover, that every text of meaning implies a historical context. The hermeneutic model shows how the multiple meaning of words (polysemy) derives not just from the world of the text itself but from a double historical reference *both* to the original conditions of inscription (the world of the author) *and* to the subsequent conditions of reception (the world of

---

[24] Ibid.

[25] Ibid.

[26] Ricoeur, 'Phenomenology and Hermeneutics', p. 101f.

[27] Ricoeur, 'Appropriation', 1981, in *Hermeneutics and the Human Sciences*, p. 182f.

the addressee). When Ricoeur keeps reminding us that *language always speaks to somebody about something,* he means that, at the most basic level, the workings of language are substantially determined by their particular 'dialectical' situation. 'It is with this selective function of context', affirms Ricoeur, 'that interpretation, in the most primitive sense of the word, is connected. Interpretation is the process by which, in the interplay of question and answer, the interlocutors collectively determine the contextual values which structure their conversation.'[28]

Consequently, interpretation can no longer be construed as the exclusive activity of the reflective philosopher. It is now recognized as the primordial condition of our being-in-the-world *qua* language-users. Ricoeur thus endorses the view of Heidegger and Gadamer that human existence (*Dasein*) is in and of itself language (*Sprachlichkeit*). We exist in language for we are always situated within the historical context of an intersubjective dialogue with others.

But this dialogue, Ricoeur explains, is not reducible to the immediacy of conversation. It is more than a *face-à-face* exchange between two interlocutors whose intentional meanings could be unambiguously limited to a direct 'ostensive' reference *vis-à-vis* an actual situation here and now. The hermeneutic model of dialogue extends beyond the 'direct reference' of two interlocutors immediately co-present one to the other in a commonly identifiable situation. In a broader sense, it embraces a historical horizon where meanings can outlive the 'here and now' of interpersonal conversation and endure over time, in the written texts, documents, monuments, institutions and traditions of a culture. And so this historical activity of language (*Geschichtesbewirkung*) involves an expropriation of the author's original meaning which, in turn, allows for a reappropriation of meaning by subsequent interpreters. This is what Ricoeur terms the detour through the 'long' intersubjective relation:

> Conversation . . . is contained within the limits of a *vis-à-vis* which is a *face-à-face*. The historical connection which encompasses it is singularly more complex. The 'short' intersubjective relation is intertwined, in the interior of the historical connection, with various 'long' intersubjective relations, mediated by diverse institutions, social roles and collectivities (groups, nations, cultural traditions, etc.). The long intersubjective relations are sustained by an historical tradition, of which dialogue is only a segment. Explication therefore extends much further than dialogue, coinciding with the broadest historical connections.[29]

Ricoeur likens the transmission of meaning in historical tradition (or 'sedimentation' as Merleau-Ponty termed it) to the mediating function of the text. The liberation of meaning from its original range of reference is analogous to the written text where meaning endures in the absence of the original author and addressee of spoken conversation. The meaning of the text is thus granted a

---

28 Ricoeur, 'Phenomenology and Hermeneutics', p. 101f.
29 Ibid.

significant autonomy with respect to (i) the author's original intention; (ii) the initial situation of discourse; and (iii) the original addressee. Hermeneutics approximates, in this manner, to the condition of textual exegesis where meaning enjoys a certain independence from an original first-order reference and opens up a 'second-order reference' *in front of the text.* It is this new order of reference carried by the 'autonomous' text which invites in turn a multiplicity of readings – that is, an open horizon of interpretations.

The historical transmission of meaning thus places us in a hermeneutic circle where each interpretation is both preceded by a semantic horizon inherited from tradition and yet exposed to multiple subsequent rereadings by other interpreters. Indeed it is precisely because all interpretation places the reader *in medias res* – in a dialectical circle of intersubjectivity rather than at a fixed beginning or end – that the idealist appeal to a presuppositionless foundation is doomed to failure. To interpret history is, Ricoeur submits, to arrive in the middle of a dialogue which has already begun and in which we try to orientate ourselves in order to make some new sense of it. (A similar point was humorously expressed by T. S. Eliot in relation to literary tradition when he remarked that while immature poets 'imitate', mature poets 'steal' – his argument being that no poet can lay claim to the absolute originality of a *creatio ex nihilo*.) Husserl's attempt to forego the hermeneutic circle in favour of an absolute intuition of self-consciousness is thus refuted by Ricoeur's model of the text. Idealist phenomenology, declares Ricoeur, 'can sustain its pretension to ultimate foundation only by adopting, in an intuitive rather than a speculative mode, the Hegelian claim to absolute knowledge. But the key hypothesis of hermeneutic philosophy is that interpretation is an open process which no single vision can conclude.'[30]

Accordingly, if Husserl's phenomenology was first advanced as a critique of the empirical sciences' claim to ultimate objectivity, Ricoeur's hermeneutics is advanced as a critique of Husserl's and Hegel's idealist claim to absolute subjectivity. Hermeneutics debunks the claims of the transcendental ego; it demonstrates that understanding always labours within the historical horizon of an intersubjective communication where we interpret meanings that have been 'distantiated' from subjective consciousness. For it is, paradoxically, in so far as we *belong* to a historical tradition that meaning is always at a *distance* from us in the immediate here and now. 'Distantiation' is the dialectical counterpart of 'belonging'. These two movements, as noted in our Introduction, represent the twin arches of the hermeneutic bridge. The text thus becomes, for Ricoeur, the model for a belonging to communication in and through distance. In interpretation we endeavour to reappropriate those meanings that have been disappropriated from understanding. We strive to recover that which has been removed.

---

[30] Ibid.

Ricoeur fully recognizes the rapport between the hermeneutic function of 'distantiation' and the controversial phenomenon of ideology understood as the 'alienation' of meaning from the human subject. But hermeneutics also provides the possibility of a critique of ideology in its project to restore a new form of self-understanding by means of the 'long' detour of interpretation. The 'self' thus retrieved from the ideological distantiation of 'false consciousness' is not, however, the self-identical *cogito* coveted by idealism. Here again the analogy of textual distantiation is rewarding. To read a text is to expose oneself to a horizon of 'other' or 'alien' meanings that exceed my subjective consciousness. The text requires the reader, just as much as the original author, to transcend his own subjective intentions. It opens us to a world of *possible* meanings, to new modes of being-in-the-world and of being-interpreted. This new world of being brought to language by the text is what Ricoeur calls the 'second-order reference' which removes us from the 'first-order reference' of the familiar world we inhabit here and now (that is, prior to our exposure to the hermeneutic circle of the text).

In contrast, then, to the idealist thesis of a self-positing subject, hermeneutics divests subjectivity of its presumption to be the origin of meaning. Instead it proposes subjectivity as a goal to be reached *after* the intersubjective detour of interpretation. In the process, of course, the very concept of subjectivity is radically altered. For, as Ricoeur never tires of reminding us, it is only by means of the distancing of the self from its original ego that the interpreter can hope to recover a new sense of subjectivity: enlarged, decentred and open to novel possibilities of self-interpretation. Once more, we find Ricoeur invoking the theory of the text as his guideline:

> It shows that the act of subjectivity is not so much what initiates understanding as what terminates it. This terminal act can be characterised as appropriation. [But] it does not purport ... to rejoin the original subjectivity which would support the meaning of the text. Rather it *responds* to the matter of the text, and hence to the proposals of meaning which the text unfolds. It is thus the counterpart of the distanciation which establishes the autonomy of the text with respect to its author, its situation and its original addressee. Thus appropriation can be integrated into the theory of interpretation without surreptitiously reintroducing the primacy of subjectivity.[31]

To take a concrete example, if I read Tolstoy's novel *Anna Karenina*, I expose myself to an alien consciousness, time and place (that is, the sensibility of the various characters of Russian society in the late nineteenth century described by the author). I am thus invited to extend my actual horizons of experience here and now by imaginatively reliving the world represented in Tolstoy's text. And in so doing, I am disappropriated from my given assumptions regarding

---

[31] Ibid.

my immediate world at the same time as I seek to reappropriate this 'other' world for my contemporary understanding. But in this dialectical movement between disappropriation and appropriation, what is ultimately revealed is a 'possible world' which results from the encounter between my world and Tolstoy's world – a new horizon of experience which is opened up by the *matter of the text itself* and which exceeds both Tolstoy's original consciousness as an author and my contemporary consciousness as a reader. In this dialectical encounter in and through the text, the meanings intended by both author and reader find themselves mutually transformed.

Ricoeur's notion of appropriation does not, it should now be clear, imply some triumphalist return of a sovereign subject to itself. If the goal of hermeneutics remains 'self-understanding', this must be reinterpreted in the altered sense of understanding oneself *in front of the text*. 'What the interpreter says is a re-saying which reactivates what is said by the text.'[32] And what is appropriated is the matter of the text – a new horizon of possible meanings opened up by the language of the text. But the matter of the text only becomes my own, insists Ricoeur, 'if I disappropriate myself, in order to let the matter of the text be. So I exchange the *me* (*moi*), *master* of itself, for the *self* (*soi*), *disciple* of the text.'[33] In this way, concludes Ricoeur, hermeneutics may serve as a double critique. It is a critique of egology as expressed in the illusion that the self can constitute itself as absolute origin. But it is equally a critique of ideology which rests on the obverse illusion that self-understanding has no role to play – particularly in a socio-historical or political context. The former results from the extreme of appropriation (total self-possession by the exclusion of the other), the latter from the extreme of disappropriation (the total alienation of my meaning by some anonymous other).

Ricoeur's critical hermeneutics bids us to surmount these twin illusions by reinstating a complementary dialectic of self and other.

---

32 Ricoeur, 'What is a Text?', p. 145f.
33 Ricoeur, 'Phenomenology and Hermeneutics', p. 101f.

Between Imagination and Language*

Are we not ready to recognise in the power of imagination, no longer the faculty of deriving 'images' from our sensory experience, but the capacity for letting new worlds shape our understanding of ourselves? This power would not be conveyed by images, but by the emergent meanings in our language. Imagination would thus be treated as a dimension of language.[1]

In this second study I will explore and evaluate the particular significance of Ricoeur's contribution to a philosophy of imagination. Before Ricoeur's hermeneutic approach, most phenomenological accounts of imagination concentrated on its role as vision, as a special or modified way of *seeing* the world. Imagination was thus defined in terms of its relation to perception, be it positive or negative, continuous or discontinuous. Husserl described the act of imagining as a 'neutralized' mode of seeing, Sartre as an 'unrealized' mode of quasi-seeing, and Merleau-Ponty as a dialectical counterpart of the visible.

This privileging of the visual model is no doubt related to the primary role granted to 'description' in the phenomenological method. With the hermeneutic turn in phenomenology, however, this privilege is significantly revised. As one moves from description to interpretation, from *Wesensschau* to *Verstehen*, the imagination is considered less in terms of 'vision' than in terms of 'language'. Or, to put it more exactly, imagination is assessed as an indispensable agent in the creation of meaning in and through language – what Paul Ricoeur calls 'semantic innovation'.

Ricoeur provides us with a cogent model of such a hermeneutics of imagination. While his early works – *Freedom and Nature* in particular – conformed to the descriptive conventions of eidetic phenomenology, the publication of *The Symbolism of Evil* in 1960 introduced a 'hermeneutic' model of analysis which opened up the possibility of a new appreciation of the linguistic functioning of imagination. This was to be the first of a number of works in which Ricoeur would explore the creative role of imagination in language – be it in the guise of symbols, myths, poems, narratives or ideologies. Our present study proposes to isolate some of the key steps in Ricoeur's hermeneutic exploration of imagination – an exploration which, it

---

* Earlier versions of this study appeared as 'Paul Ricoeur and the Hermeneutic Imagination', in D. Rasmussen and P. Kemp (eds), *The Narrative Path. Paul Ricoeur* (Cambridge, MA: MIT Press, 1989), and as 'The Hermeneutical Imagination', in our *Poetics of Imagining* (New York: Edinburgh University Press and Fordham University Press, 1998).

[1] P. Ricoeur, 'Metaphor and the Central Problem of Hermeneutics', in Paul Ricoeur, *Hermeneutics and the Human Sciences* (Cambridge: Cambridge University Press, 1981), p. 181.

should be noted at the outset, is less systematic than episodic in nature. Ricoeur's tentative and always provisional probing of a poetic hermeneutic of imagination represents, we believe, the ultimate, if discreet, agenda of his entire philosophical project. That, at least, is the hypothesis that guides our reading of his work below – our own hermeneutic wager regarding his hermeneutic wager.

The link between imagination and language had been hinted at by phenomenological thinkers before Ricoeur. Bachelard's suggestive remarks about a linguistic imagination in *The Poetics of Reverie* already pointed in this direction – while not actually delivering any consistent theory. But the most decisive anticipation of Ricoeur's hermeneutic reformulation of imagining was surely Martin Heidegger's analysis of Kant's concept of 'transcendental imagination' in *Kant and the Problem of Metaphysics* (1929) – a 'destructive' rereading of *The Critique of Pure Reason* from the point of view of an existential ontology. Heidegger's controversial reading opened the way for a hermeneutic re-examination of imagining, including ontological considerations of action, time and language.[2] But Heidegger himself did not develop these insights under the heading of a new hermeneutic of *imagining*. When he spoke of

---

[2] Martin Heidegger, *Kant and the Problem of Metaphysics* (1929), English trans. J. Churchill (Bloomington, IN: Indiana University Press, 1962), pp. 140, 149. Heidegger comes close to a hermeneutics of imagination in this work, as does H. G. Gadamer in *Truth and Method* (1960). However, both thinkers offer more of a commentary on the Kantian theory of transcendental imagination than a distinctively hermeneutic development of it as attempted by Ricoeur. I examine Heidegger's interpretation in *The Wake of Imagination* (London/Minneapolis: Hutchinson/University of Minnesota Press, 1988), pp. 189–95, 222–4. Other useful and more detailed readings of the Heideggerian interpretation of the Kantian imagination include W. J. Richardson's *Heidegger: From Phenomenology to Thought* (The Hague: Nijhoff, 1963), and Calvin O. Schrag, 'Heidegger and Cassirer on Kant', *Kantstudien*, vol. 58 (1967), pp. 87–100. See also Hannah Arendt's reading of the Kantian imagination in *Kant's Political Philosophy* (Chicago, IL: University of Chicago Press, 1982), pp. 79–89. Heidegger's analysis of imagination also posed disconcerting questions for the inherited metaphysical conceptions of Being. Referring to Kant's claim for a 'pure productive imagination', independent of experience, which first renders experience possible, Heidegger explains that Being must henceforth be understood as a temporal horizon of human existence (*Dasein*). 'The imagination', he writes, 'forms in advance and before all experience of the object, the aspect in the pure form (*Bild*) of time and precedes this or that particular experience of an object.' And he adds: 'As a faculty of intuition, imagination is formative in the sense that it produces a particular image. As a faculty not dependent on objects of intuition, it produces, that is forms and provides, images. This "formative power" is at one and the same time receptive and productive (spontaneous). In this "at one and the same" is to be found the true essence of the structure of imagination' (*Kant and the Problem of Metaphysics*, pp. 140f). Moreover, since for Heidegger receptivity is identified with sensibility and spontaneity with understanding, imagination can now be ultimately understood as the source of all human knowledge – or, as Kant put it, the 'common root' of the two stems of sensible and intelligible experience. But the subversive implications of this discovery were, Heidegger argues, to prove intolerable for Kant – who revised his initial claims in the second edition of *The Critique of Pure Reason* – and for subsequent metaphysicians who stubbornly clung to the traditional divide of knowledge into sensation (the empirical–corporeal–aesthetic) and understanding (the analytic–logical–conceptual).

imagination he did so exclusively in the Kantian context. And the fact that its functions were subsumed, in Heidegger's other works, into the more generic and 'fundamental' term *Dasein* means effectively that a hermeneutics of imagining was ultimately abandoned in favour of a hermeneutics of existence in general. Though the parallels remain highly instructive, we would have to await the later works of Paul Ricoeur for a properly hermeneutical treatment of imagination. What is indisputable is that Heidegger's rereading of the Kantian concept of imagination blazed the trail for the subsequent hermeneutic acknowledgement of imagination as a pathway leading to, rather than away from, the truth of being.

The fact, however, that the term 'hermeneutic' did not feature in the post-Heideggerian phenomenologies of imagination up to Ricoeur did not prevent the analyses of imagining proposed by Sartre, Merleau-Ponty and Bachelard from registering the influence of Heidegger's radical ontological concerns.[3] Ricoeur was the first phenomenologist after Heidegger actually to espouse a hermeneutic rereading of imagination.[4] It is our view that Ricoeur's hermeneutic discussion of the imaginative function – ranging from *La Symbolique du mal* (1960) and *La Métaphore vive* (1975) to *Temps et récit* (3 vols, 1983–5), *Ideology and Utopia* (1986) and *Du texte à l'action* (1986) – represents the most powerful reorientation of a phenomenology of imagining towards a hermeneutics of imagining.

---

[3] See the chapter on Sartre, Merleau-Ponty and Bachelard in our *Poetics of Imagining* (1998).

[4] Gadamer, though much preoccupied with problems of art, creativity and aesthetics, has not yet, to my knowledge, addressed the concept of imagination directly or comprehensively; it is, for example, only mentioned in two brief passages of his *magnum opus*, *Truth and Method* (1960), and these both refer to Kant's treatment of this term. This may have been due to a strategic resolve on Gadamer's part to avoid identification with the German Idealist and Romantic movements – characterized by the extravagant claims made for the 'productive imagination' by thinkers such as Schelling, Fichte and Jacobi. Or it could have been prompted by a fidelity to his two main philosophical mentors – Hegel and Heidegger – both of whom sublated the formative (*bildende*) and projective (*entwerfende*) powers of imagining into more inclusive concepts such as *Geist* or *Dasein*. There is, however, one tantalizing passage in Gadamer's essay, 'The universality of the hermeneutial problem' (1966) where the author touches on the central role of imagination in hermeneutic enquiry:

It is imagination (*Phantasie*) that is the decisive function of the scholar. Imagination naturally has a hermeneutitical function and serves the sense for what is questionable. It serves the ability to expose real, productive questions, something in which, generally speaking, only he *who* masters all the methods of his science succeeds. (*Philosophical Hermeneutics*, Berkeley, CA: University of California Press, 1976, p. 12).

Unfortunately, Gadamer does not develop this insight, though there are some additional hints in his essay 'Intuition and vividness', in *The Relevance of the Beautiful* (Cambridge: Cambridge University Press, 1986), pp. 157–69.

The Linguistic Imagination

In so far as hermeneutics is concerned with multiple levels of meaning, it is evident that images can no longer be adequately understood in terms of their immediate *appearance* to consciousness. Replacing the visual model of the image with the verbal, Ricoeur affirms the more *poetical* role of imagining: its ability to say one thing in terms of another, or to say several things at the same time, thereby creating something *new*. The crucial role played by imagination in this process of 'semantic innovation' was to become one of the abiding concerns of Ricoeur's later philosophy.

The problem of semantic innovation remained unresolved for Sartre who argued in *L'Imaginaire* that imagination was condemned to an 'essential poverty'. The imaginary could not teach us anything new since it was held to be a 'nothingness' projected by consciousness. The cognitive content of an image presupposed our prior contact with the perceptual world (from which all our knowledge arises). The imaginary world, for Sartre, was considered a *negation* of the perceptual world. Ricoeur would retort to Sartre that imagining is a simultaneous juxtaposing of two different worlds – real and unreal – which produces new meaning.

Before proceeding to a more detailed account of Ricoeur's original contribution to the philosophy of imagination, it may be useful first to cite his critical summary of the available theories of images. In an essay entitled 'L'imagination dans le discours et dans l'action' in *Du texte à l'action*, Ricoeur refers to the problematic and often confused nature of modern philosophies of the image. He argues that the radical equivocity at the very heart of the imaginative activity has led to a series of rival, and often mutually exclusive, accounts. These accounts are located by Ricoeur in terms of two opposite axes. On the one hand, they explain the process of imagining in terms of the *object*, a typical example of this being Hume's empiricist account of the image as a faded trace of perception (a weakened impression preserved and represented in memory). Towards this pole of explanation gravitate the theories of the *reproductive* imagination. On the other hand, we find theories which explain our imaginative activity in terms of the *subject*, that is, in terms of a human consciousness that is fascinated or freed by its own images. An example of this latter theory would be the German Idealist and Romantic accounts of the *productive* imagination from Kant and Schelling to the existentialist descriptions of Sartre in *L'Imaginaire*. But this basic distinction between the reproductive and productive roles of imagination does not resolve the aporetic nature of our inherited understanding of imagining. Ricoeur extends the problematic horizons of this debate as follows:

> The productive imagination, and even the reproductive to the extent that it comprises the minimal initiative concerning the evocation of something

absent, operates … according to whether the subject of imagination is capable or not of assuming a critical consciousness of the difference between the real and the imaginary. The theories of the image here divide up along an axis which is no longer noematic but noetic, and whose variations are regulated by degrees of belief. At one end of the axis, that of a non-critical consciousness, the image is confused with the real, mistaken for the real. This is the power of the error denounced by Pascal; and it is also, *mutatis mutandis*, the *imaginatio* of Spinoza, contaminated by belief for as long as a contrary belief has not dislodged it from its primary position. At the other end of the axis, where the critical distance is fully conscious of itself, imagination is the very instrument of the critique of reality. The transcendental reduction of Husserl, as a neutralization of existence, is the most complete instance of this. The variations of meaning along this second axis are no less ample than the above. What after all could be in common between the state of *confusion* which characterizes that consciousness which unknown to itself takes for real what for another consciousness is not real, and the *act of distinction* which, highly self-conscious, enables consciousness to posit something at a distance from the real and thus produce the alterity at the very heart of existence? Such is the knot of aporias which is revealed by an overview of the ruins which today constitute the theory of imagination. Do these aporias themselves betray a fault in the philosophy of imagination or the structural feature of imagination itself which it would be the task of philosophy to take account of?[5]

Ricoeur appears to answer yes to both parts of the question. The 'fault' of most philosophies of imagination, in other words, has been their failure to develop a properly hermeneutic account of imagining in terms of its most basic structural feature of semantic innovation.

The adoption of hermeneutics – as the 'art of deciphering indirect meanings' – acknowledges the innovative power of imagination. This power, to transform given meanings into new ones, enables one to construe the future as the possible theatre of one's liberty, as a horizon of hope. The implications of this approach are crucial. The age-old antagonism between will and necessity (or, in Sartre's terms, between *l'imaginaire* and *le réel*) is now seen to be surmountable. 'We have thought too much', observes Ricoeur, 'in terms of a will which submits and not enough in terms of an imagination which opens up.'[6]

Ricoeur's preference for a semantic model of imagination over a visual one makes possible a new appreciation of this properly creative role of imagination. If images are *spoken* before they are *seen*, as Ricoeur maintains, they can no longer be construed as quasi-material residues of perception (as empiricism believed), nor indeed as neutralizations or negations of perception (as eidetic

---

[5] Paul Ricoeur, 'L'imagination dans le discours et dans l'action', in *Du texte à l'action* (Paris: Éditions du Seuil, 1986), pp. 215–16.

[6] Ricoeur, 'Herméneutique de l'idée de Révélation', in *La Révélation* (Brussels: Facultés Universitaires Saint-Louis, 1977), p. 54.

phenomenology tended to believe). Ricoeur's privileging of the semantic functioning of images illustrates his conviction that the productive power of imagination is primarily verbal. The example of a verbal metaphor in poetry epitomizes the way in which imagination conjoins two semantic fields, making what is predicatively impertinent at a literal level into something predicatively pertinent at a new (poetic) level. Or, to use Ricoeur's graphic phrase: 'Imagination comes into play in that moment when a new meaning emerges from out of the ruins of the literal interpretation.'[7]

Taking up Aristotle's definition of a good metaphor in the *Poetics* (1495x: 4–8) as the apprehension of *similarity*, Ricoeur points out that what is meant here is not similarity between already similar ideas (for such a role would be redundant) but similarity between semantic fields hitherto considered *dissimilar*. It is the 'semantic shock' engendered by the coming together of two different meanings which produces a *new* meaning. And imagination, Ricoeur claims, is precisely this power of metaphorically reconciling opposing meanings, forging an unprecedented semantic pertinence from an old impertinence. So that if one wants to say with Wittgenstein, for example, that imagining is a 'seeing-as' (seeing one thing in terms of another), this is only the case in so far as the linguistic power of conjoining different semantic fields is already at work – at least implicitly.

This is a decisive point. Ricoeur claims that what matters in imagination is less the *content* than the *function* of images. This specific function is understood here in terms of both an intentional projection of possible meanings (the hermeneutic model) and a schematizing synthesis of the many under the guise of the same (the Kantian model). It is this twin function of projection and schematism which accounts for imagination as 'the operation of grasping the similar in a predicative assimilation responding to a semantic clash between dissimilar meanings'.[8] Ricoeur thus links the productive power of language and that of imagination. For new meanings to come into being they need to be spoken or uttered in the form of new verbal images. And this requires that the phenomenological account of imagining as *appearance* be supplemented by its hermeneutic account as *meaning*.

Imagination can be recognized accordingly as the act of responding to a demand for new meaning, the demand of emerging realities to *be* by *being said* in new ways. And it is for this reason that Ricoeur frequently invokes Bachelard's famous phrase that 'a poetic image, by its novelty, sets in motion the entire linguistic mechanism. The poetic image places us at the origin of the speaking being.'[9]

---

[7] Ricoeur, 'L'imagination dans le discours et dans l'action', pp. 213–19.

[8] Ibid.

[9] G. Bachelard, *Poetics of Space*, trans. Maria Jolas (Boston, MA: Beacon Press, 1964), p. xlx. Cited by Ricoeur in *The Rule of Metaphor*, trans. R. Czemy (Toronto: University of Toronto Press, 1977), pp. 214–15.

A poetic imagination is one that creates meaning by responding to the desire of being to be expressed. It is a Janus facing in two directions at once – back to the being that is revealed and forward to the language that is revealing. And at the level of language itself it also does double duty, for it produces a text which opens up new horizons of meaning for the reader. The poetic imagination liberates the reader into a free space of possibility, suspending the reference to the immediate world of perception (both the author's and the reader's) and thereby disclosing new ways of being in the world.[10] The function of semantic innovation – which is most proper to imagination – is therefore, in its most fundamental sense, an *ontological* event. The innovative power of linguistic imagination is not some 'decorative excess or effusion of subjectivity, but the capacity of language to open up new worlds'.[11] The function of imagination in poetry or myth, for example, is defined accordingly as the 'disclosure of unprecedented worlds, an opening onto possible worlds which transcend the limits of our actual world'.[12]

To account for this phenomenon of ontological novelty, Ricoeur's hermeneutics of imagination looks beyond the first-order reference of empirical reality which ordinary language discourse normally entails to a second-order reference of possible worlds. A hermeneutic approach to imagination thus differs from a structuralist or existentialist one in its concentration on 'the capacity of world-disclosure yielded by texts'. In short, hermeneutics is not confined to the *objective* structural analysis of texts, nor to the *subjective* existential analysis of the authors of texts; its primary concern is with the *worlds* which these authors and texts open up.[13]

An understanding of the possible worlds uncovered by the poetic imagination also permits a new understanding of ourselves as beings-in-the-world. But, for Ricoeur, the hermeneutic circle precludes any short cut to immediate self-understanding. The human subject can only come to know itself through the hermeneutic detour of interpreting signs – that is, by deciphering the meanings contained in myths, symbols and dreams produced by the human imagination. The shortest route from the self to itself is through the images of others.

The hermeneutic imagination is not confined, however, to circles of *interpretation*. By projecting new worlds it also provides us with projects of *action*. In fact the traditional opposition between *theoria* and *praxis* dissolves to the extent that 'imagination has a projective function which pertains to the

---

[10] Paul Ricoeur, 'Myth as the bearer of possible worlds', see 'Dialogue I' below and our *Debates*, (New York: Fordham, 2004). See also my 'Note on the hermeneutics of dialogue', in the same volume, pp. 127–33; and Paul Ricoeur's 'The hermeneutical function of distanciation', in *Hermeneutics and the Human Sciences*, p. 139f.

[11] Ricoeur, 'Myth as the bearer of possible worlds', p. 44.

[12] Ibid., p. 45.

[13] Ibid.

very dynamism of action.[14] The metaphors, symbols or narratives produced by imagination all provide us with 'imaginative variations' of the world, thereby offering us the freedom to conceive of the world in other ways and to undertake forms of action which might lead to its transformation. Semantic innovation can thus point towards social transformation. The possible worlds of imagination can be made real by action. This is surely what Ricoeur has in mind when he says that there can be 'no action without imagination'. We shall return to this crucial aspect of Ricoeur's argument in our discussion of the 'social imagination' below.

The Symbolic Imagination

Having outlined the key features of Ricoeur's hermeneutic account of imagination, we now take a more systematic approach by examining three categories which broadly correspond to consecutive phases in the later philosophy of Paul Ricoeur: (1) the symbolic imagination; (2) the oneiric imagination; (3) the poetic imagination.

The publication of *The Symbolism of Evil* marked Ricoeur's transition from a phenomenology of will to a hermeneutics of symbol. It signalled a departure from descriptive phenomenology, as a reflection on intentional modes of consciousness, towards the hermeneutic conviction that meaning is never simply the intuitive possession of a subject but is always mediated through signs and symbols of our intersubjective existence. Henceforth an under-standing of consciousness would involve an interpretation of culture and society.

In *The Symbolism of Evil* Ricoeur shows that a rigorous interpretation of the founding myths of Western culture (for example, Adam, Prometheus, Oedipus) enables us to disclose the symbolic relation of the human subject to meaning. Suspending the conventional definition of myth as a 'false *explanation* by means of fables', Ricoeur attempts to recover myth's genuinely *exploratory* function. Once we accept that myth cannot provide us with a scientific account of the way things really are, we can begin properly to appreciate its creative role as a *symbolizing* power. As already noted, Ricoeur defines a symbol as a double intentionality, wherein one meaning is transgressed or transcended by another. As such, it is a work of imagination which enables being to emerge as language (signification) and, by extension, as thought (interpretation). There are three principal categories of symbol examined by Ricoeur in *The Symbolism of Evil*: *cosmic*, *oneiric* and *poetic*.

---

[14] Ricoeur, 'L'imagination dans le discours et dans l'action'. See also Theoneste Nkeramihigo's discussion of Ricoeur's theory of imagination in *L'Homme et la transcendance selon Paul Ricoeur* (Paris: Le Sycamore, 1984), pp. 241–4.

Cosmic symbols refer to a human's primary act of reading the sacred *on* the world. Here the human imagination interprets aspects of the world – the heavens, the sun, the moon, the waters – as signs of some ultimate meaning. At this most basic level, the symbol is both a thing and a sign: it embodies and signifies the sacred at one and the same time.[15] Or, to put it another way, when dealing with cosmic symbols the imagination reads the things of the world as signs, and signs as things of the world. As such, the symbolic imagination is already, at least implicitly, *linguistic.* Ricoeur makes this clear in the following passage from *Freud and Philosophy*:

> These symbols are not inscribed *beside* language, as modes of immediate expression, directly perceptible visages; it is in the universe of discourse that these realities take on a symbolic dimension. Even when it is the elements of the world that carry the symbol – earth, sky, water, life – it is the word (of consecration, invocation or mythic narrative) which says their cosmic expressivity thanks to the double meaning of the *words* earth, sky, water, life' [that is, their obvious literal meaning as reference to things *and* their ulterior meaning, for example, water as a symbol of renewed spiritual life].

Ricoeur can thus affirm that the 'expressivity of the world comes to language through the symbol as double meaning'.[16] For a cosmic symbol – like any other kind – occurs whenever 'language produces composite signs where the meaning, not ' content to designate something directly, points to another meaning which can only be reached (indirectly) by means of this designation'.[17] Illustrating this linguistic property of symbols, Ricoeur comments on the phrase from the Psalms, 'The skies tell of the glory of God', as follows: 'The skies don't speak themselves; rather, they are spoken by the prophet, by the hymn, by the liturgy. One always needs the word to assume the world into a manifestation of the sacred (hierophany).'[18]

In the second category of symbols – the *oneiric* or dream image – we witness a shift from the cosmic to the psychic function of imagination. Here Ricoeur talks of complementing a phenomenology of religious symbols (*à la* Eliade) with a psychoanalysis of unconscious symbols. To this end, he invokes the works of Freud and Jung, who investigated links between the symbols of the individual unconscious and symbols as 'common representations of the culture or folklore

---

[15] Ricoeur, *The Symbolism of Evil* (Boston, MA: Beacon Press, 1969), p. 1011.

[16] Ricoeur, *De l'Interprétation: essai sur Freud* (Paris: Éditions du Seuil, 1965), pp. 23–4; English trans. *Freud and Philosophy: An Essay on Interpretation* (New Haven, CT: Yale University Press, 1970).

[17] Ibid., p. 24.

[18] Ibid., p. 25. At this point, Ricoeur cites the view of the structural anthropologist Dumézil that it is under the sign of the *logos* and not under that of *mana* that research in the history of religions takes its stand today (preface to M. Elude, *Traité d'histoire des religions*).

of humanity as a whole'.[19] Ricoeur spells out the rapport between cosmic and oneiric symbols as follows: 'To manifest the "sacred" *on* the "cosmos" and to manifest it *in* the "psyche" are the same thing ... Cosmos and psyche are two poles of the same "expressivity": I express myself in expressing the world.'[20] It is precisely this expressive function of the psychic or oneiric image which establishes its intimate relation to language. As Ricoeur remarks, dream images must be 'originally close to words since they can be told, communicated'.[21]

The third modality of symbols – the *poetic* imagination – completes the double 'expressivity' of cosmos and psyche. It is here that the creative powers of imagination are most evident and receive explicit acknowledgement from Ricoeur. In fact it is only in this third category that Ricoeur (at least in *The Symbolism of Evil*) uses the term 'imagination' in any systematic sense. It is the poetical perspective, he argues, which enables us to draw back from both the religious images of cosmology and the dream images of psychoanalysis, disclosing the symbolic function of the image in its nascent state. In poetry, Ricoeur maintains, the symbol reveals the welling up of language – 'language in a state of emergence' – instead of regarding it in its hieratic stability under the protection of rites and myths as in the history of religion, or instead of deciphering it through the resurgences of a suppressed infancy.[22] In this sense, the poetical is the epitome of the symbolic imagination.

Ricoeur insists, however, that these three levels of symbolism are not unconnected. The structure of poetic imagination is also that of the dream as it draws from fragments of our past and future; and it is also at bottom that of hierophanies which disclose the heavens and the earth as images of the sacred. In all three instances what is at issue is not the image-as-representation but the image-as-sign. Ricoeur returns to this crucial distinction again and again. In *The Symbolism of Evil* he does so in terms of a differentiation between the static image as 'portrait' and the dynamic image as 'expression'. In *Freud and Philosophy* he uses the opposition *image-representation* and *image-verb*. But, whatever the particular formulation, what Ricoeur is concerned with is a critique of the representational model of the image as mere negation or modification of perceptual reality. This critique is levelled most explicitly at Sartre. The following passage from the introduction to *The Symbolism of Evil* makes this clear:

> It is necessary firmly to distinguish imagination from image, if by image is understood a function of absence, the annulment of the real in an imaginary unreal. This image-representation, conceived on the model of a portrait of the absent, is still too dependent on the thing that it makes unreal; it remains a process for *making present* to oneself the things of the world. A poetic image is much closer to a word than to a portrait.[23]

---

[19] Ricoeur, *Symbolism of Evil*, p. 12.
[20] Ibid., pp. 12–13.
[21] Ibid., p. 13.
[22] Ibid., p. 14.

To be fair to Sartre, however, one would have to recall that while most of his examples of the 'unrealizing' function of imaging are drawn from visual representation (picturing Peter in Berlin, the portrait of King Charles, and so on), he is at pains to establish the image as a dynamic act of consciousness rather than a quasi-perceptual thing in consciousness. But, that said, it is true that Sartre, like Husserl before him, fails adequately to grasp the fact that signification and imagination are not two opposed modes of intentionality but are inextricably related through their common belonging to language. It is for this reason that Ricoeur clearly prefers the position of Bachelard, which he approvingly cites: 'The poetic image becomes a new being of our language, it expresses us in making us that which it expresses'.[24]

The Symbolism of Evil concentrates, as noted, on the first category of symbol – the cosmic. This initial phase of the hermeneutic project is described by Ricoeur as a 're-enactment in sympathetic imagination' of the foundational myths where Western man sought to communicate his first experiences of the cosmos. Myths are understood as symbolic stories – or, to be more precise, as 'species of symbols developed in the form of narration and articulated in a time and a space that cannot be co-ordinated with the time and space of history and geography'.[25] This hermeneutic act of sympathetically re-imagining the cosmic images of our foundational myths demands that Ricoeur abandon the original phenomeno-

---

[23] Ibid., p. 13.

[24] Ibid.

[25] Ricoeur, *De l'Interprétation*, p. 25. But to say that a symbol is always a sign – or a mode of linguistic signification – is not to say that every sign is a symbol. The sign always stands for something (idea, meaning, object, person); but a symbol contains a double intentionality – it can aim at two or more meanings at the same time. This is evident in the ability of poetic language (to take the paramount example) to have at least 'two thinks at a time', as Joyce once remarked. Symbolic images have a literal meaning and a secondary analogical meaning. Thus, to take Ricoeur's example from *Symbolism of Evil*, the biblical image of somebody being 'defiled' refers both to the *literal* function of this image as a sign of physical uncleanliness and to its *symbolic* allusion to man's impure or deviant relationship to the sacred. The literal meaning of a stain points beyond itself to the existential condition of sinfulness, which is *like* a stain. As Ricoeur puts it, 'Contrary to the perfectly transparent technical signs, which say only what they want to say in positing that which they signify, symbolic signs are opaque, because the first, literal, obvious meaning itself points analogically to a second meaning which is not given otherwise than in it' (p. 15). It is because there is no *direct* discourse for the confession of evil that symbolism becomes the privileged means of expression. In other words, the experience of evil is always conveyed by means of expressions (for example, stain, rebellion, straying from the path, bondage and so on) borrowed from the field of everyday physical existence which refer *indirectly* to another kind of experience – our experience of the sacred. Ricoeur concludes accordingly that symbolic images are 'donative' in that a primary meaning gives rise to a secondary one which surpasses the first in its semantic range and reference. Further clarifying what he means by symbol, Ricoeur contrasts it to allegory. While an allegory relates one meaning directly to another, without residue or ambiguity a symbol works by enigmatic suggestion or evocation – it designates a surplus of meaning which exceeds the obvious one. Allegories have one meaning, symbols two or more.

logical dream of a 'philosophy without presuppositions'. Indeed, it presupposes that which descriptive phenomenology often tended to ignore – language. The hermeneutics of symbols must begin from a full language, that is, from the recognition that before reflection and intuition *there are already symbols* 'It is by beginning with a symbolism already there', as Ricoeur observes, 'that we give ourselves something to think about'.[26] This hermeneutic task of recovering language in its symbolic fullness is, for Ricoeur, a singularly modern one. For it is precisely because language has become so formalized, transparent and technical in the contemporary era that the need is all the greater to rediscover language's inventive powers of symbolization. This is not a matter of nostalgia for a lost Atlantis. It is a task animated by the 'hope for a recreation of language'.[27] And it also involves a critical project. For it is only by demythologizing the abuses of myth (as a false explanation of reality) that we can remythologize our contemporary language – restore to it the poetic and symbolic powers of imagination. 'The dissolution of the myth as (false) explanation is the necessary way to restoration of the myth as symbolism,' writes Ricoeur. 'If demythologization is the possible gain of modern attention to objective truth, this should not prevent the positive hermeneutic task of reunifying the various fields of meaning by renewing 'contact with the fundamental symbols of consciousness.'[28] In short, we need to combine the critical gesture of modernity with the symbolizing gesture of myth if we are to develop an adequate hermeneutic of human imagination. Instead of adopting the reductive approach of an 'allegorical' reading – which would seek to uncover a disguised message beneath the image-symbols of myth – Ricoeur advances a hermeneutic imagination which would, on the contrary, 'start from the symbols and endeavor to promote the meaning, to form it, by means of creative interpretation'.[29] This is, I suspect, what Ricoeur has in mind when he suggests that it is by 'interpreting that we can hear again'. The essential point to retain from Ricoeur's hermeneutic analysis of the three kinds of symbol – cosmic, oneiric and poetic – is that they all find expression in a *linguistic* imagination. For 'it is always in language that the cosmos, that desire, and that the imaginary, come into words'.[30]

The Oneiric Imagination

Whereas Ricoeur concerned himself in *The Symbolism of Evil* with one particular field of symbols – those related primarily to mythic accounts of evil

---

[26] Ricoeur, *Symbolism of Evil*, p. 18.

[27] Ibid., p. 19.

[28] Ibid., p. 249. 'There is no pure philosophy without presuppositions,' Ricoeur argues. 'A hermeneutic meditation on symbols starts from speech that has already taken place … its first task is from the midst of speech to remember; to remember with a view to beginning' (pp. 348–9).

[29] Ibid, p. 351.

[30] Ibid.

– in *Freud and Philosophy* he enlarges the enquiry to analyse the 'epistemology of the symbol' as it manifests itself in the desires of the unconscious.[31] The dream image shows, in exemplary fashion, how we can say things other than what we are ostensibly saying; how behind direct meanings there are indirect ones. Because of this double intentionality, symbols are what make 'poets of every dreamer'.[32]

The poet is the dreamer writ large. And what is important here is the suggestion that symbols are essentially 'image-words' which traverse 'image-representations'. Imagination is not simply a 'power of images' to represent absent objects. The visual images of dreams are sensory vehicles for verbal images which transcend them and designate other meanings than the literal ones. Thus psychoanalysis recognizes that dream images call forth narrative interpretation. It is precisely because dreams – like myths and poems – operate according to a depth language of layered meanings that they can be recounted and deciphered. Dreams want to *tell* themselves. They give rise to speech, to narration, to thought. The dreamer feels closed off in a private world until the dream is recounted. And this power of recounting is exemplified, for Ricoeur,

---

[31] Ricoeur, *De l'Interprétation*, p. 23. Ricoeur tightens his definition of the symbolic image by distinguishing it from two competing models, one too expansive, the other too restrictive. The restrictive definition – which Ricoeur equates with the Platonic and Neoplatonic model of formal analogy – reduces the symbol to a one-to-one correspondence between preexisting meanings. This relation of proportional correspondence between meanings can be assessed from *without* at a purely intellectual level. It thus ignores the inner creative power of symbolism to generate a surplus of meaning within itself – a semantic surplus which calls for interpretation in order to make sense of the new meaning, a second meaning which emerges from the first (ibid., pp. 26–7). The expansive definition, by contrast, equates the symbolic function with the function of mediation in general – that is, with the function of human consciousness to construct a universe of meaning ranging from perception to language. This expansive model was given common currency by Ernst Cassirer, whose three-volume *The Philosophy of Symbolic Forms* was published in the 1950s. According to this model, the symbolic (*das Symbolische*) designates the basic precondition of all modes of giving meaning to reality. For Cassirer the symbolic refers to the universal activity of 'mediating' between consciousness and reality, an activity which operates in art, religion, science, language, and so on. Ricoeur's objection to this expansive definition is that in including all mediating and objectifying functions under the title of 'symbolism' the concept of symbol becomes so amplified as to refer both to real and imaginary worlds, that is, to virtually *everything*. Thus Cassirer appears to dissolve the distinction – so fundamental to hermeneutics – between univocal and multivocal expressions. Ricoeur insists, on the contrary, on a strict hermeneutic division between different fields of meaning – the field of signification in general (which Cassirer equates with the symbolic) and the more specific field of double or multiple meanings – where a literal meaning calls forth other meanings. It is only this latter field which, Ricoeur argues, deserves the designation 'symbolic' proper to hermeneutics. In short, the symbolic image is one which says something more than what it appears to say. It opens up an indirect or oblique meaning on the basis of a direct one – thus provoking the hermeneutic activity of *interpretation*. Hermeneutics is devoted to the specific investigation of symbolic images which contain 'the relation of one level of meaning to another' (ibid., p. 22).

[32] Ibid., p. 24.

in the poetic imagination which exposes the 'birth of the word such as it was buried within the enigmas of . . . the psyche'.[33]

But, if poetry represents the positive pole of dreams, dissimulation represents its negative pole. The basic hermeneutic lesson to be gleaned from dreams, according to Ricoeur, is that images can serve to mask as well as to disclose meanings. The work of dream images provides ample evidence of the fact that the symbolic levels of sense are far more complex and oblique than the traditional models of analogy and allegory would allow. Along with Marx and Nietzsche, Freud was to champion a modem hermeneutics of suspicion alert to the distorting and falsifying potential of images. Psychoanalysis was considered accordingly as a means of detecting the censoring function of dream images – the primary function of this method being to 'disclose the variety of elaborate procedures which interpose between apparent and latent meanings'.[34]

Psychoanalysis calls for the hermeneutic function of critical interpretation by showing how images are not innocent, how they conceal as well as reveal meaning, how they deform as well as disclose intentions. It is the double texture of dream images – the internal transgression of one meaning by another – that invites our critical interpretation. Or, as Ricoeur puts it, 'every *mythos* carries a latent logos which demands to be exposed – where someone dreams . . . another rises up to interpret'.[35]

But, if psychoanalysis promotes a hermeneutics of suspicion, it also points towards a hermeneutics of affirmation. While the former examines how images disguise meanings drawn from our private or collective past, by means of an 'archaeological' reference back to an experience which precedes them, the latter shows how dream images can open up new dimensions of meaning by virtue of a 'teleological' reference to new worlds of possibility. Because desire is the basic motivation of all such dream images, as Freud argued, these images are ways of *saying* this desire. And they do this either by dissimulating it in other guises or by expressing a passion for possibilities not yet realized.

As far as this second option is concerned, the desire of dream images invents a future and thus aspires to a condition of creation, *poiesis*, poetry. It generates a surplus of meaning (*surcroît du sens*) – proof of a level of meaning which is irreducible to a retrospective correspondence between the image of one's

---

[33] Ibid., p. 28.

[34] Ibid., p. 26.

[35] Ibid., p. 24. Ricoeur remarks here on the suggestiveness of the Greek term *enigma* – 'The enigma does not block [hermeneutic] intelligence but provokes it: there is something to unfold, or unwrap in the symbol' (ibid., p. 26). It is precisely the double meaning, the intentionality of a second sense in and through a primary sense, which solicits critical interpretation. It is because dream images involve an internal transgression of one meaning by another that Ricoeur concludes that hermeneutic interpretation belongs organically to the hermeneutic process.

dream and a literal event of one's past experience.[36] Or, as Bachelard put it, 'you cannot explain the flower by the fertilizer'. It is this productive power of images – which Freud recognized in the *eros* of dreams -which ensures that any adequate hermeneutic of imagination must extend beyond an 'archaeology of the unconscious' to include both a 'teleology of desire' and an 'eschatology of the sacred'.

In *The Conflict of Interpretations*, Ricoeur elaborates on this dual function of the hermeneutic imagination – as *recollection* and *projection*.

> We may fully comprehend the hermeneutic problem [he writes] if we are able to grasp the double dependence of the self on the [symbolic images of the] *unconscious* and the *sacred* – since this dependence is only made manifest through the modality of symbolism. In order to illustrate this double dependency, reflection must humble consciousness and interpret it through symbolic significations, rising up from *behind* or in *front* of consciousness, *beneath* or *beyond* it. In short, reflection must include an archaeology and an eschatology.[37]

Ricoeur argues, moreover, that prophecy always needs demystification. By unmasking the falsifying function of certain dream images, with the help of a psychoanalytic model of 'suspicion', we may find ourselves in a better position to restore aspects of these images as 'signs of the sacred'. Without the hermeneutic detour of suspicion we would not be able to discriminate between those images which are merely a 'return of the repressed' (in Freud's phrase) and those which serve as symbols of an eschatological horizon of possibility.

But it is rarely a simple matter of discriminating between regressive and progressive images. Every utopian image contains an archaic element and vice versa. Images of the mythic past are often used to allude prophetically to an *eschaton* still to come; and the eschatology of imagination is always a creative repetition of its archaeology. 'The progressive order of symbols', as Ricoeur puts it, 'is not external to the regressive order of phantasms; in plunging into the archaic mythologies of the unconscious new signs of the sacred rise up.'[38]

A critical hermeneutic of imagination, for Ricoeur, is one that demystifies the dissimulating property of phantasms in order to release the innovative power of images. Idols must be unmasked so that symbols may speak. And an additional reminder which hermeneutics receives from psychoanalysis is that the images of the unconscious are charged with multiple associations which are irreducible to the level of a one-to-one conceptual correspondence. Dreams provoke rational interpretation, but such interpretation never exhausts them. For, even when infantile or archaic images are deciphered in terms of their

---

[36] Ibid., p. 27.

[37] Paul Ricoeur, *Le Conflit des interprétations* (Paris: Éditions du Seuil, 1969); English trans. *The Conflict of Interpretations* (Evanston, IL: Northwestern University Press, 1974), pp. 328–9.

[38] Ibid., p. 328.

regressive reference to the past, there always remains a surplus which points towards an inexhaustible creativity of meaning. This is where Ricoeur locates his wager that new meanings *can* emerge, that things as they are *can* change: 'liberty according to hope', he writes, 'is nothing other when understood psychologically, than this creative imagining of the possible'.[39]

It is this double axis of archaeological and eschatological reference which signals the failure of all theories which seek to reduce the oneiric imagination to a system of speculative reason. There is always more to dream images than has ever been dreamed of in our philosophies. Moreover, it is due to this excess of imagination over reason that symbols call forth a multiplicity of meanings which in turn give rise to a multiplicity of readings – psychoanalytic (Freud), religious (Eliade), speculative (Hegel). This is why a hermeneutic of imagination culminates not in absolute knowledge but in a crossroads of interpretations.

The Poetical Imagination

Having concentrated on a hermeneutics of mythic and oneiric symbols in his three major works of the 1960s – *The Symbolism of Evil*, *Freud and Philosophy* and *The Conflict of Interpretations* – Ricoeur devoted much of his attention in the 1970s and 1980s to the 'poetical' expressions of imagination. This more recent phase of Ricoeur's hermeneutic project includes *The Rule of Metaphor* (1975) as well as his three-volume *Time and Narrative*. Ricoeur comments on this phase as follows:

> In *The Rule of Metaphor* I try to show how language could extend itself to its very limits forever discovering new resonances within itself. The term *vive* in the French title *La Métaphore vive* is all important, for it was my purpose to demonstrate that there is not just an epistemological and political imagination, but also, and perhaps more fundamentally, a *linguistic imagination* which generates and regenerates meaning through the living powers of metaphoricity.

Of his three-volume study of narrative he adds:

> *Time and Narrative* develops this inquiry into the inventive power of language. Here the analysis of narrative operations in a literary text, for instance, can teach us how we formulate a new structure of 'time' by creating new modes of plot and characterization ... how narrativity, as the construction or deconstruction of paradigms of story-telling, is a perpetual search for new ways of expressing human time, a production or creation of meaning.[40]

---

[39] Ibid., p. 399.
[40] Ricoeur, 'The creativity of language', p. 17.

In *The Rule of Metaphor*, as in other works, Ricoeur deals with imagination in a fragmentary rather than systematic fashion. It is, as it were, a hidden prompter guiding and motivating his delivery without ever occupying centre stage in the process of explication. Describing the innovative power of metaphorical imagination in terms of the ability to establish similarity in dissimilarity, Ricoeur points out that he has now progressed from an analysis of the creative tension between meanings in words (symbols) to that between meanings in sentences (metaphors). Or, to put it in another way, in metaphor the productive unit is no longer the *word* but the *sentence.* It is at the level of the sentence that metaphor expresses the power of imagination to create a new semantic unit out of two different ideas. 'It is in the moment of the emergence of a new meaning from the ruins of literal predication that imagination offers its specific mediation.'[41]

In this context Ricoeur tenders one of his most useful formulations of the distinction between verbal and non-verbal imagination. Borrowing Kant's terminology, he identifies the former with the productive imagination and the latter with the reproductive. 'Would not imagination have something to do with the conflict between identity and difference?' he asks. And he makes it clear that he is not speaking here of 'imagination in its sensible, quasi-sensual aspect' – the *non-verbal* imagination. On the contrary, he argues that the

> only way to approach the problem of imagination from the perspective of a semantic theory, that is to say on a verbal plane, is to begin with productive imagination in the Kantian sense, and to put off reproductive imagination or imagery as long as possible. Treated as a schema, the image presents a verbal dimension; before being the gathering-point of faded perceptions, it is that of emerging meanings.

Placing himself thus in the camp of Kant rather than of Hume, Ricoeur goes on to demonstrate how the metaphor works in the same way as the schema in so far as it functions as 'the matrix of a new semantic pertinence that is born out of the dismantling of semantic networks caused by the shock of contradiction'. The metaphoric function of imagination', he explains, involves a verbal aspect to the extent that it involves 'grasping identity within differences', establishing the 'relatedness of terms far apart' in such a way that they confront each other rather than fuse together. This schematism of metaphor 'turns imagination into the place where the figurative meaning emerges in the interplay of identity and difference'.[42]

And yet the imagination needs images. Without any visual aspect, the verbal imagination would remain an invisible productivity. So what remains to be

---

[41] Ricoeur, 'The function of fiction in shaping Reality', *Man and World*, vol. 12, no. 2 (1979), p. 130. Quoted in G. Taylor, introduction to P. Ricoeur, *Lectures on Ideology and Utopia* (New York: Columbia University Press, 1986), p. xxviii.

[42] Ricoeur, *The Rule of Metaphor* (London: Routledge, 1978), pp. 199–200.

demonstrated is the sensible moment of metaphoric imagination. And this is where Ricoeur calls for a phenomenological psychology of *seeing-as* to complement a semantics of creative *saying*. If the productive imagination were confined to a purely verbal innovation, it would cease to be *imagination*. Ricoeur seeks accordingly to graft a psychology of the imaginary on to a semantic theory of metaphor. 'Seeing-as' provides a key as the sensible aspect of poetic imagination. It holds sense and image together in an intuitive manner. It selects from the quasi-sensory mass of imagery, producing a certain semantic order. And it can also work, contrariwise, to bring conceptual meaning to intuitive fullness, as in the example of reading:

> The *seeing-as* activated in reading ensures the joining of verbal meaning with imagistic fullness. And this conjunction is no longer something outside language since it can be reflected as a relationship. *Seeing-as* contains a ground, a foundation, this is precisely, resemblance.

Ricoeur can thus conclude that seeing-as plays the role of a schema which unites the *empty* concept and the *blind* impression: 'Thanks to its character as half thought and half experience, it joins the light of sense with the fullness of the image. In this way, the non-verbal and the verbal are firmly united at the core of the image-ing function of language.'[43]

But the metaphorical imagination not only combines the verbal and the non-verbal; it also produces a new meaning by confronting a literal with a figurative sense. This *tensional* theory of metaphor, as Ricoeur terms it, is most obvious in the case of a living metaphor in poetry. For example, in Gerard Manley Hopkins's line 'Oh! The mind, mind has mountains', we find a literal *is not* (the reader knows that literally the mind does not have mountains) accompanied by a metaphorical *is*. This power to transform such a contradiction into a new poetic meaning is evident in the metaphorical function of seeing x as y – for while we know x is not y, at a literal level, we affirm that it is, at an imaginative level. Metaphor thus thrives by virtue of the fact that it introduces the spark of imagination into a 'thinking more' (*penser plus*).[44] And this thinking more – which is at root a seeing more and a saying more – attests to the curious paradox that the 'concept of imagination, in the context of a theory of metaphor centred around the notion of semantic innovation' , is also a 'logic of discovery'.[45]

Having brought his semantic theory of imagination to its limits – to the frontier of exchange between *saying* and *seeing-as* – Ricoeur invokes once again Bachelard's phenomenology of imagination as an avenue to explore the

---

[43] Ibid., pp. 207–8.

[44] Ibid., p. 303.

[45] Ibid., p. 22 and 'Imagination in discourse and action', in A.-T. Tymieniecka (ed.), *Analectica Husserliana*, 7:3 (Boston: D. Reidel, 1978).

ontological depths of this interaction between the verbal and non-verbal. Bachelard, he writes, 'has taught us that the image is not a residue of impression, but an aura surrounding speech ... The poem gives birth to the image'; the poetic image 'is at once a becoming of expression and a becoming of our being. Here expression creates being ... one could not meditate in a zone that preceded language'.[46] The poetic image thus points to the very 'depths of existence' where 'a new being in language' is synonymous with a 'growth in being' itself. It is because there is poetical imagination that words dream being.

Ricoeur's analysis of imagination's role of the metaphorical play of language leads him to the ontological paradox of *creation-as-discovery*. 'Through the recovery of the capacity of language to create and recreate, we *discover* reality itself in the process of being *created* ... Language in the making celebrates reality in the making.'[47] Ricoeur can thus conclude that 'the strategy of discourse implied in metaphorical languages is ... to shatter and to increase our sense of reality by shattering and increasing our language ... with metaphor we experience the metamorphosis of both language and reality'.[48] At this point in his reflections on metaphor Ricoeur might be said to approximate to the Aristotle of the *Poetics*, for whom it was vain to ask whether the universal that poetry 'teaches', already existed *before* it was *invented*. It is as much found as invented.'[49]

In *Time and Narrative*, Ricoeur develops the ontological implications of 'metaphorical' reference. He shows how poetical language – be it lyrical or narrative – reveals a capacity for non-descriptive reference which exceeds the immediate reference of our everyday language. While poetical reference suspends literal reference and thereby appears to make language refer only to itself, it in fact reveals a deeper and more radical power of reference to those ontological aspects of our being-in-the-world that cannot be spoken of *directly*. *Seeing-as* thus not only implies a *saying-as* but also a *being-as*. Ricoeur relates this power to redescribe being to the narrative power of 'emplotment' (*mise-en-intrigue*). Borrowing François Dagognet's term *iconic augmentation*, he points out that the role of the image (*Bild*) is to bring about an increase in the being of our world impoverished by quotidian routine.

---

[46] Ricoeur, *Rule of Metaphor*, p. 215, quoting Bachelard, *Poetics of Space*, p. xix. Ricoeur goes on to quote a further passage from Bachelard (p. xx) later in *Rule of Metaphor*, p. 351: 'The essential newness of the poetic image poses the problem of the speaking being's creativeness. Through this creativeness the imagining consciousness proves to be, very simply, very purely, an origin. In a study of the imagination, a phenomenology of the poetic imagination must concentrate on bringing out this quality of origin in various poetic images.'

[47] Ricoeur, 'Poetry and possibility', *The Manhattan Review*, vol. 2, no. 2 (1981), pp. 20–21.

[48] Ricoeur, 'Creativity in Language', in C. Regan and D. Stewart (eds), *The Philosophy of Paul Ricoeur* (Boston, MA: Beacon, 1973), pp. 122–33 (quoted in G. Taylor, in *Lectures*).

[49] Ricoeur, *Rule of Metaphor*, p. 306 (quoted in G. Taylor, *Lectures*, p. xxxii).

> We owe a large part of the enlarging of our horizon of existence to poetic works. Far from producing only weakened images of reality – shadows, as in the Platonic treatment of the *eikon* in painting or writing (*Phaedrus* 274e–277e) – literary works depict reality by *augmenting* it with meanings that themselves depend upon the virtues of abbreviation, saturation and culmination, so strikingly illustrated by emplotment.[50]

Ricoeur here rejoins the ontological hermeneutics of Heidegger and Gadamer which, in contradistinction to Romantic hermeneutics, aims less at restoring the author's intention than at making explicit the movement by which the text unfolds a world in front of itself.[51] The poetical imagination at work in a text is one which augments my power of being-in-the-world. 'What is interpreted in a text', says Ricoeur, 'is the proposing of a world that I might inhabit and into which I might project my ownmost powers.'[52] Ricoeur thus places the referential capacity of narrative works under those of poetic works in general. For if the poetic metaphor redescribes the world, 'poetic narrative resignifies the world in its temporal dimension to the extent that narrating, telling, reciting is a way of remaking action following the poem's invention'.[53]

Every historical *narrative* borrows from this imaginative power of redescription since, as a 'reference through traces', 'the past can only be reconstructed by the imagination'.[54] But it is clearly in *fictional narrative* that the productive power of human imagination to configure and refigure human time is most dramatically evident. Presupposed by both historical and fictional narrative, however, is the pre-narrative capacity of human imagination to act in the world in a symbolically significant manner. For human being-in-the-world in its most everyday sense – as Kant and Heidegger realized – involves a process of *temporalization* which makes our present actions meaningful by interpreting them in terms of a recollected past and a projected future. This capacity of temporal interpretation is none other than that of transcendental imagination. Ricoeur can thus claim:

---

[50] Paul Ricoeur, *Time and Narrative* (Chicago, IL: University of Chicago Press, 1984), p. 80.

[51] Ibid., p. 81.

[52] Ibid.

[53] Ibid.

[54] Ibid., p. 82. See also Ricoeur's discussion of the role of imagination in historical narrative, pp. 183–8. Here Ricoeur explores the analogy between narrative emplotment, which is 'a probable imaginary construction', and the equally 'imaginary constructions' of 'probabilist' theories of historical causation as proposed by Max Weber or Raymond Aron (for example, Aron's statement in *Introduction to the Philosophy of History* that 'every historian, to explain what did happen, must ask himself what might have happened'; see also Weber: 'In order to penetrate the real causal relationships, we construct unreal ones'). But while Ricoeur argues for a certain continuity between narrative explanation and historical explanation, in so far as both deploy imagination to construct unreal relationships, he also acknowledges a discontinuity: 'historians are not simply narrators: they give reasons why they consider a particular factor rather than some other to be the sufficient cause of a given course of events … Poets produce, historians argue' (*Time and Narrative*, p. 186).

What is resignified by narrative is what was already presignified at the level of human acting. Our preunderstanding of the world of action ... is characterized by the mastering of a network of intersignifications constitutive of the semantic resources of human acting. Being-in-the-world according to narrativity is being-in-the-world already marked by the linguistic practice leading back to this preunderstanding. The iconic augmentation in question here depends upon the prior augmentation of readability that action owes to the interpretants already at work. Human action can be oversignified, because it is already presignified by all modes of its symbolic articulation.[55]

It is in his analysis of the *configurative* function of narrative, however, that Ricoeur most explicitly identifies the role of productive imagination. By narrative configuration he means the temporal synthesis of heterogeneous elements – or, to put it more simply, the ability to create a plot which transforms a sequence of events into a story. This consists of 'grasping together' the individual incidents, characters and actions so as to compose a unified temporal whole. The narrative act of emplotment, which configures a manifold into a synthesis, enacts what Kant defined as the productive power of imagination. As a power of grasping the many under the rules of the same, the narrative imagination is one which introduces recollection and repetition into a linear sequence of events (natural time), thus making it into a recapitulative story (narrative time). 'In reading the ending in the beginning and the beginning in the ending', explains Ricoeur, 'we also learn to read time itself backwards, as the recapitulation of the initial conditions of a course of action in its terminal conditions.'[56]

In this manner Ricoeur translates the schematism of imagination from the metaphorical act to the larger scenario of the narrative act. He extends his analysis of the functioning of the poetical imagination from the unit of the *word* (symbol) and the *sentence* (metaphor) to that of the *text* as a whole (narrative). 'We ought not to hesitate', he says,

to compare the production of the configurational act to the work of the productive imagination. This latter must be understood not as a psychologizing faculty but as a transcendental one. The productive imagination is not only rule-governed, it constitutes the generative matrix of rules. In Kant's first *Critique*, the categories of the understanding are first schematized by the productive imagination. The schematism has this power because the productive imagination fundamentally has a synthetic function. It connects understanding and intuition by engendering syntheses that are intellectual and intuitive at the same time. Emplotment, too, engenders a mixed intelligibility between what has been called the point, theme or thought of a story, and the intuitive presentation of circumstances, characters, episodes, and changes of fortune that make up

---

[55] Ibid., p. 81.
[56] Ibid., p. 67.

the denouement. In this way we may speak of a schematism of the narrative function.[57]

This analysis of the schematizing function of narrativity brings us to one of the most problematic issues of *Time and Narrative* – the relationship between *tradition* and *innovation.* Imagination, once again, comes to the rescue by operating in a double capacity. In so far as it secures the function of reiterating types across discontinuous episodes, imagination is on the side of tradition. But, as noted in our Introduction, in so far as it fulfils its equally essential function of projecting new horizons of possibility, imagination is committed to the role of semantic – and indeed ontological – innovation. As soon as one recognizes the schematizing and synthesizing power of imagination at work in narrative, the very notions of tradition and innovation become complementary. Thus Ricoeur can claim that the term tradition must be understood not as the 'inert transmission of some already dead deposit of material but as the living transmission of an innovation always capable of being reactivated by a return to the most creative moments of poetic activity'.[58] So interpreted, tradition can only survive, can only pass itself on from one generation to the next, by fostering innovation in its midst. The function of tradition plays a role analogous to that of narrative paradigms: they not only constitute the grammar that directs the composition of new works, but they also do not and cannot eradicate the role of *poiesis* which in the last analysis is what makes each work of art different, singular, unique – an 'original production, a new existence in the linguistic kingdom'.[59] But the reverse is equally true. If tradition cannot survive without innovation, neither can innovation survive without tradition. Once again, it is imagination which plays this reciprocal role. 'Innovation remains a form of behaviour governed by rules', writes Ricoeur.

> The labour of imagination is not born from nothing. It is bound in one way or another to the tradition's paradigms. But the range of solutions is vast. It is deployed between the two poles of servile application and calculated deviation, passing through every degree of rule-governed deformation.[60]

While myth, folk-tale and traditional narratives in general gravitate towards the first pole, the more modem and postmodern exercises in narrative tend towards deviation with regard to the inherited paradigm. We shall return to this dialectic of tradition and innovation in our next study.

---

[57] Ibid., p. 68. Ricoeur's hermeneutic reading of this schematizing–temporalizing–productive power of imagination, as first outlined by Kant in the first edition of *The Critique of Pure Reason* (1781), bears interesting parallels to Heidegger's reading in *Kant and the Problem of Metaphysics* (1929), pp. 135–49, 177–92; and to the analyses of two of Heidegger's most brilliant students in Freiburg in the late 1920s, Hannah Arendt (*Kant's Political Philosophy*, 1982, pp. 78–9) and Herbert Marcuse (*Eros and Civilization*, 1955, p. 174f.).

[58] Ricoeur, *Time and Narrative*, p. 68.

[59] Ibid., p. 69.

[60] Ibid., p. 70.

In short, the schematizing function of productive imagination involves both a sedimentaton and inauguration of meaning. And this dual function of imagination as a poetic creation of the new by reference to the old is not just a property of writing but also and equally of *reading*. Indeed, Ricoeur goes so far as to claim that in many contemporary works it is the imaginative task of the reader to complete the narrative sketched out and often deliberately fragmented by the written work: 'If emplotment can be described as an act of the productive imagination, it is insofar as this act is the joint work of the text and reader.' For it is the reading which accompanies the interplay of the innovation and sedimentation of paradigms that schematizes emplotment. 'In the act of reading, the receiver plays with the narrative constraints, brings about gaps, takes part in the combat between the novel and the anti-novel, and enjoys the pleasure that Roland Barthes calls the pleasure of the text'.[61] Taking the example of Joyce's *Ulysses* as a narrative full of holes and indeterminacies, Ricoeur concludes that such a text serves as an added invitation to the creative power of the reader's imagination: 'It challenges the reader's capacity to configure what the author seems to take malign delight in defiguring. In such an extreme case, it is the reader, almost abandoned by the work, who carries the burden of emplotment'.[62]

Conclusion

It is at this final stage of narrative imagination – the reader's reception of the text – that the hermeneutic circle returns to the world of action. The act of reading is the ultimate indicator of the 'refiguring of the world of action under the sign of the plot'. Narrative plots are not, of course, confined to literature. Ricoeur is well aware of this. There is a whole set of collective stories and histories which need not bear the signature of any individual author, and which exercise a formative influence on our modes of action and behaviour in society. This is what Ricoeur calls the 'social imaginary'. And this social function of imagination is constitutive of social reality itself.[63] Ricoeur examines it under two limit ideas – *ideology* and *utopia* – which we will explore in some detail in Study 4 below.

The indispensable role of hermeneutical imagination – at both an individual and collective level – is acknowledged by the author himself in this revealing statement of his fundamental philosophical project in an *Esprit* interview in 1981. Despite appearances, says Ricoeur,

---

[61] Ibid., p. 77.

[62] Ibid.

[63] Paul Ricoeur, *Lectures on Ideology and Utopia*, lecture 1, p. 64.

my single problem since beginning my reflections has been creativity. I considered it from the point of view of individual psychology in my first works on the will, and then at the cultural level with the study on symbolisms. My present research on the narrative places me precisely at the heart of this social and cultural creativity, since telling a story ... is the most permanent act of societies. In telling their own stories, cultures create themselves ... It is true that I have been silent from the point of view of practice, but not at all the theoretical level, because the studies I have already published on the relation between ideology and utopia are entirely at the centre of this preoccupation.[64]

Is this not testimony to the hypothesis, observed throughout our current study, that Ricoeur's ultimate wager remains a hermeneutics of creative imagination?

---

[64] Paul Ricoeur, 'L'histoire comme récit et comme pratique', Interview with Peter Kemp, *Esprit*, no. 6 (Paris, June 1981), p. 165. George Taylor provides a brief, lucid, unprecedented summary of the role of imagination in Ricoeur's work in his introduction to *Lectures on Ideology and Utopia*, pp. xxvii–xxxv. See also the concluding notes, 39 and 47, to G. B. Madison's *The Hermeneutics of Postmodernity* (Bloomington, IN: Indiana University Press, 1988), pp. 194–5, where he also acknowledges the central role played by imagination in Ricoeur's overall hermeneutic project.

Between Myth and Tradition*

One of the most pressing tasks facing our contemporary culture, suggests Ricoeur, is to ensure a creative relationship between tradition and the future.[1] In this study we will examine (a) what precisely Ricoeur means by tradition and (b) how tradition may be positively related to history through a critical hermeneutics of myth. Taking up Ricoeur's view that myth is a primordial expression of the collective social imaginary, we will investigate its often neglected resources for a 'poetics of the possible'.

Hermeneutics of Tradition

In the third volume of *Time and Narrative*, entitled *Narrated Time* (1985), Ricoeur offers a comprehensive account of key concepts of tradition. The analysis is concentrated in the seventh chapter, 'Toward a Hermeneutics of Historical Consciousness'. Having renounced the Hegelian claim to a 'totalizing mediation' of history in the form of Absolute Knowledge, Ricoeur proposes this alternative:

> An open-ended mediation, incomplete and imperfect, made up of a network of perspectives split between the expectancy of the future, the reception of the past, and the living experience of the present – but without the *Aufhebung* into a totality where the reason of history and its effectiveness would coincide.[2]

Only by acknowledging this split character of history may we surmise the possibility of a 'plural unity' emerging from these divergent perspectives. The open play of perspectives, extending between past and future, requires us to

---

* Earlier and shorter versions of this study appeared as 'Between Tradition and Utopia: The Hermeneutical Problem of Myth', in *On Paul Ricoeur: Narrative and Interpretation*, ed. D. Wood (London: Routledge, 1992) and 'Hermeneutics of Myth and Tradition', in our *Poetics of Modernity* (New Jersey: Humanities Press, 1995).

[1] 'Entretien avec Paul Ricoeur', *Le Monde*, February 1987. See also Ricoeur's discussion in *Temps et récit III: Le temps raconté* (Paris: Editions du Seuil, 1985), Chap. 7; 'L'Idéologie et L'utopie', in *Du texte à l'action* (Paris: Editions du Seuil, 1986), pp. 379–93; and 'The Creativity of Language: An Interview', in my *Dialogues with Contemporary Continental Thinkers: The Phenomenological Heritage* (Manchester: Manchester University Press, 1984), pp. 29–31.

[2] Ricoeur, *TR*, p. 300; *TN*, p. 207. My translations refer and correspond to pages in the original French edition of *Temps et récit* (hereafter *TR*), cited above in note 1. A parallel reference is also provided for the English translation: *Time and Narrative* (hereafter *TN*), Vol. 3, trans. K. McLaughlin and D. Pellauer (Chicago: University of Chicago Press, 1988).

revise the accepted view of tradition as a *fait accompli*. Tradition is now to be understood as an ongoing dialectic between (a) our being-affected-by-the-past and (b) our imaginative projection of history-yet-to-be-made (*la visée de l'histoire à faire*).

The futural project of history runs into trouble as soon as it slips its mooring in past experience. History loses direction when cut adrift from all that preceded it. Arthur Rimbaud was no doubt announcing the modernist manifesto when he proclaimed, in his *Lettre du Voyant*, written in the revolutionary year of the Paris Commune, 1871, '*Libre aux nouveaux d'exécrer les ancêtres*'. But such a view, applied literally to the realm of history and pushed to extremes, runs the risk of schismatic negation.

> If it is true [writes Ricoeur] that the belief in *des temps nouveaux* contributed to the shrinking of our experiential space, even to the point of banishing the past to the shades of oblivion – the obscurantism of the Middle Ages! – whereas our horizon of expectancy tended to withdraw into a future ever more vague and indistinct, we may ask ourselves if the tension between *expectancy* and *experience* was not already beginning to be threatened the very day that it was acknowledged.[3]

Ricoeur recommends that we resist this slide toward schism. What form should such resistance take? First, we should realize that the project of the future cancels itself out as soon as it loses its foothold in the 'field of experience' (past and present); for it thereby finds itself incapable of formulating a path toward its ideals. Ricoeur counsels, accordingly, that our dreams must remain determinate (and therefore finite) if they are to become historically realizable. Otherwise they forfeit their capacity to solicit responsible political commitment. In order to prevent the future from dissolving into fantasy, Ricoeur counsels that we bring it closer to the present by means of intermediary projects within the scope of social action. Invoking what he terms a 'post-Hegelian Kantianism', Ricoeur advances three conditions which the utopian imagination of expectancy must observe: (i) it must project a hope for all of humanity and not just one privileged community or nation; (ii) this humanity is only worthy of the name to the extent

---

[3] Ricoeur, *TR*, p. 311 (my italics), and TN, p. 215, where Ricoeur explains the paradox as follows:

> If the newness of the *Neuzeit* is only perceived in the light of the growing difference between (past) experience and (future) expectancy, in other words, if the belief in modernity rests on expectancies which become removed from all anterior experiences, then the tension between experience and expectancy could only be recognized when its point of rupture was already in view. The idea of progress which still related a better future to the past, rendered even closer by the acceleration of history, tends to give way to the idea of utopia, as soon as humanity's hopes lose all reference to acquired experience and are projected into a future completely without precedent. With such utopia, the tension becomes schism.

that it possesses a history; and (iii) in order to possess a history, humanity must be the subject of history in the sense of a 'collective singular' (*un singulier collectif*).[4]

Warning against the contemporary diminution of the experiential space of tradition, Ricoeur resists the tendency to dismiss tradition as something complete in itself, impervious to change. On the contrary, he urges us to rediscover tradition as an ongoing history, thereby reanimating its still unaccomplished potentialities. 'Against the adage which claims that the future is in all respects open and contingent and the past univocally closed and necessary,' writes Ricoeur, we must make our expectancies more determinate and our experience more indeterminate.'[5] Only when future imaginings are rendered determinate in this way can we retroactively reveal the past as a 'living tradition.'

Critical reflection on the project of 'making history' thus calls for an interrogation of our relation to tradition, broadly understood as our 'being affected by history' (*Wirkungsgeschichtlichkeit*, in Gadamer's phrase). At this decisive point in his argument, Ricoeur calls for a 'step back from the future toward the past'. In keeping with Marx's dictum that man makes history according to circumstances which he has inherited, Ricoeur declares that we are only the *agents* of history to the degree that we are also its *patients*. To exist in history means that 'to act is to suffer and to suffer is to act'. The countless victims of history who are acted upon by forces beyond their control epitomize this condition of suffering – in both senses of the term. But this is only the extreme case. Even those we consider the active initiators of history also suffer history to the extent that their actions, however calculated, almost invariably produce certain non-intended consequences. (This was admirably demonstrated by Sartre in his descriptions of 'inverted *praxis*' in the first book of the *Critique of Practical Reason*, for example, the counterproductive effects of imported gold from the American colonies on the Spanish economy in the seventeenth century, or of mountain deforestation on the Chinese harvests.)

---

[4] Ibid. Kant identified this common project with the constitution of 'a civil society administering universal rights'. Ricoeur grants this as a necessary condition of the historical rapprochement between utopia and tradition. Without the 'right to difference', the claim of universal history may be monopolized by one particular society or grouping of dominant societies, thereby degenerating into hegemonic oppression. On the other hand, the many examples of torture and tyranny still found in modern society remind us that social rights and the right to difference are not in themselves a sufficient condition for the realization of universal justice. One also requires the existence of a constitutional state (*un état de droit*), where both individuals and collectivities (*non-étatiques*) remain the ultimate subjects of right. In this respect, Ricoeur observes, it is important to recall that the Kantian project of a 'civil society administering universal rights' has not yet been achieved. This project remains for us a fitting guide in our efforts to give practical shape to our utopian expectancies.

[5] Ricoeur, *TR*, p. 313; *TN*, pp. 216, 228.

However, to avoid the pitfall of fatalism, Ricoeur points to the necessity of always interpreting our 'being-affected-by-the-past' in positive dialectical tension with our horizon of expectancy. Once this tension is lost sight of we easily succumb to a sterile antithesis between a reactionary apologism of the past and a naïve affirmation of progress. Ricoeur posits a third way, beyond this either/or.

To respect the demands of historical continuity and discontinuity, we must preserve the idea of a consciousness perduring through history while at the same time heeding the 'decentring of the thinking subject' carried out by the hermeneutics of suspicion. The ethical demand to remember the past does not oblige us to rehabilitate the idealist model of a sovereign mind commanding a total recapitulation of historical meaning. What does need to be retained, however, is the idea of tradition itself. But retention is only permissible on the basis of a critical reinterpretation of this idea. Here Ricoeur distinguishes among three different categories of historical memory: (1) traditionality, (2) traditions, and (3) Tradition (with a capital 'T').

Ricoeur describes *traditionality* in the first and second volumes of *Time and Narrative* as a dialectic between 'sedimentation and innovation.' Here he relates the category to the realm of fictional narrative (what he calls *mimesis* 2). But in the third volume of *Time and Narrative* Ricoeur extends the range of reference. He now argues that traditionality is to be understood in the general sense of a formal style which transmits the heritages of the past. This means extending the discussion from *mimesis* 2 to *mimesis* 3, that is, to the rapport between narrative and the historical time of action and suffering that we, readers and receivers of tradition, inhabit. In this enlarged context, traditionality is defined as a temporalizing of history by means of a dialectic between the effects of history upon us (which we passively suffer) and our response to history (which we actively operate). Traditionality, in other words, is the precondition for transmitting actual historical meaning.

Ricoeur claims that this dialectical category enables us to obviate certain erroneous attitudes to the past. First, it refuses to accept that the past can be abolished in the manner of a schismatic utopianism or Nietzschean 'active forgetting' (an attitude which dissolves history into an arbitrary multiplicity of incommensurable perspectives). But the dialectic of traditionality equally resists the idealist temptation to synchronize past and present, thereby reducing the diversity of history to the identity of contemporaneous understanding (the error of Hegel and Romanticism). Avoiding both extremes, the model of traditionality proposes a fusion of horizons (*à la* Gadamer). It suggests how we may have access to history without imposing our present consciousness onto the past. The past is thus opened up as a historical horizon which is at once detached from our contemporary horizon and included in it.

> It is in *projecting* an historical horizon [notes Ricoeur] 'that we experience, in its tension with the horizon of the present, the effect of the past on us ... This effect [*efficience*] of history on us is something which,

as it were, takes effect without us. The fusion of horizons is that which we labor toward. And here the labor of history and the labor of the historian come to each other's aid.[6]

Traditionality means, in short, that 'the temporal distance which separates us from the past is not a dead interval but a *generative transmission* of meaning'.[7]

The second category outlined by Ricoeur is that of *traditions*. Whereas traditionality is a formal concept, the second category comprises the material contents of tradition. The transition from form to content is necessitated by the activity of interpretation itself. Interpretation reveals that tradition is essentially linguistic (*langagière*) and so cannot be divorced from the transmission of acquired meanings which precede us. Moreover, the identification of traditions with language is to be understood not just in the sense of natural languages (French, Greek, English, and so on) but in the sense of things already said by those who existed in history before we arrived on the scene. This takes into account the complex set of social and cultural circumstances which each one of us presupposes as a speaking and listening being.

Ricoeur insists that the linguistic character of historical meaning is central to the entire argument of *Time and Narrative*. The first relation of narrative to action (*mimesis* 1) discloses the primordial capacity of human action to be symbolically mediated. The second (*mimesis* 2), operating in the structural emplotment of fiction and historiography, reveals how imitated action functions in terms of a text. The third mode of *mimesis* – the effects that historical meaning has on our present acting and suffering – is shown to coincide in large part with the transmission of meaning via the textual mediations of the past. Moreover, this parallel between a *hermeneutics of history* and a *hermeneutics of texts* is corroborated by Ricoeur's demonstration that historiography, as a knowledge by means of traces, depends largely on texts that give to the past the status of documentary witness. Our consciousness of being, exposed to the effectiveness of history, finds its complement in our interpretative response to the texts which communicate the past to us. All comprehension of historical tradition entails historical traditions of comprehension. Ricoeur sums up:

> As soon as one takes *traditions* to refer to those *things said* in the past and transmitted to us through a chain of interpretations and reinterpretations, we must add a material dialectic of contents to the formal dialectic of temporal distance [that is, traditionality]. The past puts us into question before we put it into question. In this struggle for the *recognition of meaning,* the text and the reader are each in their turn familiarized and defamiliarized.[8]

---

[6] *TR*, p. 320; *TN*, p. 221.

[7] Ibid. Ricoeur stresses that before tradition is allowed to congeal into an inert deposit, it 'is an activity which can only be comprehended *dialectically* in the exchange between the past which is interpreted and the present which interprets' (my italics). See also my 'Myth and the Critique of Tradition', in *Reconciling Memories*, ed. A. Falconer (Dublin: Columbia Press, 1988), pp. 8–24.

[8] *TR*, p. 322; *TN*, p. 222.

Drawing thus from the Gadamer/Collingwood model of question–response, Ricoeur relates the essence of traditions to the fact that the past interrogates and responds to us to the degree that we interrogate and respond to it. Traditions are proposals of meaning that call for our interpretative response.

Ricoeur defines the third category of the historical past as *Tradition* with a capital 'T' (*La Tradition*). This last move from traditions to Tradition is motivated by the observation that every proposal of meaning is also a claim to truth. Gadamer's famous defence of Tradition, as Ricoeur reminds us, stemmed largely from the conviction that our historical consciousness of the past refers to some truth (that is, is not purely arbitrary or subjective). Gadamer argued that this claim to historical truth does not come from us alone but is a voice from the past that we seek to reappropriate. The Gadamerian defence of Tradition–Authority–Prejudgement presupposes that we are carried by the meanings of the past before we find ourselves in a position to judge them. Put in other terms, we are spoken to before we speak; we are posited in tradition before we posit tradition; we are situated before we are free to criticize this situation. Whence Gadamer's conclusion that the Enlightenment claim to neutral, ahistorical judgement, residing above all prejudice, is itself a prejudice. Hermeneutic understanding is auditory understanding: it listens to the truth-claims of memory.

In an influential essay entitled 'Hermeneutics and the Critique of Ideology', first published in 1973, Ricoeur suggests that the opposition between Gadamerian Tradition and Habermasian critique is not insurmountable. The hermeneutic of tradition, he points out, already contains within itself the possibility of a critique of the historical imaginary. As soon as we acknowledge that tradition is not some monolith of homogeneous dogma but an ongoing dialectic made up of different rival traditions, internal crises, interruptions, revisions and schisms – as soon as we acknowledge this, we discover that there exists an essential dimension of distance at the very heart of tradition which actually invites critical interpretation. On this issue *critical hermeneutics* differs radically from *Romantic hermeneutics*. It rejects the idea that we understand the past by reproducing in the present some original production of meaning, as if the temporal distantiation of meaning could be magically wished away. A critical hermeneutics of tradition insists on the necessity to discriminate between true and false interpretations of history.

This raises the crucial question of legitimation. To resolve this problem, Habermas had declared it necessary to move beyond the 'interest in communication', exemplified by the hermeneutic sciences, to the 'interest in emancipation', exemplified by the critical social sciences. Since the social imaginary of tradition is by its nature subject to ideological distortion, Habermas appealed to an ahistorical ideal of undistorted communication. The danger here, however, is that this criterion of legitimacy may be deferred to an indefinite future without any grounds in history. It may prove to be *too utopian* – idealizable but not realizable.

One could, of course, appeal to a transcendental reflection in order to provide universal norms of validation. But this move runs the risk of enclosing us in a monological transcendental deduction *à la* Kant. Without a dialogical rootedness in history, the critical moment of transcendental self-reflection cannot provide adequate grounds for the ideal of undistorted communication. In short, the validation of universal norms must itself be located in a historical dialectic between a determinate horizon of expectancy and a specific space of experience. Ricoeur's argument runs as follows:

> It is on this return journey of the question of foundation to the question of historical effectiveness that the hermeneutics of tradition makes itself heard again. To avoid the endless flight of a perfectly a-historical truth, we must try to discern signs of this truth in the anticipations of agreement operative in every successful communication, in every communication where we actually experience a certain reciprocity of intention and recognition. In other words, the transcendence of the idea of truth, which is a dialogical idea from the outset, must be perceived as already at work in the practice of communication. Thus reinstated in our horizon of expectancy, the dialogical idea is compelled to rejoin the buried anticipations of tradition itself. So understood, the pure transcendental standpoint may legitimately assume the negative status of a *limit-idea* with regard to both our determinate expectancies and our hypostasized traditions. But, short of being divorced from the effectiveness of history, this limit-idea must also become a *regulative idea* which directs the concrete dialectic between the horizon of expectancy and the space of experience.[9]

Ricoeur recommends, accordingly, that we interpret tradition's pretension to truth in the non-absolutist sense of a 'presumption of truth'. This means that we respect truth-claims of tradition until such time as a better argument prevails. The 'presumption of truth' refers to our basic attitude of credit or trust in the propositions of meaning legacied by the past – a primary response which precedes the critical moment of distantiation and reminds us that we are not the originators of truth but already belong to a context of 'presumed truth'. Ricoeur believes that this model bridges the gap between the finitude of hermeneutic facticity (stressed by Heidegger and Gadamer) and the validity of the ideal undistorted communication (championed by Habermas).

In like manner, Ricoeur proposes to mediate between Gadamer's *backward look* of inherited pre-understanding and Habermas's *forward look* of communicative action. Ricoeur inserts Habermas's critique of ideology into the heart of Gadamer's hermeneutics of tradition, thereby opening the latter to a novel project. But he insists that such a project requires in turn a fundamental

---

[9] *TR*, p. 328; *TN*, p. 226.

respect for tradition if it is to safeguard itself against the danger of arbitrary or ahistorical voluntarism – that is, a future project completely divorced from the historical heritage of the past. Ricoeur's final assessment of the Gadamer–Habermas debate in 'Hermeneutics and the Critique of Ideology' is most instructive:

> How can [Habermas's] interest in emancipation remain anything other than a pious vow, save by embodying it in the reawakening of communicative action itself? And upon what will you concretely support the reawakening of communicative action, if not the creative renewal of cultural heritage?[10]

Here Ricoeur compels us to acknowledge an intimate link between the reawakening of political responsibility and the reactivation of traditional sources of communicative action. The apparently insurmountable opposition between the hermeneutic and a critical attitude is thus overcome. Where the hermeneutic consciousness (in Gadamer's sense) invokes a common understanding that precedes us, the critical consciousness reinterprets it in terms of a regulative idea: the ideal of unrestricted and unconstrained communication. But this antithesis disappears if one endorses, with Ricoeur, a critical hermeneutics that realizes that critical theory cannot 'speak from' the basis of a transcendental subject – because it too must presuppose some kind of historical memory. For critical theory, historical memory is not a prerogative of tradition (as it tended to be for Gadamer) but remains an ally of the Enlightenment, understood as a project of emancipation. In this way, critique as a project of freedom nourishes itself from a historical heritage that finds its modern impetus in the *Aufklärung* but that actually dates back much further to include some of the oldest mythic narratives of liberty. As Ricoeur puts it:

> Critique is also a tradition. I would even say that it plunges into the most impressive tradition, that of liberating acts, of the Exodus and the Resurrection. Perhaps there would be no more interest in emancipation, no more anticipation of freedom, if the Exodus and the Resurrection were effaced from the memory of mankind ... If this is so then nothing is more deceptive than the alleged antinomy between a [hermeneutic] ontology of prior understanding and a [critical] eschatology of freedom ... As if it were necessary to choose between reminiscence and hope! In theological terms, eschatology is nothing without the recitation of acts of deliverance from the past ... It is the task of philosophical reflection to eliminate deceptive antinomies which would oppose the interest in the reinterpretation of cultural heritages received from the past, and the interest in the futuristic projections of a liberated humanity.[11]

---

[10] See Paul Ricoeur, 'Hermeneutics and the Critique of Ideology', in *Hermeneutics and the Human Sciences*, ed. John B. Thompson (Cambridge: Cambridge University Press, 1981), pp. 63–100.

[11] Ibid.

Tradition, Ricoeur concludes, must be understood in the dynamic perspective of our being-affected-by-the-past, which in turn is related to our historical horizon of expectancy. In this larger dialectic between tradition and expectation we rediscover suppressed potentialities of past meaning which give flesh to the ideal of undistorted communication. Indeed, it is only in terms of such an interplay between memory and anticipation that the ideal image of a reconciled humanity can be invested with an effective history.[12]

But Ricoeur rounds off his analysis with a warning. This indispensable interplay between past and future is becoming increasingly threatened in our time. As our horizon of expectation becomes ever more distant, our inherited space of experience becomes more restricted. And this growing discrepancy between expectation and heritage lies at the root of our crisis of modernity. 'The entire present is in crisis,' notes Ricoeur, 'when expectancy takes refuge in utopia and tradition congeals into a dead residue.'[13] Our contemporary task is to confront this crisis and prevent the tension between expectation and tradition from further degenerating into schism.

This task – which Ricoeur does not hesitate to describe as an 'ethical duty'[14] – is twofold. On the one hand, we must bring the expectancies for the future closer to the present by a strategic *praxis* sensitive to the concrete steps that need to be taken toward realizing what is 'desirable and reasonable'. On the other, we must try to halt the shrinking of our experiential space by liberating the still untapped potentialities of inherited meaning. 'All initiative on the historical plane', Ricoeur concludes, 'consists in the perpetual transaction between these two tasks.'[15] Such transaction is a charge for hermeneutic understanding.

We might add a cautionary comment here, however, to Ricoeur's perceptive analysis. Is there not a sense in which the crisis of modernity also has a positive value, in so far as the gap between past and future that it opens up serves to heighten our consciousness of the problem of historical meaning? Would Ricoeur himself have devoted so much attention to the question of narrative continuity and transmission if the crucial link between tradition and historical expectation was unproblematically assured? For just as the cultural crisis of modernity has given rise to a proliferation of new literary forms, from Virginia Woolf and Joyce to Beckett and Borges, has this same crisis not also given rise to a new urgency of philosophical questioning about the nature of historical truth – of which *Time and Narrative* is itself an exemplary witness? I am reminded here of Hannah Arendt's observation in her preface to *Between Past and Future*:

---

12 *TR*, p. 329; *TN*, p. 228.
13 *TR*, p. 339; *TN*, p. 235.
14 *TR*, p. 370; *TN*, p. 258.
15 *TR*, p. 339; *TN*, p. 235.

The call to thought makes itself heard in that strange in-between period which sometimes inserts itself into historical time when not only the later historians but actors and witnesses, the living themselves, become conscious of an interval in time which is entirely determined by things which are no longer and are not yet. History has often shown that it is such intervals which may contain the moment of truth.[16]

Ricoeur's hermeneutic analysis of tradition and expectation is written, it would seem, from such an interval.

Hermeneutics of Myth

I shall now examine how the dialectic between tradition and history has often found expression in the mediational role of myth. By taking myth as a specific instance of the dialectic I hope to make the argument more concrete. The function of myth was first analysed by Ricoeur in *The Symbolism of Evil*, where it was defined as a foundational narrative of a community. By means of a reference to the origins of its history, the mythic narrative seeks to account for how a particular culture or community came to be. Most civilizations possess their own cosmogenies or 'creation myths'. And these are in turn usually supplemented by 'anthropological myths' (for example, the myths of Adam and Prometheus), which tell the story of the genesis of human value. In this respect myth is closely bound up with tradition as a recollection, transmission and reinterpretation of past values. Such is the function of 'mythopoetic imagination'.

But myth also contains another crucial dimension: a poetical anticipation of the future. And it is here that a critical hermeneutics of myth can help to relate tradition to the ongoing project of history understood as *history-making*, that is, as a positive activity of social *poiesis*.

Hermeneutic understanding, as noted in our preceding studies, discriminates between positive and negative symbols. And so myth, as a narrative of symbolic events, can be salvaged as a constructive mediation between tradition and history, maintaining both elements in a relationship of creative tension. So salvaged, myth may legitimately fulfil its dual potential of creation and critique: the hermeneutic disclosure of possible worlds which are suppressed in our present reality and whose very otherness provides alternatives to the established order. By projecting ulterior modes of understanding, albeit on an imaginary plane, myth can function as a salutary indictment of the status quo.

The project of modernity, as we saw above, has frequently been predicated upon a rupture with the past. In contemporary movements of science, philosophy and theology, we find repeated calls for a demythologization of

---

[16] Hannah Arendt, Preface to *Between Past and Future* (London: Faber, 1961), p. 9.

tradition. The critical demand to demystify and debunk is, of course, an indispensable corrective to the conservative apotheosis of Tradition as monolith of truth. But as Ricoeur keeps reminding us, it can easily be pushed to extremes.

The need to continually reevaluate one's cultural imaginary raises the central question of myth as narrative. Narrative understanding, considered as the human endeavour to make sense of history by telling a story, relates to tradition in two ways. By creatively reinterpreting the myths of the past, narrative can release new and hitherto concealed possibilities of understanding one's history. And by critically scrutinizing the past, it can, in Walter Benjamin's words, wrest tradition from the conformism that always threatens to overpower it.[17] To properly attend to this dual capacity of narrative is, therefore, to resist the facile opposition between the 'eternal values' of tradition, on the one hand, and the free inventiveness of critical understanding, on the other. Every narrative interpretation, as Alasdair MacIntyre observes, whether it involves a literary or a political reading of history, 'takes place within the context of some traditional mode of thought, transcending through criticism and invention the limitations of what had hitherto been reasoned in that tradition ... Traditions when vital embody continuities of conflict.'[18] This implies that the contemporary act of rereading and retelling tradition can actually disclose uncompleted and disrupted narratives which open up unprecedented possibilities of imagining –

---

[17] Walter Benjamin, 'Theses on the Philosophy of History', in *Illuminations*, ed. Hannah Arendt (London: Fontana, 1973), p. 57. Ricoeur makes a similar point in *Time and Narrative*, Vol. I, pp. 68–70:

> Let us understand by the term tradition not the inert transmission of some already dead deposit of material but the living transmission of an innovation always capable of being reactivated by a return to the most creative moments of poetic activity ... A tradition is constituted by the interplay of innovation and sedimentation ... Innovation remains a form of behavior governed by rules. The labor of imagination is not born from nothing. It is bound in one way or another to tradition's paradigms. But the range of solutions is vast. It is deployed between the two poles of servile application and calculated deviation, passing through every degree of 'rule-governed deformation.' The folklore, the myth and in general the traditional narrative stand closest to the first pole. But to the extent that we distance ourselves from traditional narrative, deviation becomes the rule ... It remains, however, that the possibility of deviation is inscribed in the relation between sedimented paradigms and actual works. Short of the extreme case of schism, it is just the opposite of servile application. Rule-governed deformation constitutes the axis around which the various changes of paradigm through application are arranged. It is this variety of applications that confers a history on the productive imagination and that, in counterpoint to sedimentation, makes a narrative tradition possible.

[18] Alasdair MacIntyre, *After Virtue* (London: Duckworth Press, 1981), p. 206.

and, by extension, acting. No text exists in a vacuum. No narrative operates in splendid isolation from social and historical contexts. Moreover, Tradition itself is not some seamless monument existing beyond time and space. It is itself a narrative construct requiring ongoing interpretation. To examine one's culture, consequently, is also to examine one's conscience – in the sense of critically discriminating between value-interpretations.

Ricoeur's critical hermeneutics interprets myth as a masked discourse concealing hidden meaning behind apparent meaning, and the task it sets itself is to remove the mask.[19] In the remainder of this study, we will briefly mention some consequences of this approach for a contemporary understanding of myth.

According to a hermeneutics of suspicion, myths are not innocent, as Romantic ethnology would have us believe. They become authentic or inauthentic according to the 'interests' they serve. These interests, as Habermas recognized in *Knowledge and Human Interests*, can be those, broadly, of emancipation or domination. Hence religious myths of a kingdom may be interpreted either as an opiate of the oppressed or an antidote to such oppression. Likewise, national myths can be used to liberate a community or to incarcerate that community in tribal bigotry. In this respect, we may say that the founding myths of most nation-states call for critical discrimination between authentic and inauthentic uses.

A hermeneutic evaluation of myth involves not just *epistemological* considerations but *ethical* ones. It asks about questions of justice and injustice in addition to questions of truth and falsehood. And it is precisely here, as Ricoeur admits, that hermeneutics can be complemented by the critique of concealed interests advanced by Habermas and the Frankfurt School.[20] This does not require us to crudely deconstruct figurative myths into literal facts. It calls rather for a critical distinction between what Ricoeur refers to as the explicatory function of doctrinaire myths, which justifies the status quo in a dogmatic or irrational manner, and a genuinely exploratory function, which puts the status quo into question and opens us to an ethical poetics, to possible worlds of justice.

What is required, to put it in other terms, is a hermeneutic dialectic between the claims of *logos* and *mythos*. Without the constant vigilance of *logos*,

---

[19] Ricoeur, 'The Critique of Religion', in *The Philosophy of Paul Ricoeur: An Anthology of His Work*, ed. Charles E. Reagan and David Stewart (Boston, MA: Beacon Press, 1978), p. 215.

[20] For further discussion of this relationship between ideology and utopia see Ricoeur, 'Science and Ideology', in *Hermeneutics and the Human Sciences*, pp. 222–47, as well as the Ricoeur texts cited in note 1. See also Karl Mannheim, *Ideology and Utopia* (London: Routledge and Kegan Paul, 1936); and Frederic Jameson, 'The Dialectic of Utopia and Ideology', in *The Political Unconscious* (London: Methuen, 1981).

mythos remains susceptible to all kinds of perversion. (One need only consider, for instance, the way fascist movements unscrupulously exploited Germanic or Roman myths.) Ricoeur claims that the hermeneutic critique of *mythos* is indispensable because ideological representations are neither good nor bad in themselves but become so by virtue of their ongoing reinterpretation by each generation. That is why the hermeneutic imagination cannot afford to approach myths in a naive or uncritical manner:

> We are no longer primitive beings living at the immediate level of myth. Myth for us is always mediated and opaque and ... several of its recurrent forms have become deviant and dangerous, e.g., the myth of absolute power (fascism). We are no longer justified in speaking of 'myth in general.' We must critically assess the content of each myth and the basic intentions which animate it. Modern man can neither get rid of myth nor take it at its face value. Myth will always be with us, but we must always approach it critically.[21]

The movement from the poetical to the ethical critique of myth signals a convergence of imagination and reason. It is only when *mythos* and *logos* conjoin in a common project of universal liberation that we can properly speak of authentic symbols. Whenever a particular myth is considered the founding act of one community to the exclusion of all others, the possibility of corruption inevitably arises. Ricoeur argues accordingly:

> The potential of any authentic myth goes beyond the limits of any single community. The *mythos* of a community is the bearer of a meaning which extends beyond its own particular frontiers; it is the bearer of other possible worlds ... Nothing travels or circulates as widely and effectively as myth. Whence it follows that even though myths originate in particular cultures, they are also capable of emigrating and developing in other cultural parameters ... Only those myths are genuine which can be reinterpreted in terms of liberation, as both a personal and collective phenomenon. We should perhaps sharpen this critical criterion to include only those myths which have as their horizon the liberation of mankind as a whole. Liberation cannot be exclusive ... In genuine reason (*logos*) as well as in genuine myth (*mythos*), we find a concern for the universal emancipation of man.[22]

Conclusion

The critical task of hermeneutics, as Ricoeur sees it, is not to reduce great myths of tradition to one-dimensional tracts. Rather it entails the scrupulous

---

[21] See Ricoeur, 'Myth as the Bearer of Possible Worlds: An Interview', in my *Dialogues with Contemporary Thinkers*, pp. 36–45.

[22] Ibid.

disentangling of enabling interests from disabling ones operative within mythologies. And this necessary act of critical discrimination should not be confused with 'demythizing,' which would lead to a positivistic impoverishment of our culture.[23]

The crisis of modernity is characterized by a sharp separation between myth and history: a divorce exemplified in what Weber called the desacralization (*Entzauberung*) of tradition. But while this divorce has several negative consequence it has at least the virtue of offering us a certain critical distance. And this means, for example, that we are no longer subject to the illusion that myth 'explains' reality. Because of our condition of crisis, we are far less prone today to believe that myth provides a true account of history. Indeed, it is arguable that it is the very demythologization of myth that permits us to rediscover its genuine, emancipatory function. Or to put it another way: having eliminated the abuse of myth as mistaken *explanation* of how things are, we are free to appreciate its role as inventive *exploration* of how things might be. We thus begin to recognize that the value of myth resides in its ability to contain more meaning than a narrow history of facts. Ricoeur calls this 'saving myth' by demythologizing it. To save myth, in short, is to safeguard it as a poetics of the possible.[24]

What is needed, Ricoeur concludes, is a hermeneutic dialectic between a critical *logos* and a creative *mythos*. Deprived of hermeneutic vigilance, myth remains susceptible to all kinds of misuse.[25] Every mythology implies a conflict of interpretations with important ethical stakes. For it is our ethical responsibility to ensure that *mythos* is always conjoined with *logos* in order to

---

[23] On this distinction between the 'explanatory' and 'exploratory' functions of myth and the critical procedures of demythologization and demythization see Paul Ricoeur, *The Symbolism of Evil,* trans. Emerson Buchanan (Boston, MA: Beacon Press, 1969), and 'The Language of Faith', *Union Seminary Quarterly Review*, 28 (1973), pp. 213–24. See also Rudolf Bultmann, *The Theology of the New Testament* (London: SCM, 1952), p. 295f. See Bultmann and Jaspers, *Myth and Christianity* (New York: Noonday Press, 1957); and René Girard, 'Qu'est-ce qu'un mythe?' in *Le bouc émissaire* (Paris: Grasset, 1982). I have outlined a critique of Girard's position in 'René Girard et le mythe comme bouc émissaire', in *Violence et vérité*, ed. P. Dumouchel (Paris: Grasset, 1985), pp. 35–49. For an application of the demythologizing project to the national myths of Irish culture and politics see my 'Myth and Motherland', in *Postnationalist Ireland* (London: Routledge, 1998) and *Navigations* (Dublin: Lillput, 2004).

[24] See further discussion of this theme in Richard Kearney, *Poétique du Possible* (Paris: Beauchesne, 1984), pp. 190–99.

[25] 'Paul Ricoeur, 'Myth as the Bearer of Possible Worlds', in my *Dialogues*, pp. 39–42. See also Paul Ricoeur, 'Science and Ideology', in *Hermeneutics and the Human Sciences*, p. 245. See also Ricoeur's discussion of the Habermas/Gadamer debate on the rapport between belonging and critical distance in 'Hermeneutics and the Critique of Ideology', ibid., pp. 63–100. Also of interest would be his more recent analyses in *Lectures on Ideology and Utopia* (New York: Columbia University Press, 1986); and *Du Texte à L'action: essais d'herméneutique, II* (Paris: Éditions du Seuil, 1990), especially Part III, 'Idéologie, utopie et politique', pp. 281–406.

prevent narratives of tradition from glorifying one specific community to the exclusion of all others. If tradition is to be ethical, it must be inclusive. Ethical *logos* shares with poetic *mythos* the desire for freedom – our freedom to imagine others and others' freedom to imagine us.

In maintaining a poetical fidelity to the great (and small) myths of tradition, we retain a questioning attitude. Without fidelity we become disinterested spectators of a cultural void; without questioning we become slaves to prejudice. If myth is to remain true to its promise it must pass through the detour of critical enlightenment. To belong authentically to the myths of tradition is also to be *elsewhere* – to be here and not here at once. For hermeneutic imagination to be inside tradition is to be simultaneously outside it. This is one of Ricoeur's most compelling insights: to imagine ourselves as we truly are is to imagine ourselves otherwise.

Between Ideology and Utopia*

In this study we will explore in detail Ricoeur's concept of the *social imaginary*. This comprises the interplay of ideals, images, ideologies and utopias informing our political unconscious. Here we are concerned with ways in which a politics of imagination operates in our everyday lives, often anonymously, to produce collective narratives – stories we tell ourselves in order to explain ourselves to ourselves and to others. These narratives, as Ricoeur argues in his *Lectures on Ideology and Utopia* (1985), exceed the limits of individual imagination and extend into the realm of a communal imaginary with both ideological and utopian dimensions.

One of the most controversial aspects of the social imaginary is the role of ideology. Much of critical theory – from Marx and Engels to Althusser and Barthes – has equated ideology with *false consciousness*. And the opening chapters of Ricoeur's *Lectures* chart the course of this equation. In order to disclose our social reality it was first deemed necessary to expose our ideological fantasies. One of the first steps in such disclosure was to demystify the ways in which ideology alienates human consciousness by attributing the origin of value to some illusory absolute outside of the human. For humanity to return to itself and rediscover its own powers of making (*poiesis*) it must first debunk the pseudo-world of fetish images.

This standard equation of ideology with false consciousness was not always the case, however. The first recorded use of the term ideology was by Destutt de Tracy at the end of the eighteenth century – and then he defined it as the 'science of the genesis of ideas'. But the initial claim of ideology to provide a scientific foundation for social law was soon dismissed. *Idéologue* became a word of abuse for those engaged in lofty abstractions rather than facing up to the truths of reality. Napoleon set his seal on this derogatory connotation when he denounced as 'ideologues' all who opposed his ambitions by letting idealist principles take priority over the exigencies of *la politique réelle*.[1]

It was this negative sense of ideology as abstract unreality which, Ricoeur argues, was later taken up by philosophers. Hegel invoked it summarily in his

---

* Earlier versions and sections of this chapter appeared in *Phenomenology of the Truth Proper to Religion,* ed. D. Guerriere (Albany, NY: SUNY Press, 1990), pp. 126–45; *Irish Philosophical Journal* 2, 1 (1985); pp. 37–55; *The Irish Theological Quarterly*, 52, 1 and 2 (1986); pp. 109–26, and in more extensive form as 'Ideology and Utopia: The Social Imaginary', in our *Poetics of Modernity* (New Jersey: Humanities Press, 1995).

[1] Raymond Boudon, *L'Idéologie* (Paris: Fayard, 1986), p. 40f.

Philosophy of History; but it was Marx who went on to analyse its workings in detail in the now famous passage of *The German Ideology*, where he spoke of a *camera obscura* that reverses the proper rapport between the real and the illusory. I shall return to Ricoeur's discussion of this analysis below. The main point to be made at this stage is that it was the negative definition of ideology as false consciousness that dominated most subsequent theories. Lenin, it is true, used it in the more positive sense of a propaganda weapon, but, so defined, the question of truth was considered irrelevant. What mattered was its efficacity as an instrument of class warfare. Most other modern critics of ideology mentioned by Ricoeur – Mannheim, Aron and Althusser – take it for granted that scientific truth is alien to ideology. To describe something as ideological is generally to describe it as false, or at least epistemologically neutral.

Of course, once the epistemological question is bracketed, it is possible to conceive of ideology as serving a symbolic function in society. It may then be analyzed as illustrating the social imaginary of a culture, its myths, ideals and rhetorics. But it is no longer considered a science of social truth in the sense originally proposed by de Tracy.

In his critical genealogy of the term, Ricoeur traces the various ways in which ideology came to mean the very opposite of science. Where scientific reason dealt with truth, the role of the social imaginary was increasingly dismissed as ideological mystification. The task of science, especially after the Enlightenment, was to unmask this ideological imaginary and return humanity to itself. Science, in short, promised to convert false consciousness into true consciousness, to transform the imaginary into the real and the rational. It is just this stark opposition between ideology and science which Ricoeur challenges in his *Lectures on Ideology and Utopia*. Resisting the reduction of the social imaginary to ideological distortion he argues instead for an affirmation of its utopian potentials.[2]

The Critique of Ideology

We have observed that most critiques of ideology focused on its negative role as a purveyor of falsehood. Ricoeur labels this approach a hermeneutics of suspicion: a practice of interpreting (*hermeneuein*) discourse as 'masked'. Above all, this suspicion was directed to a specifically *religious* consciousness, considered by Marx and others as the most extreme example of human subservience and the most primordial expression of ideology.

---

[2] Ricoeur, *Lectures on Ideology and Utopia* (New York: Columbia University Press, 1985); and Section III, 'Idéologie, utopie et politique', of *Du Texte à l'action: essais d'herméneutique, II* (Paris: Éditions du Seuil, 1986), and especially 'L'Idéologie et l'utopie: deux expressions de l'imaginaire social', pp. 379–93.

As noted in our previous studies, the hermeneutic strategy of removing the mask to uncover repressed meanings was developed in the nineteenth century by the 'three masters of suspicion' – Marx, Nietzsche and (later) Freud. The first of these, Marx, developed a hermeneutics of false consciousness, which discerned the hidden connection between ideology and the historical phenomenon of class domination. He interpreted religion, in particular, as a coded system of submission, where the myth of a supernatural paradise becomes the opium of the people, totally concealing its own socioeconomic motivation. In this respect, Ricoeur shows how Marx's denunciation of the religious character of the great money fetish in the first book of *Capital* constitutes one of the central planks of his critique of ideology (to which we shall return). Nietzsche, for his part, advanced a genealogical hermeneutics of the will, which interpreted the religious attitude as a distortion whose intention is to replace a strong will-to-power with passivity, resentment, and self-abnegation. Dismissing religion as 'Platonism for the people', Nietzsche endeavoured to expose religious cults of otherworldly transcendence as no more than disguised negations of life. Finally, Freud championed a genetic hermeneutics of desire. Religion, he held, is an imaginary substitute for lost primitive or infantile objects. It represents an 'obsessional neurosis' whereby human desire is repressed through a complex of unconscious, self-concealing mechanisms. Thus, in *Moses and Monotheism* and *Totem and Taboo*, Freud explained the origin of the religious imaginary as a symbolic compensation for prohibited pleasures.

Ricoeur argues accordingly that Marx, Nietzsche and Freud all share the suspicion that religious ideology remains ignorant of itself as a production of false values. For them, it is a 'myth' in the sense that it inverts the real and the imaginary, compensating for historical injustice with some ahistorical and otherworldly justice. It is no more than a fantasy projection – an illusory system of relations where man finds himself degraded, imprisoned or abandoned.[3]

Ricoeur acknowledges the legitimacy – even the necessity – of such a hermeneutics of suspicion. There is always a need to unmask the ideological content of the religious imaginary. Indeed, this critique is an indispensable component of modern culture in general and of modern theology in particular. As Ricoeur typically observes in 'The Critique of Religion' (1973):

> The reading of ideology as a symptom of the phenomenon of domination will be the durable contribution of Marxism beyond its political applications. From this point of view Marx does not belong solely to the Communists. Marxism, let it not be forgotten, appeared in Germany in the middle of the last century at the heart of the departments of Protestant

---

[3] Karl Marx and Frederick Engels, *On Religion* (Moscow: Foreign Languages Publishing House, 1955), p. 50.

theology. It is, therefore, an event of Western culture, and I would even say, of Western theology.[4]

We shall reconsider this point in more detail below.

A common task of critical hermeneutics, atheistic or theistic, is to debunk ideological inversions of the original relationship between the real and the imaginary. But it is not the only task. Ricoeur proposes to go further than the masters of suspicion in arguing that critique must itself be subject to critique. This extension of the hermeneutic critique makes it possible to recognize, in the symbolizing activities of ideology, the possibility of a more positive function obscured by the falsifying function. The hermeneutics of doubt may in this way be preserved and also supplemented by a hermeneutics of invention. But before exploring how this might be done, let us take a closer look at Ricoeur's analysis of the three functions of ideology: *integration, dissimulation* and *domination*.[5]

Integration

Ideology expresses a social group's need for a communal set of images whereby it can represent itself to itself and to others. It is an essential aspect of the social imaginary, which enables any particular society to identify itself. Each society, explains Ricoeur, invokes a tradition of mythic idealizations through which it may be aligned with a stable predictable, and repeatable order of meanings. This frequently assumes the form of an ideological reiteration of the founding act of the community. It seeks to redeem society from the crises of the present by justifying actions in terms of some sanctified past, some sacred beginning.[6] We could cite here the role played by the Aeneas myth in Roman society or the cosmogony myths in Greek society, or, indeed, the Celtic myths of Cuchulain and the Fianna in Irish society. Where an ancient past is lacking, a more recent past will suffice – the Declaration of Independence for the United States, the October Revolution for the former Soviet Union, and so on.

Ideology thus serves to relate the social imaginary of a historical community to some inaugural act that founded it and can be repeated over time in order to preserve a sense of social integration. The role of ideology, writes Ricoeur,

---

[4] Ricoeur, 'The Critique of Religion' (1973), in *The Philosophy of Paul Ricoeur: An Anthology of His Work*, ed. Charles Regan and David Stewart (Boston, MA: Beacon Press, 1978), p. 215.

[5] Ricoeur, 'Science and Ideology' (1974), in *Hermeneutics and the Human Sciences*, ed. and trans. John B. Thompson (Cambridge: Cambridge University Press, 1981), pp. 222–46.

[6] Mircea Eliade, *Myths, Dreams, and Mysteries* (London: Fontana, 1968), p. 24: 'Myth is thought to express the absolute truth because it narrates a sacred history; that is, a trans-human revelation which took place in the holy time of the beginning ... By imitating the exemplary acts of mythic deities and heroes man detaches himself from profane time and magically re-enters the Great Time, the Sacred Time.'

is not only to diffuse the conviction beyond the circle of founding fathers, so as to make it the creed of the entire group; its role is also to perpetuate the initial energy beyond the period of effervescence. It is into this gap, characteristic of all situations *après coup*, that the images and interpretations intervene. A founding act can be revived and reactualized only in an interpretation which models it retroactively, through a representation of itself.[7]

It is arguable, moreover, that no social group could exist without this indirect relation to its own inaugural event. 'The ideological phenomenon thus begins very early; for domestication by memory is accompanied not only by consensus, but also by convention and rationalization (in the Freudian sense) ... At this point, ideology ... continues to be mobilizing only insofar as it is justificatory'.[8]

The ideological recollection of foundational images has the purpose, therefore, of both integrating and justifying a social order. While this can accompany a cultural or national revival, it can also give rise to a 'stagnation of politics', a situation where each power rehearses an anterior power: 'Every prince wants to be Caesar', as Ricoeur wryly notes, 'every Caesar wants to be Alexander, every Alexander wants to Hellenise an Oriental despot.'[9] Either way, ideology entails a process of schematization and ritualization that stereotypes social action and permits a social group to recollect itself through rhetorical maxims and idealized self-images. In this respect, Ricoeur endorses Durkheim's identification of ideology as the inner mechanism of the 'national spirit',[10] a notion also pursued by Althusser, who sees it as the political vacuum of conservative nation-states turned in upon their own fetishized images. (This is what Lacanian psychoanalysis, on which Althusser drew, would call the narcissistic imaginary of the 'mirror-phase'.)[11]

Dissimulation

If the schematic 'rationalizations of ideology' bring about social integration, they do so paradoxically, at a 'pre-rational' level. The ideology of foundational myths operates 'behind our backs', as Ricoeur puts it, rather than appearing as a transparent theme. We think *from* ideology rather than *about* it. Moreover, it is precisely because the codes of the ideological imaginary function in this oblique manner that the practice of distortion and dissimulation can occur. This was the epistemological reason for denouncing ideology as 'an inverted image of our

---

[7] Ricoeur, 'Science and Ideology', p. 225.

[8] Ibid.

[9] Ibid., p. 229.

[10] Boudon, *L'Idéologie*, p. 85f.

[11] See Louis Althusser, 'Freud and Lacan', in *Lenin and Philosophy, and Other Essays*, trans. B. Brewster (London: New Left Books, 1971).

own position in society'. Ideology is by its nature an 'uncritical instance' and thus easily susceptible to deceit, alienation, and, by extension, intolerance. All too frequently, ideology functions in a reactionary or at least socially conservative fashion. 'It signifies that what is new can only be accommodated in terms of the typical, itself stemming from the sedimentation of social experience.'[12]

Consequently, the future – understood as opening up that which is unassimilable and unprecedented *vis-à-vis* the pre-existing order – is often translated back into the established 'types' of the past. This accounts for the fact that many social groups display traits of ideological orthodoxy that render them intolerant toward what is marginal, different or alien. Pluralism and permissiveness are the *bêtes noires* of social orthodoxy. They represent the intolerable. The phenomenon of the intolerable arises when the experience of radical novelty threatens the possibility of the social group's recognizing itself in a retrospective reference to its hallowed traditions, as observed in our preceding study.

But Ricoeur demonstrates how ideology can also function in a dissimulating capacity to the extent that it conceals the gap between what is and what ought to be – that is, between our currently lived reality and the ideal world of our traditional self-images.[13] By hiding the gulf that separates contemporary historical experience from inherited memory, ideology often justifies the status quo by presuming that nothing has changed. Self-dissimulation expresses itself as a resistance to change – as a closure to new possibilities of self-imagination. While it is virtually impossible for a social consciousness to endure otherwise than through some kind of interpretative detour via ideological codes, there is always the danger of reducing the challenge of the new to the acceptable limits of an established heritage. With this in mind, Ricoeur proceeds to analyze how the ideological functions of integration and dissimulation may become joint allies of domination.

Domination

This third major function of the ideological imaginary raises the vexed question of the hierarchical organization of society – the question of authority. As Ricoeur observers, citing both Max Weber and Jürgen Habermas, social systems tend to legitimize themselves through an ideology that justifies their right to secure and retain power.

The process of legitimation is inherently problematic, however, in so far as there exists a disparity between the nation-state's ideological claim to authority

---

[12] Ricoeur, 'Science and Ideology', p. 227.

[13] I have applied this critique of ideology as it operates in Irish myth and religion in two lengthy studies: 'Faith and Fatherland', *The Crane Bag*, 8, 1 (1984), pp. 55–67, and 'Myth and Motherland', *Field Day* (Derry), 5 (1984), pp. 61–83, reprinted in *Ireland's Field Day* (London: Hutchinson, 1985).

and the answering belief of the public. Ideology thus entails a surplus-value of claim over response, of power over freedom. Put in another way, if a system's claim to authority were fully consented to by those whom it governs, there would be no urgent need for the persuasive/coercive strategies of ideology. Ideology operates, accordingly, as a 'surplus-value' symptomatic of a discrepancy between the legitimizing 'ought' of normative codes, on the one hand, and the 'is' of lived social existence, on the other. It is because there is no transparent coincidence between the claim to authority and the response to this claim that ideology is deemed necessary to preserve the semblance of a united social consensus. Ideology thus assures what Weber termed the 'charismatic' function of the social imaginary. And, as such, it is a direct consequence of modernity, for it seeks to fill the gap left by the diminution of tradition. Ideology attempts to compensate for the modern 'disenchantment' of society.

Ricoeur's analysis of domination re-engages at this point with Marx's celebrated critique of ideology. Marx, as mentioned above, identified the ideological function of domination as a distorting inversion of the true relation of things. In *The German Ideology* he wrote that 'if in all ideology men and their circumstances appear upside down as in a *camera obscura*, this phenomenon arises just as much from their historical life-process as the inversion of objects on the retina does from their physical life-process'.[14] Marx developed Feuerbach's suggestion that religion is ideology *par excellence*: by projecting a heavenly otherworld beyond the historical world, religion inverts the true relation between the imaginary and the real – superstructure and infrastructure – and makes man stand on his head. This inversion represents, for Marx, the fundamental form and content of all ideological systems, ranging from the ancient mythological cosmogonies to the metaphysical idealisms of Plato, Descartes, and even Hegel. Ideology is thus considered the prime agency of false consciousness in so far as it gives priority to the imaginary over the material, to superstructural abstraction over infrastructural *praxis*. Ricoeur places Marx's critique of ideology accordingly firmly within the hermeneutic of suspicion which proposes to *invert the inversion* – that is, to liberate us from our false idealizations so that we may repossess ourselves as we are in reality. In this respect it constitutes what Ricoeur calls an 'archeological' interpretation that relocates the origin (*arche*) of meaning in the material forces and relations of production.

Ricoeur goes along with Marx – up to a point. He concedes that Marxist critique serves the useful purpose of negating the negative function of ideology. It exposes illusory representations that serve the interests of the dominant class by keeping the dominated class servile. Any genuine commitment to religion must, Ricoeur insists, be prepared to expose itself to the risk of this purgative hermeneutic. A critique of religion nourished by Feuerbach and Marx, as he

---

[14] Boudon, *L'Idéologie*, p. 85f.

puts it, 'pertains to the mature faith of modern man'.[15] A genuine theistic hermeneutic does well then to appropriate to itself the demystification of religion as a 'mask of fear, a mask of domination, a mask of hate'. A Marxist critique of ideology may be embraced therefore as 'a view through which any kind of mediation of faith must pass ... To smash the idols is also to let [authentic] symbols speak.'[16]

Having acknowledged as much, Ricouer then proceeds to take his departure from Marx. The Marxist critique of religion has serious shortcomings to the extent that its equation of the form of ideology with a specifically religious content, and its equation of the latter with the sole function of inversion and domination, lead to a reductive understanding of religion. While it is true that religion can serve the interests of class domination, it can also serve *other interests* – for example, the interest in emancipation. Marx's exclusive equation of ideology with the distorting practice of religious inversion is much too limited in Ricoeur's view. Ideology is a broader and more extensive phenomenon than Marx realized. With the demise of religion as the dominant superstructure of society, other discourses come to serve as the ideological means of justifying and integrating new orders of domination. In the modern era, science frequently fulfils the role of ideological legitimation even though it was, paradoxically, science that claimed to overcome ideology for Marx and several Enlightenment thinkers. A profound irony indeed.

While indebted to Marx, therefore, for exposing a specifically religious version of ideological inversion, Ricoeur resolves to supplement this critique with a further critique of the claim of scientific reason itself to have discovered some *post-ideological* vantage point of total knowledge. The positivist claim to non-ideological rationality is, Ricoeur argues, both naive and deceptive. In fact, taking a cue from the Frankfurt School, he even suggests that such a claim *itself constitutes a new form of ideology* – for it justifies a new social order dominated by principles of disinterested objectivism that cover a system of technological manipulation. Many so-called Marxist societies, founded largely on the critique of ideology, often laid claim to a scientific materialism that becomes an ideology of domination in its own right.

The critique of ideology must, then, itself be exposed to critique lest the rule of positivist reason degenerate into an uncritical dogmatism that conceals its own ideological legitimation. In short, the unchallenged cult of science can also become an opium of the people in the modern technological era.

To the extent, finally, that Marxism after Marx dogmatically invokes the model of scientific materialism to legitimize the official doctrine of the party and, by extension, of the ruling group within the party, it performs the role of

---

[15] Ricoeur, 'The Critique of Religion', p. 219.
[16] Ibid.

ideological domination denounced by Marx himself. Whence it follows that the critical potential of Marxism can be realized only if the use of Marx's work is 'completely disassociated from the exercise of power and authority, and from judgments of orthodoxy'.[17] This can occur only, Ricoeur suggests, when Marxism extends its critique of the religious ideology of dominion to its own tendency to replace this with a scientific ideology of dominion. Ricoeur sums up his critique of Marx's critique thus:

> That religion ... reverses the relation of heaven and earth, signifies that it is no longer religion, that is, the insertion of the Word in the world, but rather the inverted image of life. Then it is nothing more than the (narrow) ideology denounced by Marx. But the same thing can happen, and undoubtedly does happen, to science and technology, as soon as their claim to scientificity masks their justificatory function with regard to the military–industrial system.[18]

Ideology, in the broad sense of social self-representation which Ricoeur affords it, is an unsurpassable phenomenon of socio-historical existence. Social reality always presupposes some sort of symbolic constitution, and it frequently includes an 'interpretation in images and representations of the social bond itself'.[19] Ricoeur concludes, therefore, that it is impossible to discover some *ideologically free zone* from which to speak in any absolute scientific manner about ideology. Ideology is an indispensable dimension of the hermeneutic circle in which our historically situated consciousness is obliged to operate. Hence, while reaffirming the need for a perpetual critique of the deforming function of ideology, Ricoeur flatly rejects the assumption that we can totally abolish ideology – understood in the general sense of a symbolic constitution and interpretation of the social bond.[20] The best response to ideological

---

[17] Ricoeur, 'Science and Ideology', p. 236.

[18] Ibid., p. 231.

[19] Ibid. See Claude Lévi-Strauss, *Structural Anthropology* (New York: Basic Books, 1963), and Cornelius Castoriadis, *L'Institution imaginaire de la société* (Paris: Éditions du Seuil, 1976). For a detailed critical commentary on Castoriadis's and Ricoeur's notion of ideology as a 'social imaginary', see John B. Thompson, *Studies in the Theory of Ideology* (Berkeley: University of California Press, 1985).

[20] Boudon makes this point in *L'Idéologie*, p. 183f. It is also Ricoeur's conclusion. The hermeneutics of suspicion runs the danger of assuming that it remains unscathed by the defects that it denounces. A totally non-ideological science could be only a non-historical science – that is, a form of total and timeless knowledge disengaged from historical interests and limits. And, for Ricoeur, this is impossible, as it is for Heidegger, Sartre, Merleau-Ponty and other exponents of the new, phenomenological finitude of understanding. All understanding of history – no matter how scientific – is itself historically conditioned and therefore incapable of ever escaping from ideology in any absolute manner. Moreover, the historical character of understanding accounts for the primacy of symbolic consciousness, that is, of mediated, indirect, and multilayered consciousness, over and above transparent scientific knowledge. Because human understanding operates in a hermeneutic circle, it cannot represent meaning in a timeless univocal fashion; it can represent

imagination is not pure negation but a hermeneutic imagination capable of critical discrimination. Such a critical hermeneutic, Ricoeur believes, would be able to operate *within* the social imaginary, while refusing any absolute standpoint of knowledge (Hegelian or positivist). Even the most scientific critique works within the limits of a hermeneutic circle.

Toward a Hermeneutic of Invention

Ideology is indeed a creation of false consciousness. But it is not only that. Once the work of demystification has taken place, once the archeological unveiling of the concealed meaning behind the apparent meaning has removed the masks of falsehood, there remains another task. This supplementary practice of interpretation involves what Ricoeur terms a *hermeneutics of*

---

meaning only through a temporalizing process of representation. This means that our understanding of present reality is mediated by a recollection of the past (*wiederholen*) and a projection of the future (*entwerfen*). Perhaps the central discovery of phenomenological hermeneutics has been the priority of the figurative over the literal; the recognition that there can be no access to reality except through the hermeneutic detour of our intentional and symbolizing representation. I shall return to this question later. Suffice it to cite Ricoeur's outline of the implications of this discovery for the relationship between ideology and our understanding of social reality. To quote a key passage from 'Science and Ideology':

> If it is true that the images which a social group forms of itself are interpretations which belong immediately to the constitution of the social bond; if, in other words, the social bond is itself symbolic, then it is absolutely futile to seek to derive the images from something prior which would be reality, *real* activity, the process of real life, of which there would be secondary reflections and echoes. A non-ideological discourse *on ideology* here comes up against the impossibility of reaching a social reality prior to symbolization. This difficulty confirms me in the view that the phenomenon of inversion cannot be taken *as* the starting point for an account of ideology, but that the former must be conceived as a specification of a much more fundamental phenomenon which pertains to the representation of the social bond in the after-event of its symbolic constitution. Travesty is a second episode of symbolization. Whence, in my opinion, the failure of any attempt to define a social reality which would be initially transparent and then obscured, and which could be grasped in its original transparence, short of the idealizing reflection. What seems to me much more fecund in Marx's work is the idea that the transparence is not behind us, at the origin, but in front of us, at the end of a historical process which *is* perhaps interminable. But then we must have the courage to conclude that the separation of science and ideology is itself a limiting idea, the limit of an internal work of differentiation, and that we do not currently have at our disposal a non-ideological notion of the genesis of ideology ... Such is the fundamental reason why social theory cannot entirely free itself from the ideological condition: it can neither carry out a total reflection, *nor* rise to a point of view capable of expressing the totality; and hence cannot abstract itself from ideological mediation into which the other members of the social group are subsumed. (pp. 237–9)

invention. Such a hermeneutics seeks to discriminate between falsifying and emancipating modes of symbolization. Having shattered the fetishes of false consciousness, it labours to identify genuine symbols of liberation. This is the second function of hermeneutic understanding – the utopian function – which Ricoeur sees as indispensable for a proper appreciation of our social imaginary.

Symbolizations of utopia pertain to the futural dimension of our social imaginary. The hermeneutics of affirmation focuses not on the origin behind such symbols but on the end (*utopos*) in front of them – that is, on the horizon of aspiration opened up by symbols. In this way, it is possible to rescue social symbolizations from the distorting strategies of reactionary politics. The social imaginary can thus be divested of its deluding function and reinterpreted in terms of a genuine symbolic anticipation of liberty, truth, or justice. To extend an archeological hermeneutics of doubt into such utopian hermeneutics of hope is to offer the possibility of redeeming symbols from the ideological abuses of doctrinal prejudice, racist nationalism or totalitarian domination; and to do so in the name of a utopian project of freedom that excludes no creed, community or class. Utopian symbols differ from most archeological symbols, explains Ricoeur, in that they tend to be inclusive rather than exclusive modes of representation; they free us from the narrow security of conservativism.[21]

The distinction between archeological and utopian interpretations of symbols has important epistemological implications. The archeological tends to treat symbolic expressions as surface representations of some reality that pre-exists representation. By contrast, utopian hermeneutics, while acknowledging that symbols operate according to a double intentionality, discerns a deep reference that is not exhaustively determined by anterior causes.[22] This utopian reference is a 'second-order' signification, wherein a symbol can refer not just to some reality before the representation but some future horizon of value: some 'surplus' meaning that transcends the limits of ideology. Here value is ahead of the symbol rather than behind it. It unfolds as a horizon of possibilities. As Ricoeur explains:

> Hermeneutics is concerned with the permanent spirit of language ... not as some decorative excess or effusion of subjectivity, but as the creative capacity of language to open up new worlds. Poetic and mythic symbols (for example) do not just express nostalgia for some forgotten world. They constitute a disclosure of unprecedented worlds, an opening onto other

---

[21] On the distinction between 'archeological' and 'eschatological' (and 'teleological') aspects of hermeneutics, see Paul Ricoeur, 'Existence and Hermeneutics', in *The Conflict of Interpretations*, ed. Don Ihde (Evanston, IL: Northwestern University Press, 1974), pp. 22–4.

[22] On the analysis of symbol as a 'double intentionality', see Paul Ricoeur, 'The Hermeneutics of Symbols and Philosophical Reflection', in *The Philosophy of Paul Ricoeur*, p. 36f.; and *The Symbolism of Evil*, trans. Emerson Buchanan (New York: Harper and Row, 1967), Introduction and Postscript.

possible meanings which transcend the established limits of our actual world ... and [function as] a recreation of language.[23]

Ricoeur warns that the critical moment of demystification is not to be confused with desymbolization. Instead of reducing symbols to some putatively 'literal' content, hermeneutic reason exposes the perversion of symbols in order to recover their genuine value. To the extent, therefore, that certain social symbols play the role of ideological domination, they have already abandoned their 'exploratory' role as disclosures of possible worlds. One could even say that the abuse of the social imaginary usually occurs when such symbols are interpreted as literal facts rather than figurative intentions – for example, when a particular nation argues that it and it alone possesses absolute truth. This leads to sectarian triumphalism. This, for Ricoeur, is ideology at its worst – the misrepresentation of a utopian project as a literal possession. It occurs when a church declares that it is the kingdom; or when a state declares that it is utopia (the sole possessor of freedom or equality). This is the language of religious wars and cold wars: the language of ideological closure. The critical function of hermeneutic understanding is not therefore to dispense with the social imaginary, but rather to debunk the alienations of the social imaginary in order to restore its genuinely utopian projects of liberty.[24]

---

[23] Ricoeur, in interview with Kearney, 'The Symbol as Bearer of Possible Worlds', in *The Crane Bag Book of Irish Studies*, ed. Kearney and Hederman (Dublin: Blackwater Press, 1982), and republished in an edited version in Kearney, *Dialogues with Contemporary Continental Thinkers* (Manchester: Manchester University Press, 1984). In this dialogue, Ricoeur distinguishes three modes of language: (i) ordinary language, as identified by much contemporary analytic philosophy (for example the late Wittgenstein and Austin); (ii) scientific language, as practised by the structuralist model of textual autonomy and codification; and (iii) the symbolic language of myth, religion and ideology privileged by phenomenological hermeneutics. Ricoeur argues that the third mode is indispensable. The philosophy of ordinary language recognizes the importance of communication, but often reduces meaning to a one-dimensional realm (as Marcuse recognized) by not taking sufficient account of language as a place of prejudice and dissimulation. The scientific language of structuralism, for its part, exposes the immanent arrangements of texts and textual codes, but virtually ignores the meaning created by these codes. A phenomenological hermeneutics, taking its inspiration from Husserl and Heidegger, addresses this central question of meaning. It acknowledges both the critical and creative functions of language, by disclosing how human self-understanding occurs in and through the mediating detour of signs, whereby we understand ourselves as projects of possibility. Ricoeur concludes that we need a hermeneutic approach to language, directed neither toward scientific verification nor ordinary communication but toward the disclosure of possible worlds ... 'The decisive feature of hermeneutics is the capacity of world disclosure yielded by symbols and texts. *Hermeneutics* is not confined to the *objective* structural analysis of texts nor to the *subjective* existential analysis of the authors of texts; its primary concern is with the worlds which these authors and texts open up. It is by an understanding of the worlds, actual and possible, opened up by language that we may arrive at a better understanding of ourselves.'

[24] In so far as religion is based on a 'divine revelation' that can be transmitted only through history, it too belongs to a cultural and mythologizing heritage that requires critical interpretation. Because religious traditions involve historical mediation and distantiation, they participate to greater or lesser degrees in the ideological process.

We have already observed how ideology expresses a disparity between symbolic representations and reality. But this disparity need not always entail an alienating inversion of the true relations of things. It may also express a fundamental, if congealed, aspiration toward utopian images of universal justice, peace, and beauty – images that, as Herbert Marcuse and Ernst Bloch have pointed out, endorse the categorical imperative of imagination: things as they are must *change*. We could cite here the eschatological image of the Last Days or the creation of a City on the Hill in which we may poetically dwell.

Not all utopian dreams are, of course, liberating. All too often they have served the millennial ambitions of megalomaniacs. But abuses do not make for good law. Here again Ricoeur reminds us how important a certain ethical critique is for a poetics of utopia. Such critique would enable us to show, for example, that the utopian imaginary is authentic when it serves to explode ideologies that disguise present injustice. Differently stated, the social imaginary is liberating to the degree that its utopian forward look critically reappropriates its archeological backward look, in such a way that history itself may be creatively transformed.[25]

Here it is a question of the social imaginary taking the form of a projection whereby a community expresses aspirations for a better world. If one can say, therefore, that without the backward look a culture is deprived of its *memory*, without the forward look it is deprived of its *dreams*. At best, hermeneutic interpretation functions as a creative interplay between the claims of ideology and utopia. Ricoeur spells out the implications of this interplay thus:

> Every society possesses … a socio-political *imaginaire* – that is, an ensemble of symbolic discourses that can function as a rupture or a reaffirmation. As reaffirmation, the *imaginaire* operates as an 'ideology' which can positively repeat and represent the founding discourse of a society, what I call its 'foundational symbols,' thus preserving its sense of identity. After all, cultures create themselves by telling stories of their past. The danger is, of course, that this reaffirmation can be perverted, usually by monopolistic elites, into a mystificatory discourse which serves to uncritically vindicate or justify the established political powers. In such instances, the symbols of a community become fixed and fetishized; they serve as lies. Over against this, there exists the *imaginaire* of rupture, a discourse of 'utopia' which remains critical of the powers that be out of fidelity to an 'elsewhere,' to a society that is not-yet.[26]

[25] Ricoeur, 'Science and Ideology', p. 224. Ricoeur calls for a surpassing of the conventional polar opposition between ideology (*mythos*) and science (*logos*) by placing the critique of ideology within the framework of an interpretation 'which knows itself to be historically situated but which strives to introduce as far as it can a factor of distantiation into the work that we constantly resume in order to re-interpret our cultural heritage'.

[26] Ricoeur, 'The Creativity of Language', in *Dialogues*, ed. Kearney, pp. 29–30.

But this utopian discourse, as Ricoeur points out, is not always positive either. If ideology has its pathological expression, so does utopia. For besides the authentic utopia of liberating rupture there can also exist a dangerously schizophrenic discourse which projects a static future cut off from the present and the past – a mere alibi for the consolidation of the repressive powers that be. In short, ideology as a symbolic confirmation of the past, and utopia as a symbolic opening towards the future, are complementary. If cut off from each other, they can lead to political pathology.[27]

Conclusion

Ricoeur concludes his study by showing how the social imaginary vacillates in the gap between memory and projection. In so far as we remain aware of this gap, it can remind us that society's self-representation is an open-ended process. The gap is an indispensable and unsurpassable horizon of our finite hermeneutic understanding. To deny its existence would be absurd, even ethically dangerous.

Ideologies are gaps or discordances in relation to the real course of things, but the death of ideologies would be the most sterile of lucidities. For a social group without ideology and utopia would be without a plan, without a distance from itself, without a self-representation. It would be a society without a project, consigned to a history fragmented into events which are all equal and insignificant.[28] In other words, if the gap between the historical and the ideal becomes too rigid, the ideological function regresses to sterile conservatism or an escapism that denies reality altogether. In both instances, ideology functions as alienation and precludes the possibility of authentic historical action. Ideology can be considered retrievable, therefore, only when it knows itself to be ideology – namely, a figurative–symbolic representation rather than a literal fact – and only when it ensures that the ideal is kept in close and creative relationship with the real, thereby motivating social action. Action is impossible when the disparity between the real and the ideal precludes the adaptation of our hermeneutic imagination to a historical reality constantly in flux.

In the final analysis, critical hermeneutics provides a satisfactory basis for a dialectical rapport between imagination and reason. The model of the hermeneutic circle (outlined by the phenomenological hermeneutics of Heidegger, Gadamer and Ricoeur) can be extended to include both our *belonging* to the traditional representations of history and our critical *distance* from them. The phenomenon of belonging involves the recognition that our

---

[27] Ibid.
[28] Ricoeur, 'Science and Ideology', p. 241.

understanding always presupposes a historically situated pre-understanding; it rules out the possibility of reaching some non-ideological vantage point where scientific reason could assume absolute knowledge beyond the limits of historical imagination. All objective knowledge about our position in a social class, historical epoch, or cultural tradition presupposes a relation of prior belonging, from which we can never totally extricate ourselves. The claim to total knowledge is a fatal illusion – another example of inauthentic ideology. 'Before any critical distance', insists Ricoeur, 'we belong to a history, to a class, to a nation, to a culture, to one or several traditions. In accepting this belonging, which precedes and supports us, we accept the very first role of ideology – the *mediating function of the image or self-representation.*'[29] Of course, it is precisely because of this belonging that we are also subject to the alienating possibilities of the ideological imaginary – to wit, dissimulation and domination. Hence the need for the second hermeneutic function of critical 'distantiation'.

Critical distance, as noted in our preceding studies, is itself integral to the hermeneutic circle. This is so because the gap between the present (which is real) and the future or past (which are often ideal) provides the possibility of historical distantiation. Historical distancing implies self-distancing, a distancing of the subject from itself, which allows for a critical self-imagining. Ricoeur thus compares the historical phenomenon of critical self-questioning with the textual model of interpretation: both concern a mediation of the subject through the distancing detour of signs and images.[30]

The dialectic of belonging and distancing allows for the transition from prejudice to critical self-reappraisal. In this dialectical passage, we can detach ourselves partially from our anchorage in historical inheritance, but we cannot do so in any final sense. The notion of a disinterested, free-floating consciousness is a fallacy. Scientific reason, to which critique often aspires, is obliged to remain incomplete, for it is always hermeneutically founded in the unsurpassable condition of historical pre-understanding. Distantiation never dissolves belonging. And a positive feature of this limitation is, of course, the refusal of totalitarian knowledge.

Ricoeur concludes accordingly by suggesting that what is needed is a hermeneutic imagination of non-totalization, capable of disabusing us of the twin extremes of dogmatic detachment and attachment. This requires a proper balance between ideology and utopia. Philosophical examples of this would be

---

[29] Ibid., p. 243.

[30] Ibid., p. 244: 'The mediation by texts has an exemplary value. To understand a saying is first to confront it as something said, to receive it in its textual form detached from its author; this distancing is intimately part of any reading whereby the matter of the text is rendered near only in and through a distance. This hermeneutics of the text … contains crucial indications for a just reception of the critique of ideology … Distantiation, dialectically opposed to belonging, is the condition of possibility of the critique of ideology, not outside or against hermeneutics, but within hermeneutics.'

Habermas's reinterpretation of the socialist tradition as motivated by a utopian goal of unrestricted communication, or Ricoeur's own reinterpretation of the Judaeo-Christian promise as an eschatological project of universal liberty. Both readings involve a critique of ideology that distances us from historical prejudice while acknowledging our continued belonging to a specific historical interest in liberation. To completely renounce our hermeneutic bond to historical traditions is to relapse into the illusion of absolute knowledge. There is no short-cut out of ideology that does not lead back into ideology. When reason pretends to surmount all ideological mediation it simply becomes a new ideological function in its own right. That is why the critique of ideology is a task that 'must always be begun, but which in principle can never be completed'.[31]

---

[31] Ibid., p. 245. There has been much written in recent times about the 'end of ideology'. Curiously, this sense of an ending has been registered by intellectuals of both left and right. While Daniel Bell and the neo-conservatives have hailed the end of ideology as a victory for liberal Western humanism, neo-Marxists like Althusser and Jameson equate the demise of ideology with the disintegration of bourgeois humanism (see *The End of Ideology Debate*, ed. C. Waxman [New York: Simon and Schuster, 1968]). Althusser promoted a 'science of socialism' as an 'epistemological rupture' with the 'ideological prehistory' of bourgeois thought (see Althusser, 'Ideology and Ideological State Apparatuses', in *Lenin and Philosophy and Other Essays*, trans. B. Brewster [London: New Left Books, 1971]). Jameson developed this argument stating that in our postmodern context a new 'map of knowledge' will have to replace the old humanist-inspired critique of ideology. 'The luxury of the old-fashioned ideological critique,' he notes, 'the indignant moral denunciation of the other, becomes unavailable' ('Postmodernism, or the Cultural Logic of Late Capitalism', in *New Left Review*, 145 (1984: 53–91)). What these and other 'prophets of extremity' often ignore, however, is that the end of ideology has as concomitant the end of value. In an era 'after value', the critique of ideology would become irrelevant. Questions of better and worse, truth and falsity, justice and injustice would disappear. An ethics of hermeneutic understanding cannot accept such a conclusion.

Between Good and Evil*

In an essay entitled 'Evil, A Challenge to Philosophy and Theology' (1985), Ricoeur offers a hermeneutic critique of different discursive responses to evil: lament and blame, myth, wisdom, and theodicy.[1] In the first part of this study, we will trace the main outlines of Ricoeur's genealogy of discourses before moving on, in our second part, to a discussion of Ricoeur's own hermeneutic response to the enigma of evil in terms of (a) practical understanding; (b) working-through, and (c) pardon.

I

The first discursive response – *lament* and *blame* (witnessed in the Hebrew Bible, for example) – differentiates between evil as suffering and evil as wrongdoing. Lament refers to an evil that befalls us from outside. By contrast, blame refers to evil that arises from within us and for which we are responsible. Or to put it another way, if lament sees us as victims, blame makes culprits of us.[2] Ricoeur observes that, in fact, these two categories are almost always intertwined. We can feel guilty for committing an evil act while simultaneously experiencing seduction, or invasion, by an overwhelming force outside of us. But for the moment, we'll let the distinction stand.

The next discursive genre – *myth* – allows for the incorporation of evil into 'great narratives of origin' (Mircea Eliade). These genealogical narratives seek to explain the origin of evil in terms of the genesis of the cosmos (cosmogony). They offer a 'plot' which configures the monstrosity of evil, explaining the source of the obscene and thereby taking some of the shock out of it. Such mythic spectacles make the foreign curiously familiar, the unbearable bearable, the outrageous accessible.[3] In mythological legends, considerations of human moral choice are inextricably linked to cosmological cycles of fate, destiny, or

---

* Earlier versions of sections of this study appeared in our 'Others and Aliens: Between Good and Evil', in *Evil After Postmodernmism*, ed. Jennifer Geddes (London and New York: Routledge, 2001) and in 'Evil, Monstrosity and the Sublime', in our *Strangers, Gods and Monsters* (London and New York: Routledge, 2003).

[1] Ricoeur, *Figuring the Sacred: Religion, Narrative and Imagination* (Indianapolis, IN: Fortress Press, 1995).

[2] Ricoeur, ibid., p. 250.

[3] As Aristotle noted in *Poetics* (London: Dent, 1963), 111, 4–iv, 3: 'There is the enjoyment people always get from representations ... we enjoy looking at accurate likenesses of things which are themselves painful to see, such as obscene beasts and corpses'.

predestination. The evil figure is the alienated figure, that is, a self determined by some force beyond itself.

Myth then proceeds towards *wisdom* – Ricoeur's next discursive category – to the extent that we not only recount the origins of evil but also seek to justify why such is the case for each one of us. In short, while myth narrates, wisdom argues.[4] It seeks to address the question not only of *why* but *why me?* The wisdom genre turns lament into a legal complaint. It tries to make moral sense of the monstrous. An exemplary case here is the Book of Job, where God and man engage in dialogue about the nature of creation and covenant. With such wisdom literature, the enigma of evil becomes less a matter of metaphysical givenness than of interpersonal relations (human–human or human–divine). In the conclusion to Job, arguments about retribution and justice are ultimately turned to a contemplative wisdom of love: Job learns to love Yahweh 'for naught' in defiance of Satan's wager at the outset of the story.

Wisdom discourse gives way, in turn, to the fourth discursive account of evil listed in Ricoeur's critical genealogy, namely, the *speculative*. This discourse begins, Ricoeur argues, with the development of Christian theology. Augustine is the first great advocate of this position in his answer to the gnostics. In order to show that evil is not a substance implanted in the universe but a punishment (*poena*) for human sin (*peccatum*), Augustine invents a new category, 'nothingness' (*nihil*). Evil is now construed as a deficiency in being which amounts to a privation of goodness (*privatio boni*). If there is evil in the world, therefore, it can only be the result of human action – that is, an act of turning away from the benign being of God towards a lack of being. Augustine thus proposes a radically moral vision of evil which replaces the genealogical question, *Unde malum?*, with the question of wilful human wrongdoing, *Unde malum faciamus?* The cause of evil is not to be found in cosmology but in some form of willed action – the sins of the 'bad will'. This leads in turn, of course, to a penal view of history where no one, in principle, should suffer unjustly. Everyone gets his or her reward, and all pain is a recompense for sin.

The difficulty for Augustine and subsequent theology was, as Ricoeur notes, how to reconcile this extreme hypothesis of moral evil with the need to give sin a 'supra-individual' and historical–generic account in order to explain how suffering is not always justly apportioned as a retribution for individual sins. For in countless cases it is clearly excessive. In other words, if evil is something we as humans do, it is also *done to us*. It is, at least in part, something we inherit, something already there. Augustine thus sought to reinterpret the Genesis tale of original sin in order to rationalize this apparently irrational paradox: namely, we are responsible but not *entirely* responsible for the evil we commit or endure.

---

[4] Ricoeur, *Figuring the Sacred*, p. 252; see also Ricoeur, *The Symbolism of Evil* (Boston, MA: Beacon Press, 1967).

It was, Ricoeur observes, but a short step from these Augustinian speculations on original sin to the fully fledged theories of Western onto-theology. Thus we find Leibniz, for example, invoking the principle of Sufficient Reason to account for the judicious balancing of good with evil in the 'best of all possible worlds'. And if this balancing act of retribution and compensation is attributed to the infinite mind of God by Leibniz, it is dialectically humanized by Hegel and the German Idealists. Hegel's 'cunning of reason' silences the scandal of suffering by subsuming the tragic into a triumphant logic where all that is real is rational. Here the *hubris* of systematic speculation reaches its untenable extreme: 'The more the system flourishes, the more its victims are marginalized. The success of the system is its failure. Suffering, as what is expressed by the voices of lamentation, is what the system excludes.'[5]

But neither version of theodicy – Leibnizian or Hegelian – can provide a convincing answer to the protest of unjust suffering: *why me?* This protest rightly and righteously continues to echo through the memoirs of evil from Job and Gethsemene to Hiroshima and Auschwitz. Nor can theodicy resist the debunking of 'rational theology' in part three of Kant's *Critique of Pure Reason*. Indeed the greatness of Kant, for Ricoeur, was to recognize the need to pass from a purely 'theoretical' explanation of evil to a more 'practical' one. This move from speculative explanation to moral–political action liberates the insight that evil is something that ought not to be and needs to be struggled against. By de-alienating evil and making it a matter of contingency rather than necessity (cosmogonic, theological, metaphysical or historical), Kant brought us face to face with the *responsibility of action*.

Ricoeur adds that if Kant freed us from the excess of rationalist speculation on evil, he also warned against the opposite extreme of drunken irrationalism (what he called *Schwärmerei*), the sort of mystical madness which submits to evil as an alien power that invades and overwhelms us at whim. This latter view typifies not only belief in demonic possession but also the mystical profession of the 'dark side of God' running from the gnostics and Bruno to Boehme, Schelling, and Jung (for example, *Answer to Job*). By taking the mystique out of evil, Kant removed some of its captivating power. He enabled us to see that evil is not a property of some external demon or deity but a phenomenon deeply bound up with the anthropological condition. Evil thus ceases to be a matter of paranoid projection and sacrificial scapegoating and becomes instead an affair of human responsibility. Absolutist dualities are overcome. One's self becomes oneself-as-another and one's other becomes another-as-oneself.

But even Kant, Ricoeur is compelled to admit, could not totally ignore the aporetic character of evil. For if he clearly called for a response within the limits of practical human reason, he could never completely deny some

---

[5] Ricoeur, *Figuring the Sacred*, p. 257.

residual inscrutability (*Unerforschbarkeit*) of evil. At one point, Kant even states that there may be 'no conceivable ground from which the moral evil in us could originally have come'.[6] The lament of *Why? Why me? Why my beloved child?* remains as troublingly enigmatic as ever. Victims of evil cannot be silenced with either rational explanation (theodicy) or irrational submission (mysticism). Their stories cry out for other responses capable of addressing both the alterity and the humanity of evil.

II

But do such responses exist? How may we acknowledge the enigma of evil, laid bare by our detour through Western genres of thought, while still addressing Tolstoy's question: *What is to be done?* Ricoeur proposes a three-fold approach: (a) practical understanding (*phronesis – mimesis – praxis*); (b) working-through (*catharsis–Durcharbeitung*), and (c) pardon.

'Practical understanding' is the name Ricoeur gives to that limited capacity of the human mind to *think* the enigma of evil. He draws here from such varied models as biblical 'wisdom' (discussed above), Aristotle's 'practical wisdom' (*phronesis*), Kant's indeterminate judgement and the hermeneutic notion of 'narrative understanding'. What each of these models has in common is an ability to transfer the aporia of evil from the sphere of theory (*theoria*) – proper to the exact knowledge criteria of logic, science and speculative metaphysics – to the sphere of a more practical art of understanding (*techne/praxis*), which allows for an approximate grasp of phenomena: what Aristotle calls 'the flexible rule of the architect'. Where speculative theory, epitomized by theodicy, explained evil in terms of ultimate causal or creationist origins, practical understanding is geared towards a more hermeneutic comprehension of the enigmatic, contingent and singular characteristics of evil – while not abandoning all claims to quasi-universal criteria (that would account for at least a minimally shared sense of evil). Such practical understanding borrows from action the conviction that evil is something that ought not to be and must be struggled against. In that sense, it resists the fatalism of archaeologies of evil – mythical and theodical. And it does so in favour of a future-oriented *praxis*.

The response offered by practical understanding is to act against evil. Instead of acquiescing in the face of an origin that precedes us, action turns our understanding towards the future 'by the idea of a *task* to be accomplished'. The moral–political requirement to act does not, therefore, abandon the legitimate quest for some minimal model of reasonable discernment. It in fact

---

[6] I. Kant, *Religion within the Limits of Reason Alone* (New York: Harper Torchbooks, 1960), p. 38. Cited by Ricoeur, *Figuring the Sacred*, pp. 258–9.

demands it. For how could we act against evil if we could not identify it, that is, if we could not critically discriminate between good and evil? In this respect, the genuine struggle against evil presupposes a critical hermeneutic of discernment – and such hermeneutic understanding retains Kant's insistence on a practical reason that seeks to think somehow the unthinkable. And to do so with the 'sobriety of a thinking always careful not to transgress the limits of knowledge'.[7]

Our critical understanding of evil may never surpass the provisional nature of Kant's indeterminate (that is, 'aesthetic reflective') judgement. But it at least judges – and does so in a manner alert to both the singular alterity of evil and to its quasi-universal character as grasped by the *sensus communis*. It is not exact or adequate judgement, but a form of judgement for all that, based on the practical wisdom conveyed by narratives and driven by moral justice. We may say, accordingly, that practical judgement is not only 'phronetic' but also 'narrative' in character. This overlapping of *phronesis* (Aristotle) and judgement (Kant) is neatly captured in Ricoeur's account of the ethical role of narrative:

> Ethics as Aristotle conceived it, and as it can still be conceived today, speaks abstractly of the relation between virtue and the pursuit of happiness. It is the function of poetry in its narrative and dramatic form, to propose to the imagination and to its mediation various figures that constitute so many *thought experiments* by which we learn to link together the ethical aspects of human conduct and happiness and misfortune. By means of poetry we learn how reversals of fortune result from this or that conduct, as this is constructed by the plot in the narrative. It is due to the familiarity we have with the types of plot received from our culture that we learn to relate virtues, or rather forms of excellence, with happiness or unhappiness. These 'lessons' of poetry constitute the 'universals' of which Aristotle spoke; but these are universals that are of a lower degree than those of logic and theoretical thought. We must none the less speak of understanding but in the sense that Aristotle gave to *phronesis* ... In this sense I am prepared to speak of phronetic understanding in order to contrast it with theoretical understanding. Narrative belongs to the former and not to the latter.[8]

If practical understanding addresses the action–response to evil, it sometimes neglects the suffering–response. Evil is not just something we struggle against. It is also (as noted above) something we undergo. To ignore this passivity of evil suffered is, for Ricoeur, to ignore the extent to which evil strikes us as shockingly strange and disempowering. It is also to underestimate that irreducible alterity of evil which myth and theodicy tend to overestimate. One

---

[7] Ricoeur, *Figuring the Sacred*, p. 259.

[8] Ricoeur, 'Life in Quest of Narrative', in *On Paul Ricoeur: Narrative and Interpretation*, ed. David Wood (London: Routledge, 1991), p. 23.

of the wisest responses to evil is, on this count, to acknowledge its traumatizing effects and work through them (*durcharbeiten*) as best we can. Practical understanding can only redirect us toward action if it has already recognized that an element of alterity almost always attaches to evil, especially when it concerns illness, horror, catastrophe, or death. No matter how prepared we are to make sense of evil, we are never prepared enough. That is why the 'work of mourning' is so important as a way of not allowing the inhuman nature of suffering to result in a complete 'loss of self' (what Freud called 'melancholia'). Some kind of catharsis is necessary to prevent the slide into fatalism that all too often issues in despairing self-destruction. The critical detachment brought about by cathartic mourning elicits a wisdom that turns *passive lament* into the possibility of *active complaint*, that is, *protest.*[9]

The role played by narrative testimonies is crucial in this respect, whether it be those of survivors of the Holocaust or of trauma–abuse. For such narrative rememberings invite the victim to escape the alienation of evil, that is, to move from a position of mute helplessness to speech-acts of revolt and (where possible) self-renewal. Some kind of narrative working-through is necessary, it seems, for survivors of evil not to feel crippled by grief or guilt (about the death of others and their own survival) nor to succumb to the game of the 'expiatory victim'. What the catharsis of mourning-narrative allows is that new actions are still possible *in spite of evil suffered.* It detaches us from the obsessional repetitions and repressions of the past and frees us for a future. For only thus can we escape the disabling cycles of retribution, fate and destiny: cycles which *estrange* us from our power to act by instilling the view that evil is overpoweringly alien – that is, irresistible. Working-through the experience of evil – narratively, practically, cathartically – helps us to take the allure out of evil, and doing so enables us to distinguish between possible and impossible modes of protest and resistance. Working through is central to a hermeneutics of action in that it makes evil *resistible.* In sum, by transforming the alienation and victimization of lament into a moral response of just struggle, Ricoeur's hermeneutics of understanding and action offers a powerful, if partial, response to the challenge of evil.

Finally, there is the difficult issue of forgiveness. Against the 'never' of evil, which makes pardon impossible, we are asked to think the 'marvel of a once again', which makes it possible.[10] But the possibility of forgiveness is a 'marvel' precisely because it surpasses the limits of rational calculation and explanation. There is a certain gratuitousness about pardon due to the very fact that the evil it addresses is not part of some dialectical necessity. Pardon is

---

[9] See S. Freud, 'Remembering, Repeating, and Working-Through', in *The Standard Edition of the Complete Psychological Works of Sigmund Freud*, vol. 12. Ricoeur elaborates further on this theme in *La Mémoire, l'histoire, l'oubli* (Paris: Éditions du Seuil, 2000).

[10] Ricoeur, *La Mémoire, l'histoire, l'oubli*, especially the epilogue entitled 'Le Pardon difficile', pp. 593–658.

something that makes little sense before we give it but much sense once we do. Before it occurs it seems impossible, unpredictable, incalculable in terms of an economy of exchange. There is no science of forgiveness. And yet this is precisely where phronetic understanding, attentive to the particularity of specific evil events, joins forces with the practice of patient working through – their joint aim being to ensure that past evils might be prevented from recurring. Such prevention often requires pardon as well as protest in order that the cycles of repetition and revenge give way to future possibilities of non-evil. This is a good example of Ricoeur's claim that forgiveness gives a future to the past.

Cathartic narration can, Ricoeur concludes, help to make the impossible task of pardon that bit more possible. This is why amnesty is never amnesia. The past must be recollected, reimagined, rethought and worked through so that we can identify, *grosso modo*, what it is that we are forgiving. For if pardon is beyond reason, it is not completely blind. Or to put it in Pascal's terms, pardon has its reasons that reason cannot comprehend. Perhaps only a divinity could forgive indiscriminately. And there may indeed be some crimes that a God alone is able to pardon. Even Christ had to ask his Father to forgive his crucifiers: 'Father forgive them, for they know not what they do.' As man alone he could not do it. Impossible for us, possible for God. But here an ethics of pardon approaches the threshold of a religious hermeneutics.

If philosophy is to continue to address the perennial enigma of evil, it might do well to take a lead from Ricoeur's hermeneutic response – first, by conducting hermeneutic analyses of the principal discourses deployed in the history of theology and philosophy to represent the enigma of evil; and, second, by advancing new modes of recognition and renewal. We need both a hermeneutics of interpretation and an ethics of active forgiveness. For as Ricoeur continually reminds us, it is not enough to interpret our world of suffering and injustice, we must also try to change it.

Between Poetics and Ethics*

One of the most abiding concerns of Ricoeur's later philosophy was undoubtedly the question of narrative. But, one might ask, does narrative really have a fundamental role to play in contemporary culture, where practices of storytelling are increasingly challenged by technologies of information and simulation? And is it possible to determine which narratives are genuine and which fake, which enabling and which disabling? Moreover, does it make any sense to go on talking about a poetics of narrative in our postmodern world? Or to ask what rapport, if any, such a poetics might have with ethics?

Ricoeur's critical hermeneutics offers, we believe, a compelling response to such questions by outlining four central tasks of narrative: (i) to realize our debt to the historical past; (ii) to respect the rival claims of memory and forgetfulness; (iii) to cultivate a notion of self-identity; and (iv) to persuade and evaluate action. All four, as Ricoeur suggests, lead ultimately to a decisive hermeneutic threshold where a poetics of narrative converses with an ethics of responsibility.[1]

Narrative and History

A key power of narrative, claims Ricoeur, is to 'provide ourselves with a figure of something'.[2] So doing, we can make present what is absent. Translated into the idiom of historical time, we are dealing here with the capacity to liberate ourselves from the blind amnesia of the 'now' by projecting futures and retrieving pasts. Projection is an emancipatory function of narrative under-standing, retrieval a testimonial function. Both resist the contemporary tendency to reduce history to a 'depthless present' of 'irreference'.[3]

---

* Earlier versions or sections of this study appeared as 'Remembering the Past: The Question of Narrative', in *Philosophy and Social Criticism*, vol. 24, nos 2/3 (1998) and as 'The Narrative Imagination', in our *Poetics of Modernity* (Atlantic Heights, NJ: Humanities Press, 1995).

[1] By narrative I understand the act of imitating action which Aristotle called *mimesis* and Ricoeur redefined as a mode of emplotment which synthesizes heterogenous elements; see *Time and Narrative*, Vol. 1 (Chicago: University of Chicago Press, 1984). As such, narrative refers to all accounts, literary and historical, that tell stories involving a temporal concordance of discordance – ranging from myths, legends, and fairy tales to dramas, fiction, movie and television stories, and so on, but not including, in the strict sense, music, lyric poetry or painting.

[2] Ricoeur, *Time and Narrative,* Vol. 3 (Chicago: University of Chicago Press, 1988), pp. 184–5).

[3] See my critique of this postmodern position of 'irreference' in the conclusion to my *Wake of Imagination* (St Paul, MN: University of Minnesota Press, 1988) and Chapter 6 and 'Afterwords'

In the third volume of *Time and Narrative*, Ricoeur analyses the 'testimonial' role of narrative in historical retrieval. A poetics of narrative, he maintains, must include a sense of ethical responsibility to 'the debt we owe the dead'.[4] We would not be able to respond to the summons of historical memory were it not for the mediating/schematizing function of imagination, which provides us with 'figures' for events that happened but are suppressed from memory. The responsibility here is twofold. On the one hand, narrative provides us with figural reconstructions of the past that enable us to see and hear things long since gone. On the other, it stands in for, by standing for, these things as events that actually happened. Here we encounter the right of the past, as it once was, to incite and rectify our narrative retellings of history. We recall our debt to those who have lived, suffered and died. We remind ourselves, for example, that gas ovens and gulags did exist, that Nagasaki and Cambodia were bombed, that political crimes and injustices have been inflicted on innocent people over the centuries. These were not simulations. They actually happened.

The ostensible paradox here is, of course, that it should be narrative that responds to the ethical summons to respect the 'reality of the past'. It is ironic that it should be poetics that comes to the service of ethics as a means of recalling our debt to those who suffered and died (and are often forgotten). But in this case narrative serves to recall the neglected 'others' of history, for, as Ricoeur remarks, 'it is always through some transfer from Same to Other, in empathy and imagination, that the Other that is foreign is brought closer'.[5]

This process of transfer, however, is by no means obvious. In addition to narrative re-enactment – which reappropriates the past as present under the category of the Same – historical imagination has a duty to the *otherness* of the past by way of expressing the past precisely as past, that is, as something that is no more. We are dealing here with a dual fidelity to the past as sameness and difference. The hermeneutic act of *transfer by analogy* seeks to address this paradox. It enables us to transport ourselves into alien or eclipsed moments, refiguring them as similar to our present experience (failing which we would not be able to recognize them), while simultaneously acknowledging their dissimilarity as distinct and distant. In short, the narrative reappropriation of the past operates according to a double responsibility: to the past as *present*, and to the past as *past*.

To the extent that it remains ethically responsible to historical memory, then, imagination refuses to allow reconstruction to become a reduction of the other

---

of my *Poetics of Imagining* (London: Routledge, 1991), pp. 210–32. See also Jameson's critique in 'Postmodernism, or, the Cultural Logic of Late Capitalism', *New Left Review*, no. 145 (1984), pp. 53–9. For Baudrillard's own account of this sublime 'irreference' of simulation, see *Simulations* (New York: Semiotext(e), 1983). For Lyotard's account of sublime 'irrepresentability', see *The Inhuman*, trans. G. Bennington and R. Bowlby (Stanford: Stanford University Press, 1991), p. 136.

[4] Ricoeur, *Time and Narrative*, Vol. 3, pp. 185–6.

[5] Ibid.

to the self; it resists absorbing difference into sameness.[6] So when we talk of narrative providing us with 'analogies' of the past as it actually was, we do well to appreciate that the analogous 'as' is a two-way trope of absence/presence.

This point merits development. Narratives of the past comprise an interweaving of fiction and history. Once we recognize that historical narrative entails a refiguring of past events, we can admit that the telling of history involves the deployment of certain literary practices – plot, composition, character, point of view and so on. This is why the same text can be at once a great work of history and a great work of fiction. It can tell us about the way things actually happened in the past at the same time that it makes us see, feel and live the past as if we were there. Moreover, this 'fiction effect' of history can often enhance, rather than diminish, the task of *standing for*. One thinks, for example, of Michelet's version of the French Revolution, a historical narrative whose literary qualities, in certain respects, are almost comparable to Tolstoy's *War and Peace*. Otherwise put, fiction can serve history, and this service entails ethical as well as poetical dimensions.

The deployment of novelistic techniques by historians to place some past event or personage vividly before the reader's mind was already recognized by Aristotle in the *Rhetoric*, under the title of lexis or 'locution' – a way of making things visible *as if* they were present. The danger is, of course, that the figural 'as if' might collapse into a literal belief, so that we would no longer merely 'see as' but make the mistake of believing we are *actually* seeing. This 'hallucination of presence' (easily conducive to dogmatism and fundamentalism) calls for ethical vigilance by historians in order to sustain a proper dialectical balance between empathetic belief and critical disbelief.

But freedom from illusion is not the only ethical responsibility of narrative. Equally important is the responsibility to refigure certain events of deep ethical intensity that conventional historiography might be tempted to overlook in favour of a so-called objective explanation of things. In a case like the Holocaust, it would seem that such a practice of 'neutralization' is quite inappropriate. The biblical watchword *Zakhor*, 'Remember!', is more ethically fitting in such circumstances. This is something Primo Levi, a survivor of the camps, makes hauntingly evident in his resolve to tell the story as it happened in the most vivid fashion imaginable. The recourse to narrative tropes and devices to achieve this impact is motivated throughout by an ethical imperative: people must never be allowed to forget lest it happen again. Or as Levi himself put it in his conclusion to *Si c'est un homme*: 'The need to recount to "others," to make the "others" participate, acquired in us before and after our liberation the

---

6 Ibid.

vehemence of an immediate impulse ... and it was in response to such a need that I wrote my book.'[7]

In such cases, 'rememoration' takes on an ethical character quite distinct from the triumphalist commemoration of history's great and powerful. Where the latter tends to legitimate ideologies of conquest, the former moves in the opposite direction, namely, toward a felt reliving of past suffering as if we (readers/listeners/spectators) had actually been there. The distinction is important. The cause of the *tremendum horrendum* needs narrative to plead its case lest it slip irrevocably into oblivion. The horrible must *strike* us as horrible. 'Horror attaches to events that must never be forgotten', writes Ricoeur. 'It constitutes the ultimate ethical motivation for the history of victims. The victims of Auschwitz are, par excellence, the representatives in our memory of all history's victims. Victimization is the other side of history that no cunning of reason can ever justify and that, instead, reveals the scandal of every theodicy of history.'[8]

In such instances, the refigurative power of narrative prevents historians from neutralizing injustice. It prevents historiography from explaining history away. And this ethical task of preserving the specificity of past suffering from sanitizing homogenization applies not only to positivist historians but also to the ontodicies of certain philosophers. I am thinking particularly here of Hegel's Ruse of Reason or Heidegger's musings on the Destiny of *techne* (which put gas chambers and combine-harvesters into the same category).[9]

The ethical role of imagination in remembering the horrible is tied to a specific function of individuation: the need to respect the uniquely unique character of certain historical events. Dachau, Hiroshima, the Gulag, Mai Lai, Bloody Sunday, the Killing Fields, Sabra and Chatilla, Tiananmen Square.

---

[7] Primo Levi, *Si c'est un homme* (Paris: Julliard, 1987). For further discussion of this ethical role of narrative memory see my *Poetics of Imagining* (London: Routledge, 1991), pp. 220–8, and Claude Lanzmann's review of *Schindler's List*, 'Holocauste, la représentation impossible', in *Le Monde*, February 1994. In addition to the fictional and cinematic narratives of the Holocaust, it would be useful to consider how other narratives of traumatic events in history are retold in contemporary novels or films – for example, Oliver Stone's retelling of Vietnam in *Platoon*, Costa Gavras's retelling of the Chilean *coup* in *Missing*, Gerry Conlon's and Jim Sheridan's retelling of the Guildford Four injustice in *In the Name of the Father*, and so on. Be it a question of documentary drama, fictional history, or historical fiction, in each case we are concerned with an interweaving of fiction and history. No matter how 'empirical' and 'objective' a historical account claims to be, there is no denying its reliance on narrative strategies of selection, heightening, arrangement, invented speeches and reconstructed events, not to mention its need for coherence and connection. As Hayden White puts it, the historian 'must choose the elements of the story he would tell. He makes his story by including some events and excluding others, by stressing some :and subordinating others. This process of exclusion, stress and subordination is carried out in the interest of constituting *a story of a particular kind*. That is to say, he "emplots" his story' (*Metahistory*, p. 6).

[8] Ricoeur, *Time and Narrative*, Vol. 3, p. 187.

[9] See R. Wolin, *The Heidegger Controversy* (Cambridge, MA: MIT Press, 1992).

Such historical horrors of our century cannot be explained away as cogs in some dialectical wheel. They are more than epiphenomena of the *Zeitgeist*. Yet it is just this relativizing tendency that our current culture of simulation evinces when it reduces narrative to a play of imitation devoid of historical reference. Frederic Jameson decries this tendency to eclipse the historically unique as a 'postmodern cult of the depthless present'.[10] But other commentators, Jean Baudrillard and Jean-François Lyotard among them, seem at times to celebrate this liquidation of reference. Lyotard claims narrative forms of imagination betray the 'irrepresentable' nature of the postmodern sublime, while Baudrillard hails the postmodern condition of 'irreference' where even the reality of war is reduced to TV games of spectacle and simulation.[11] We can no longer distinguish, some postmodernists hold, between what is real and unreal in the representation of things. And one is tempted to conclude that it is a short step from Baudrillard's kind of thinking here to the claims of revisionist historians like Faurisson or David Irving that the gas chambers never existed (or Nolte's claim that the Holocaust is not a unique event but merely one of a variety of similar events). In any case, what the postmodern cult of irrepresentability and irreference appears to put in question is the power of narrative to retrieve historically real events for our ethical consideration in the here and now.

Against such a position, Ricoeur replies: the more narrative singularizes historical memories, the more we strive to understand them; and the more we understand them, the better able we are, in the long run, to explain them (rather than simply suffer them as emotional trauma). It is not then a question of opposing 'subjective' narration to 'objective' explanation. It is a question of appreciating that explanation without narration is ultimately inhuman, just as imagination without hope of explanation runs the risk of blind irrationalism. The refigurative act of standing for the past provides us with a 'figure' to experience *and* think about, to both feel *and* reflect upon. 'Fiction gives eyes to the horrified narrator,' as Ricoeur puts it, 'Eyes to see and to weep. The present state of literature on the Holocaust provides ample proof of this ... one counts the cadavers or one *tells the story* of the victims'.[12] If history-telling, therefore, forfeits this testimonial vocation, it risks becoming a spectacle of exotica or else a repository of dead fact. Neither option is acceptable. 'There are crimes that must not be forgotten, victims whose suffering cries less for vengeance than for narration,' Ricoeur protests. 'The will not to forget alone can prevent these crimes from ever occurring again.'[13]

---

[10] See Jameson, 'Postmodernism and Consumer Society', in *Postmodern Culture*, ed. H. Foster (London: Pluto Press, 1985).

[11] See Baudrillard, *Simulations*.

[12] Ricoeur, *Time and Narrative*, Vol. 3, p. 188.

[13] Ibid., p. 189.

This ethical task of testimony is not simply an individual responsibility. It is also a collective one. Here, it seems, the ethical debt to the dead joins forces with the poetical power to narrate. And we recall that the two modes of narrative – fiction and history – share a common origin in epic, which has the characteristic of preserving memories on the communal scale of societies. Placed in the service of the not-to-be-forgotten, this poetic power permits us to live up to the ethical task of collective anamnesis.

The ethical rapport of narrative to history may be summarized, accordingly, under the following aspects: (1) a testimonial capacity to bear witness to the reality of the past (with its often untold suffering); (2) an analogizing capacity to make present those who are absent and 'other' than ourselves; and (3) an eschatological capacity to project future possibilities where justice might at last prevail.[14]

Narrative and Memory

Historical communities, Ricoeur repeatedly shows, are constituted in great part by the stories they recount to themselves and to others. Hence the importance of the rectifications that contemporary historians bring to bear on the historical accounts of their predecessors. This is as true of the French debates on the meaning of the French Revolution or the German *Historikerstreit* on the Second World War. It is also true of the classic case of biblical Israel – a historic spiritual community formed on the basis of foundational narratives (especially Genesis and Exodus) – which successive generations recount and reinterpret. This is why Judaism, for Ricoeur, is considered the 'culture of the book' *par excellence*. Moreover, it is precisely because stories proceed from stories in this manner that historical communities are ultimately responsible for the formation and re-formation of their own identity. One cannot remain constant over the passage of historical time – and therefore remain faithful to one's promises and covenants – unless one has some minimal remembrance of where one comes from, of how one came to be what one is. For Ricoeur, then, identity is a form of memory. Or as Hegel put it, *das Wesen ist das Gewesene.*

But along with this ethic of responsibility to remember goes an attendant ethic of flexibility. Once one recognizes that one's identity is fundamentally narrative in character, one discovers an ineradicable openness and indeterminacy at the root of one's collective memory. Each nation, state or *societas* discovers that it is at heart an 'imagined community' (in Benedict Anderson's phrase). And that means that *qua* narrative construction it can be

---

[14] For a development of these three functions of narrative imagination see our Conclusion below and the 'Afterwords' to my *Poetics of Imagining* (New York: Edinburgh University Press/Fordham University Press, 1998).

reinvented and reconstructed. After such a discovery of one's narrative identity, it is more difficult to make the mistake of taking oneself *literally*, of assuming that one's collective identity *goes without* saying. This is why, at least in principle, the tendency of a nation towards xenophobic or insular nationalism can be resisted by its own narrative resources to imagine itself otherwise – either through its own eyes or those of others.

Fundamentalism arises when a nation forgets its own narrative origins, bearing out Adorno's adage that 'all reification is forgetting'. Thus the solution to the problem of Northern Ireland may well reside in the willingness of both British and Irish nationalists to exchange narrative memories – which ground their respective national identities – thereby learning to see each other through alter-native eyes. The same goes for Israel and Palestine, of course, where an acknowledgement of the narrative basis of their respective identities might lead to a greater willingness to re-imagine the identity of the historic enemy. In that way, reified memory (expressing itself in compulsive repetition and resentment) may find its best antidote in alternative memory – liberating one's historical consciousness by remembering *oneself-as-another.*

It is only by means of the latter kind of memory, as Ricoeur argues in *Memory, History, Forgetting* (2000), that pardon may release the historical past into a different, freer future.[15] For genuine amnesty does not and cannot come from blind forgetfulness (amnesia), but only from a remembering which is prepared to forgive the past by emancipating it from the deterministic stranglehold of violent obsession and revenge. Genuine pardon, as Ricoeur observes, involves not a forgetting of the events themselves but a different way of *signifying* a debt to the dead which paralyses memory – and, by implication, our capacity to recreate ourselves in a new future. The proper task of amnesty is not to efface the memory of crimes. It is rather to remember them so as to dissolve the debt they have accrued. 'Forgiveness is a sort of healing of memory, the completion of its mourning period. Delivered from the weight of debt, memory is liberated for great projects. Forgiveness gives memory a future.' Ricoeur claims accordingly that it is not a contradiction to say that amnesty is the strict corollary of forgiving memory even as it is the strict contrary of 'repetition memory'.[16]

Critical caution is clearly called for here. Narrative memory is never innocent. It is an ongoing conflict of interpretations: a battlefield of competing meanings. Every history is told from a certain perspective and in the light of specific prejudice (at least in Gadamer's sense). Memory, as suggested above, is not always on the side of the angels. It can as easily lead to false consciousness and ideological closure as to openness and tolerance. This

---

[15] Ricoeur, *La Mémoire, l'histoire, l'oubli* (Pans: Éditions du Seuil, 2000), especially epilogue on 'La Pardon difficile'.

[16] Ibid., p. 23.

distorting power is sometimes ignored by contemporary advocates of narrative ethics – MacIntyre, Nussbaum, Booth – who tend to downplay the need for a hermeneutic of critical suspicion. Nor is it properly appreciated by those advocates of the second of Nietzsche's *Untimely Meditations*, 'The Use and Abuse of History for Life', who believe it is sufficient to 'actively forget the past', to have done with it. Those who think they can dispense with historical memory by fiat will ultimately be dispensed with by history.

To better adjudicate the critical stakes involved in such debates, let me take the example of the Holocaust. The first-hand narratives of Lawrence Langer's *Holocaust Testimonies*, no less than the literary witnesses of authors like Primo Levi, Milena or Elie Wiesel, are reminders of just how indispensable narrative memory is for the ethical remembrance of genocide. For Primo Levi the need to recount his memories was an ethical duty to have others participate in the events which might otherwise be forgotten and, by being forgotten, repeat themselves.[17] For Wiesel the reason he tells and retells these narratives is to give the victims 'the voice that was denied them' by history. Or as one of his characters puts it, searching for a former Holocaust survivor in a New York psychiatric hospital: 'Perhaps it is not given to humans to efface evil, but they may become the consciousness of evil.'[18] Recounting is a way of becoming such an ethical consciousness. For just as the Greeks knew that virtues were best transmitted by remembering and retelling the admirable deeds of the heroes, so too the horror of moral evil must be retrieved from oblivion by means of narrative memory.[19]

It is clear that the history of victims calls for a mode of remembering different from the ritualistic commemoration of heroes and gods. And here Ricoeur recommends the 'little narratives' of the vanquished as opposed to the 'Grand Narratives' of the victors. But moralists of narrative memory such as Lanzmann and Lyotard sometimes fail fully to appreciate that reminiscence of suffering has just as much need to be felt as rememoration of glory. Historical horror requires to be served by an aesthetic (*aisthesis*: sensation) quite as powerful and moving as historical triumph – perhaps even *more* powerful if it is to compete for the attention of the public at large. It is not enough that *Shoah*, Claude Lanzmann's film about the Holocaust, be shown in an élite art-house cinema or as a late-night highbrow TV special on Arte, C4 or PBS. The story of the Holocaust demands to be heard and seen by as many people as possible in each new generation. And this is at bottom an ethical demand. Hence the importance of the decision by national public television in the USA in March 1997 to screen a vivid reminder of the Holocaust: an event that a whole new generation of young Americans

---

[17] See Levi, *Si c'est un homme*.

[18] Ricoeur, 'The Memory of Suffering', in *Figuring the Sacred: Religion, Narrative and Imagination* (Minneapolis, MN: Fortress Press, 1995).

[19] Ibid.

ignored. The film that was chosen, and which provoked widespread debate throughout the schools and media networks of the entire continent, was Spielberg's *Schindler's List* – a phenomenon that should give some pause to the moralizing elitism of Lanzmann and his fellow avant-gardists.

Sometimes an ethics of memory is obliged to resort to an aesthetics of representation. Viewers need not only to be made intellectually aware – *à la* Brecht and Lanzmann – of the horrors of history; they also need to experience the horror of that suffering *as if* they were actually there.[20] Memory not only illuminates; it also illustrates; and part of this illustration is its use of images to *strike* us – in the sense of striking home the horror of evil and the grace of goodness.

A crucial function of narrative memory, as Ricoeur often reminds us, is empathy. And empathy is not always escapism. It is, as Kant noted in his account of 'representative thinking', a way of identifying with as many fellow humans as possible – actors and sufferers alike – in order to participate in a common moral sense (*sensus communis*). In this manner, narrative imagination can assist a certain *universalization* of remembrance. Here our own memories – personal and communal – can be shared and exchanged with others of very different times and places. The familiar and the foreign can change hands.[21]

We may say, in summary, then, that if Lanzmann and Lyotard are correct in stressing memory's ability to attest to the incomparable *singularity* of a unique event like Auschwitz, Ricoeur is right to counterbalance this by emphasizing how memory also testifies to the representative *universality* of good and evil. The truth is no doubt to be found in some kind of Aristotelian mean which combines both ethical impulses in delicate tension. That is what a practical wisdom (*phronesis*) of historical narrative requires in our age of easy forgetfulness – a proper balance between the dual fidelities of memory to the *uniqueness* and *communicability* of past events. As Ricoeur observes:

> We must remember because remembering is a moral duty. We owe a debt to the victims. And the tiniest way of paying our debt is to tell and retell what happened at Auschwitz ... By remembering and telling, we not only prevent forgetfulness from killing the victims twice; we also prevent their life stories from becoming banal ... and the events from appearing as necessary.[22]

Sometimes, in some places – Northern Ireland, Bosnia, Rwanda – it is important to let go of history, to heed Nietzsche's counsel 'actively to forget' the past in order to surmount the instincts of resentment and revenge. At other

---

[20] Ricoeur, *Time and Narrative*, Vol. 3, p. 188. See here the debate by Claude Lanzmann, 'Holocaust, la représentation impossible', *Le Monde* (Paris, February, 1994) and Jean-François Lyotard, *Heidegger et les 'juifs'* (Paris: Galilée, 1988).

[21] Ibid., p. 187.

[22] Ricoeur, 'Memory of Suffering', p. 290.

times, in other places – Auschwitz being the time and place *par excellence* – it is essential to remember the past in order to honour our 'debt to the dead' and to ensure it never happens again. Narrative remembrance, as analysed by Ricoeur, can serve two functions: it can help us to represent the past as it really was, *or* to reinvent it as it might have been. In fiction, the role of reinvention is what matters most – even in historical novels like *War and Peace*. In psychotherapeutic and historical testimony, by contrast, the function of veridical recall claims primacy. Distinguishing between these two separate, if often overlapping, functions is, for Ricoeur, of crucial ethical import – as is discerning *when* it is right to remember and *when* it is better to forget. Or, indeed, *how much* we should remember or forget.[23]

Narrative and Self-identity

The very notion of selfhood (individual and social) is challenged by discourses where human subjects are increasingly defined as 'desiring machines' or 'effects of signifiers'. The best answer to this crisis of identity is not, however, to revive some substantialist notion of the person as essence, *cogito* or ego. We must look here again, Ricoeur suggests, to the resources of narrative. The most fitting response to the question 'Who is the author or agent?' is to tell the story of a life. Why? Because the enduring identity of a person, presupposed by the designation of a proper name, is provided by the narrative conviction that it is the same subject who perdures through its diverse acts and words between birth and death. The story told tells about the action of the 'who': and the identity of this 'who' is a narrative identity. This is what Ricoeur' terms an *ipse-self.*

The narrative self involves an ongoing process of self-constancy and self-rectification that requires imagination to synthesize the different horizons of past, present, and future.[24] The narrative concept of self thus offers a dynamic notion of identity (*ipse*) that includes mutability and change within the cohesion of one lifetime (what Dilthey referred to as the *Zusammenhang des Lebens*). This means, for instance, that the identity of human subjects is deemed a constant task of reinterpretation in the light of new and old stories we tell about ourselves. 'The subject becomes, to

---

[23] Ricoeur, *La Mémoire, l'histoire, l'oubli*, especially Part 3 entitled 'La Condition Historique'.

[24] This was something already recognized by Heidegger in his hermeneutic reading of Kant's transcendental imagination in the *Kantbuch* of 1929. The function of narrative imagination relates broadly to the three temporal ecstasies of Heideggerean *Dasein*, which Heidegger himself traces back to the schematizing function of transcendental imagination in Kant's First Critique. For a more detailed commentary on Heidegger's reading of Kant's concept of transcendental imagination, see my *Wake of Imagination*, pp. 189–95.

borrow a Proustian formula, both reader and writer of its own life. Selfhood is a cloth woven of stories told.'[25]

The narrative model of self-identity has been developed by a number of contemporary thinkers, from Ricoeur and MacIntyre to Taylor and Benhabib. These advance the rudimentary argument that Enlightenment models of the disembodied *cogito*, no less than the traditional models of a substance-like self (*idem*), fail to appreciate the fundamental socialization processes through which a person acquires a self-identity capable of projecting a narrative into the world in which it is both an author and an actor.[26] Moreover, the narrative model of identity suggests that the age-old virtue of self-knowledge, first promoted by Socrates and Seneca, involves not some self-enclosed ego but a hermeneutically 'examined life freed from naive archaisms and dogmatisms'. The subject of self-knowledge is, in other words, one clarified by the cathartic effect of narratives conveyed by culture. Self-constancy is the property of a subject instructed by the 'figures' of a culture it has critically applied to itself.[27]

This critical application of a self's cultural figures to itself is a necessary moment in the hermeneutics of identity. Why? Because storytelling can also be a breeding ground of illusions, distortions and ideological false-hoods. In configuring heterogeneous elements of our experience, narrative emplotment can easily serve as a cover-up. Narrative concordance can

---

[25] P. Ricoeur, *Time and Narrative*, Vol. 3, p. 246. It is worth recalling here that the story of a society, no less than that of an individual life, is also perpetually refigured by the real and fictive stories it tells about itself. A society's self-image is also a 'cloth woven of stories told'. See here our 'Ethics and the Narrative Self', in *The Modern Subject*, ed. by Otto Christensen and Siri Meyer, *Kulturtekster*, vol. 6, Bergen, Norway, 1996, pp. 48–62.

[26] See in particular S. Benhabib, *Situating the Self* (New York: Routledge, 1992), p. 5f; but also the works of Hannah Arendt, Charles Taylor, Alasdair MacIntyre and Martha Nussbaum.

[27] Ricoeur, *Time and Narrative*, Vol. 3, pp. 247–9. See also M. Nussbaum's insightful analysis of the role 'literary imagination' plays in the development of ethical self-knowledge and judgement in *Love's Knowledge,* especially the following studies: 'Flawed Crystals: James's *The Golden Bowl* and Literature as Moral Philosophy'; 'Finely Aware and Richly Responsible: Literature and the Moral Imagination'; 'Perceptive Equilibrium: Literary Theory and Ethical Theory'; 'Reading for Life'; 'Fictions of the Soul'; and 'Narrative Emotions'. These studies, Nussbaum explains,

> argue for a conception of ethical understanding that involves emotional as well as intellectual activity and gives a certain type of priority to the perception of particular people and situations, rather than to abstract rules. They argue, further, that this ethical conception finds its most appropriate expression and statement in certain forms usually considered literary rather than philosophical – and that if we wish to take it seriously we must broaden our conception of moral philosophy in order to include these texts within it. They attempt to articulate the relationship, within such a broader ethical inquiry, between literary and more abstractly theoretical elements. (p. ix).

Nussbaum goes on to make the following statements: 'the fresh imagination of particularity (provided by fiction) is an essential moral faculty' (p. 237); 'allowing oneself to be in some sense

mask discordance, its drive for order and unity displacing difference. Indeed, as Lyotard among others reminds us, even emancipatory narratives can degenerate into oppressive Grand Narratives. The question of power interests cannot, therefore, be divorced from the hermeneutic analysis of narrative. We are constantly in need of a hermeneutic critique to be applied to the deceptive proclivities of narrative. Here I concur with Edward Said, who observes in 'Permission to Narrate' (1984), and again in *Culture and Imperialism* (1993), how narratives frequently operate as representations of power: representations that must be challenged, by 'counter-narratives', in order that their abusive tendencies be exposed and, ideally, reversed. But these so-called counter-narratives, Said recognizes, are themselves forms of narrative – alternative stories to the official story, emergent stories of marginal or truncated histories, indirect stories of irony and subversion.[28] Such unofficial narratives brush history against the grain. They put the dominant power in question.

A similar argument obtains at the level of individual identity. Here the process of narrative self-critique takes the form of a cathartic clarification whereby the self comes to 'know itself' by retelling itself. This may occur, for

---

passive and malleable, open to new and sometimes mysterious influences, is a part of the transaction and a part of its value. Reading novels ... is a practice of falling in love. And it is in part because novels prepare the reader for love that they make the valuable contribution they do to society and to moral development' (p. 238); 'Novels can be a school for the moral sentiments, distancing us from blinding personal passions and cultivating those that are more conducive to community. Proust goes so far as to say that the relation we have with a literary work is the only human relation characterized by genuine altruism, and also the only one in which, not caught up in the vertiginous kaleidoscope of jealousy, the reader can truly know the mind of another person ... there is a real issue here and I do not think we can fully understand the ethical contribution of the novel without pursuing it' (p. 240). Several of Nussbaum's arguments for an ethical imagination find support in other contemporary theories – for example, Arthur Danto's idea of 'transfigurative literature', Northrop Frye's notion of 'educated imagination', Frank Lentriccia's concept of 'art for life's sake', Iris Murdoch's claim that 'art is the most educational thing we have', or Marshall Gregory's thesis of the 'vicarious imagination' inspired by Sir Philip Sidney's 'Apology' for ethical literature:

> Narratives have the power to move us because they are empirical, which is the ground of their vividness; because they provide deep companionship, which means that they are fulfilling. And what moves us, of course, also *forms us* ... History and literature both possess an immense power to educate. Since modernism's elevation of the notion of aesthetic purity and structuralism's elevation of the notion of linguistic indeterminateness, the educational power of both literature and history has nearly been forgotten, especially by critics and academics. Writers, however, continue to assert literature's and history's educational power. (Selfhood Forged and Memory Enriched: Narrative's Empirical Appeal to the Vicarious Imagination, forthcoming)

[28] Edward Said, *Culture and Imperialism* (New York: Knopf, 1993); 'Permission to Narrate', *London Review of Books*, 29 February 1984. Also on the role of narrative in nationalist movements, see Tony Judt's review essay, 'The New Old Nationalism', *New York Review of Books,* Vol. 41, no. 10 (26 May 1994), pp. 44–51.

example, when a person commits herself to working the bits and pieces of unintelligible or suppressed experience into a narrative that acknowledges a certain self-constancy through change. This model of analytic working through (*Durcharbeitung*) applies to both individual case-histories and to collective stories of communities. For, just as psychoanalysis shows how the story of a life comes to be composed through a series of rectifications applied to preceding narratives, the history of a society proceeds from the critical corrections new historians bring to their predecessors' accounts.

Thus do communities come to know themselves in the stories they tell about themselves. Returning to the case of biblical Israel, we may note that it is in the perpetual recounting of its own foundational narratives (Genesis, Exodus, Kings and so on) that the historical community bearing its name is formed. Exemplifying the hermeneutic circle of narrative identity, Israel draws its self-image from the reinterpretation of those texts it has itself created. For communal identity, no less than for personal identity, stories proceed from stories.

To sum up this third part of our argument, we could say that for narrative identity to be ethically responsible it must ensure that self-constancy is always informed by self-questioning. This requires that narrative identity never forget its origins in narrative imagination. A critical fluidity and openness pertains to narrative identity as long as we recognize that it is always something made and remade. Hence a society that willingly reconstitutes itself through a corrective process of ongoing narrative is as impervious to self-righteousness as it is to fundamentalism. Any slippage towards collective solipsism is resisted by the imaginative tendency of narrative to freely vary worlds foreign to itself. At its best, narrative imagination remains open to the possibility of its own self-deconstruction. Indeed, sometimes it is when narrative splits itself into 'little narratives' (*petits récits*), sundered narratives, even anti-narratives attesting the impossibility of Grand Narrative, that it remains most faithful to otherness.

It is, moreover, this same propulsion of narrative toward otherness that entails the corollary movement toward ethical commitment. Citing the well-known example of a subject's capacity to keep its promises over time, Ricoeur affirms that narrative identity is only equivalent to true self-constancy in the moment of decision: a moment that makes 'ethical responsibility the highest factor in self-constancy'.[29] Thus, to return to our example of biblical Israel, we might say that it is the Jewish community's ability to reimagine itself through its *own* narratives that provides it with both the coherent identity of a historical people and the ethical resource to imagine the narratives of others (for example, the Palestinians) who oppose them. The ethical moment of decision

---

[29] Ricoeur, *Time and Narrative*, Vol. 3, p. 249.

might be seen accordingly as an expression of the Hebraic constancy of narrative memory – the memory of the age-old demand to liberate the imprisoned, to care for 'the famished, the widowed, and the orphaned', to welcome the stranger as the other-than-self.

There is a hermeneutic circle here. But there are limits to this self-interpretation that prevent it from degenerating into a vicious circle. First, there is the 'decision' mentioned above, which, though profoundly informed and galvanized by narrative, ultimately cuts across the narrative circuit and stakes a claim for action as we move from text to life-world. Second, there is a moment of responsibility to the other, who, although heard and witnessed via narratives, is none the less irreducible to these narratives in the final analysis. Levinas describes this as an ethical obligation to the face of the other, while Lyotard and Adorno speak of this limit-marking alterity in terms of a willingness to surpass narrative in deference to the 'sublime'. Either way, there is a recognition that narrative understanding may indeed have full poetic licence within the imaginary, but that it encounters limits to its own free play when confronted with the irreducible otherness of the other. Narrative understanding is ethical because it is answerable to something beyond itself, so that even where it knows no censure (within the text), it knows responsibility (to the other beyond the text).

Narrative and Persuasion

The idea that narrative is ethically vacuous is further belied by its fourth major function – the evaluative dimension of persuasion. Most narratives, as Ricoeur reminds us, convey something of the Rilkean summons: Change your life! This phenomenon of persuasion has wide-ranging implications for our under-standing of the rapport between ethics and poetics (for example, rhetoric, tropology, textual exegesis, reader reception). Narrative persuasion almost always involves some element of ethical solicitation, however tacit or tangential.

We are not talking of a morality of rule here, which would be antipathetic to poetic liberty. Ricoeur's maxim that 'the imaginary knows no censorship' goes to repudiate the intrusion of moralizing dogmatism into the free space of creativity. On this view, Rushdie had full poetic licence to imagine whatever he wanted in *The Satanic Verses*, as did Kazantzakis in *The Last Temptation of Christ* or the Marquis de Sade in *L'économie du boudoir*. What Ricoeur recommends is not a moralism of abstract rules but an ethics of experience (concerned with cultural paradigms of suffering and action, happiness and dignity). As Aristotle first acknowledged, poetics teaches us essential truths about human experience (unlike history, which is confined to facts), and these essential truths are intimately related to the pursuit of possibilities of happiness or unhappiness – that is, the desire for the good life guided by practical wisdom (*phronesis*). The fictional narrator presents us with a variety of ethical possibilities that the reader is then free to choose from, discarding some, embracing others. The narrator proposes; the reader disposes. But the pact of trust and exchange struck by narrator and reader always carries some evaluative charge.

> The strategy of persuasion undertaken by the narrator [writes Ricoeur], is aimed at giving the reader a vision of the world that is never ethically neutral, but that rather implicitly or explicitly induces a new evaluation of the world and of the reader as well. In this sense, narrative already belongs to the ethical field in virtue of its claim – inseparable from its narration – to ethical justice. Still it belongs to the reader, now an agent, an intitiator of *action,* to choose among the multiple proposals of ethical justice brought forth by the reading.[30]

Here Ricoeur essays a hermeneutic retrieval of Aristotle. It is because ethical *phronesis* implies just thinking and a desire for the good that Aristotle considers it has a significant role in poetic *mimesis*. There is no 'imitation of an action' that does not give rise to approbation or reprobation relative to a scale of goodness. And so we may ask what would remain of the cathartic pity and fear that Aristotle taught us to link to unmerited misfortune, 'if aesthetic pleasure were to be totally dissociated from any sympathy or antipathy for the character's ethical quality'.[31] Even when narrative fiction subverts the established system of virtue, it is still engaged, however implicitly, in a process of evaluation. 'Poetics', comments Ricoeur, 'does not stop borrowing from ethics, even when it advocates the suspension of all ethical judgement or its ironic inversion. The very project of ethical neutrality presupposes the original ethical quality of action.'[32] We may say, then, that poetic narratives not only excite emotions of pity and fear, they also teach us something about happiness and unhappiness – that is, the good life. What we learn in the narrative 'imitation of action' we may incorporate in our return journey from text to action. This combination of emotion and learning in fiction is what prompts Ricoeur to identify narrative understanding with phronetic understanding. In a study entitled 'Life in Quest of Narrative', he writes:

> Aristotle did not hesitate to say that every well-told story *teaches* us something; moreover, he said that the story reveals universal aspects of the human condition and that, in this respect, poetry was more philosophical than history, which is too dependent on the anecdotal

---

[30] Ibid.

[31] Ricoeur, *Time and Narrative*, Vol. 1, p. 59.

[32] Ibid.

aspect of life. Whatever may be said about this relation between poetry
and history, it is certain that tragedy, epic and comedy, to cite only
those genres known to Aristotle, develop a sort of understanding that
can be termed *narrative understanding* and which is much closer to the
practical wisdom of moral judgment than to science, or more generally,
to the theoretical use of reason.[33]

The validity of Ricoeur's observation can be seen in the simple fact that
while ethics often speaks generally of the relation between virtue and the
pursuit of happiness, fiction fleshes it out with experiential images and
examples – that is, with particular stories. To understand what courage
means, we tell the story of Achilles; to understand what wisdom means, we
tell the story of Socrates; to understand what *caritas* means, we tell the story
of St Francis of Assisi. Ricoeur concludes:

> It is the function of poetry in its narrative and dramatic form to propose
> to the imagination and to its mediation various figures that constitute
> *so* many *thought experiments* by which we learn to link together the
> ethical aspects of human conduct and happiness and misfortune. By
> means of poetry we learn how reversals of fortune result from this or
> that conduct, as this is constructed by the plot in the narrative. It is due
> to the familiarity we have with the types of plot received from our
> culture that we learn to relate virtues, or rather forms of excellence,
> with happiness or unhappiness.[34]

These 'lessons' of narrative imagination constitute the 'universals' of
which Aristotle spoke. But they are universals of a more approximate (and
context-sensitive) kind than those of theoretical thought. Ricoeur speaks of
narrative understanding, then, in the sense Aristotle gave to *phronesis*, by
contrast with the abstract logic of pure *theoria.* And it is on this basis that he
makes his ultimate wager that the good life is a life recounted.

---

[33] Ricoeur, 'Life in Quest of Narrative', in *On Paul Ricoeur: Narrative and Interpretation*, ed.
D. Wood, pp. 22–3.

[34] Ibid. One might explore links here between Ricoeur's version of a phroneric understanding of
experience and Dewey's notion of 'emotional thinking'.

PART TWO

Myth as the Bearer of Possible Worlds (1978)*

RK: One of your first attempts at hermeneutic analysis concentrated on the way in which human consciousness was mediated by mythic and symbolic expressions from the earliest times. In *The Symbolism of Evil* (1960) you demonstrated how mythic symbols played an important ideological and political role in the ancient cultures of the Babylonians, Hebrews and Greeks. And in this same work you declared that 'myth relates to events that happened at the beginning of time which have the purpose of providing grounds for the ritual actions of men of today'. Are you suggesting that mythic symbols can play a relevant role in contemporary culture? And if so, could you elaborate on how they might do so?

PR: I don't think that we can approach this question directly, that is, in terms of a direct relationship between myth and action. We must first return to an analysis of what constitutes the *imaginary nucleus* of any culture. It is my conviction that one cannot reduce any culture to its explicit functions – political, economic and legal, and so on. No culture is wholly transparent in this way. There is invariably a hidden nucleus which determines and rules the *distribution* of these transparent functions and institutions. It is this matrix of distribution which assigns them different roles in relation to (1) each other, (2) other societies, (3) the individuals who participate in them, and (4) nature, which stands over against them.

RK: Does this ratio of distribution differ from one society to another?

PR: It certainly does. The particular relationship between political institutions, nature and the individual is rarely if ever the same in any two cultures. The ratio of distribution between these different functions of a given society is determined by some *hidden* nucleus, and it is here that we must situate the specific identity of culture. Beyond or beneath the self-understanding of a society there is an opaque kernel which cannot be reduced to empirical norms or laws. This kernel cannot be explained in terms of some transparent model because it is constitutive *of* a culture *before* it can be expressed and reflected in specific

* Recorded in Paris in 1978. First published in *The Cranebug Journal*, Vol. 2, Nos 1 and 2, 1978.

representations or ideas. It is only if we try to grasp this kernel that we may discover the *foundational mytho-poetic* nucleus of a society. By analyzing itself in terms of such a foundational nucleus, a society comes to a truer understanding of itself; it begins to critically acknowledge its own symbolizing identity.

RK: How are we to recognize this mythical nucleus?

PR: The mythical nucleus of a society is only *indirectly* recognizable. But it is indirectly recognizable not only by what is said (discourse), but also by what and how one lives (*praxis*), and third, as I suggested, by the distribution between different functional levels of a society. We cannot, for example, say that in all countries the economic layer is determining. This is true for our Western society. But as Lévi-Strauss has shown in his analysis of many primitive societies, this is not universally true. In several cultures the significance of economic and historical considerations would seem to be minor. In our culture the economic factor is indeed determining; but that does not mean that the predominance of economics is itself explicable purely in terms of economic science. This predominance is perhaps more correctly understood as but one constituent of the overall evaluation of what is primary and what is secondary. And it is only by the analysis of the hierarchical structuring and evaluation of the different constituents of a society (that is, the role of politics, nature, art, religion and so on) that we may penetrate to its hidden *mytho-poetic nucleus.*

RK: You mentioned Lévi-Strauss. How would you situate your own hermeneutical analyses of symbol and myth in relation to his work in this area?

PR: I don't think that Lévi-Strauss makes any claim to speak of societies in general. He has focused on certain primitive and stable societies, leaving aside considerations of history. This is important to realize so as not to draw hasty conclusions from his analyses. Lévi-Strauss has deliberately chosen to speak of societies *without history*, whereas I think that there is something specifically historical about the societies to which we in the West belong, depending on the extent to which they are affected by Hebraic, Hellenic, Germanic or Celtic cultures. The development of a society is both synchronic and diachronic. This means that the distribution of power functions in any given society contains a definite *historical* dimension. We have to think of societies in terms of both a set of simultaneous institutions (synchronism) and a process of historical transformation (diachronism). Thus we arrive at the panchronic approach to societies, that is, both synchronic and diachronic, which characterizes the hermeneutical method. And we must also realize that the kinds of myth on which our societies are founded have themselves this twofold characteristic: on the one hand, they constitute a certain system of simultaneous symbols which can be approached through structuralist analysis; but, on the other hand, they have a history, because it is always through a process of interpretation and reinterpretation that they are kept alive. Myths have a historicity of their own. This difference of history typifies, for example, the development of the Semitic, pre-Hellenistic and Celtic mythical nuclei. Therefore, just as societies are both structural and historical, so also are the mythical nuclei which ground them.

RK: In the conclusion to *The Symbolism of Evil* you state that 'a philosophy instructed by myths arises at a certain moment in reflection and wishes to answer to a certain situation in modern culture'. What precisely do you mean by this 'certain situation'? And how does myth answer to this problematic?

PR: I was thinking there of Jaspers's philosophy of 'boundary situations', which influenced me so strongly just after the Second World War. There are certain boundary situations such as war, suffering, guilt, death and so on, in which the individual or community experiences a fundamental existential crisis. At such moments the whole community is put into question. For it is only when it is threatened with destruction from without or from within that a society is compelled to return to the very roots of its identity, to that mythical nucleus which ultimately grounds and determines it. The solution to the immediate crisis is no longer a purely political or technical matter but demands that we ask ourselves the ultimate questions concerning our origins and ends: Where do we come from? Where are we going? In this way, we become aware of our basic capacities and reasons for surviving, for being and continuing to be what we are.

RK: I am reminded here of Mircea Eliade's statement in *Myths, Dreams, Mysteries* that myth is something which always operates in a society regardless of whether this society reflectively acknowledges its existence. Eliade maintains that because modern man has lost his awareness of the important role that myth plays in his life, it often manifests itself in *deviant* ways. He gives as an example the emergence of fascist movements in Europe characterized by a mythic glorification of blood sacrifice and the hero–saviour together with the equally mythical revival of certain ancient rituals, symbols and insignia. The suggestion is that if we do not explicitly recognize and reappropriate the mythic import of our existence it will emerge in distorted and pernicious ways. Do you think this is a valid point?

PR: You have hit here on a very important and difficult problem: the possibilities of a perversion of myth. This means that we can no longer approach myth *at the level of naiveté*. We must rather always view it from a critical perspective. It is only by means of a selective reappropriation that we can become aware of myth. We are no longer primitive beings, living at the immediate level of myth. Myth for us is always mediated and opaque. This is so not only because it expresses itself primarily through a particular apportioning of power functions, as mentioned earlier, but also because several of its recurrent forms have become deviant and dangerous, for example, the myth of absolute power (fascism) and the myth of the sacrificial scapegoat (anti-Semitism and racism). We are no longer justified in speaking of 'myth in general'. We must critically assess the content of each myth and the basic intentions which animate it. Modern man can neither get rid of myth nor take it at its face value. Myth will always be with us, but we must always approach it *critically*.

RK: It was with a similar scruple in mind that I tried to show in *Myth and Terror* (1978) that there are certain mythic structures operative in extreme Irish Republicanism – recurrence of blood sacrifice, apocalypse/renewal, and so on – which can become deviant manifestations of an original mythical nucleus. And I feel accordingly that any approach to myth should be as much a demythologization of deviant expressions as a resuscitation of genuine ones.

PR: Yes. And I think it is here that we could speak of the essential connection between the 'critical instance' and the 'mythical foundation'. Only those myths are genuine which can be reinterpreted in terms of *liberation*. And I mean liberation as both a personal and collective phenomenon. We should perhaps sharpen this critical criterion to include only those myths which have as their horizon the liberation of humanity *as a whole*. Liberation cannot be exclusive. Here I think we come to recognize a fundamental convergence between the claims of myth and reason. In genuine reason as in genuine myth we find a concern for the *universal* liberation of all. To the extent that myth is seen as the foundation of a particular community to the absolute exclusion of all others, the possibilities of perversion – chauvinistic nationalism, racism and so on – are already present.

RK: So in fact you suggest that the foundational power of myth should always be in some sense chaperoned by critical reason?

PR: In our Western culture the myth-making of man has often been linked with the critical instance of reason. And this is because it has had to be constantly interpreted and reinterpreted in different historical epochs.

In other words, it is because the survival of myth calls for perpetual historical interpretation that it involves a critical component. Myths are not unchanging and unchanged antiques which are simply delivered out of the past in some naked, original state. Their specific identity depends on the way in which each generation receives or interprets them according to their needs, conventions and ideological motivations. Hence the necessity of critical discrimination between liberating and destructive modes of reinterpretation.

RK: Could you give an example of such reinterpretation?

PR: Well, if we take the relation of *mythos* and *logos* in the Greek experience, we could say that myth had been absorbed by the *logos*, but never completely so; for the claim of the *logos* to rule over *mythos* is itself a mythical claim. Myth is thereby reinjected into the *logos* and gives a mythical dimension to reason itself. Thus the rational appropriation of myth becomes also a revival of myth. Another example would be the reinterpretative overlap between the mythical paradigms of the Hebraic exodus and the prophetic dimension in Hebrew literature. And then at a second level, this Hebraic *mythos* came down to us through a Hellenization of its whole history. Even for us today, this Hellenization is an important mediation because it was through the conjunction of the Jewish Torah and Greek logos that the notion of law could be incorporated into our culture.

RK: You would not agree, then, with those modern theologians, such as Moltmann and Bultmann, who suggest that the Hellenization of the Judaeo-Christian culture is a perversion of its original richness?

PR: No. The tension between the Greek logos and the Semitic nucleus of exodus and revelation is fundamentally and positively constitutive of our culture.

RK: Several critics have described your hermeneutical approach to myth and symbol as an attempt, almost in the manner of psychoanalysis, to reduce myth to some hidden rational message. In *The Symbolism of Evil* you say that the aim of your philosophy is to disclose through reflection and speculation the *rationality* of symbols. And again in *On Interpretation* you state that 'every *mythos* harbors a *logos* which requires to be exhibited'. But is it possible to extract the *logos* and yet leave the *mythos* intact? Or is myth something essentially enigmatic and therefore irreducible to rational content?

PR: This criticism must be understood in the following way. There are two uses of the concept of myth. One is myth as the *extension* of a symbolic structure. In this sense it is pointless to speak of a demythologization, for that would be tantamount to desymbolization – and this I deny completely. But there is a second sense in which myth serves as an *alienation* of this symbolic structure; here it becomes reified and is misconstrued as an actual materialistic explanation of the world. If we interpret myth *literally*, we misinterpret it. For myth is essentially *symbolic*. It is only in instances of such misinterpretation that we may legitimately speak of demythologization, not concerning its symbolic content but concerning the hardening of its symbolic structures into dogmatic or reified ideologies.

RK: Do you think that Bultmann's use of the term demythologization had something to do with this confusion between two different types of myth (as creative symbol or reductive ideology)?

PR: Yes I do. Bultmann seems to ignore the complexity of myth. And so when he speaks, for example, of the necessity to demythologize the myth of the threefold division of the cosmos into Heaven, Earth and Hell, he is treating this myth only in terms of its literal interpretation, or rather misinterpretation. But Bultmann does not realize that there is a symbolic as well as a pseudosymbolic or literal dimension in myth, and that demythologization is only valid in relation to this second dimension.

RK: Are myths *universal*, in terms of their original symbolic structures, or do they originate from *particular* national cultures?

PR: This is a very difficult problem. We are caught here between the claims of two equally valid dimensions of myth. And it is the delicate balance between them that is difficult to find. On the one hand, we must say that mythical structures are not simply universal any more than are languages. Just as man is fragmented between different languages, so also he is fragmented between mythical cycles, each of which is typical of a living culture. We must acknowledge, then, that one of the primary functions of any myth is to found the specific identity of a community. On the other hand, however, we must say that just as languages are in principle translatable one into the other, so too myths have a horizon of universality which allows them to be understood by other cultures. The history of Western culture is made up of a confluence of different myths which have been expatriated from their original community, that is, Hebrew, Greek, Germanic, Celtic. The horizon of any genuine myth always exceeds the political and geographical boundaries of a specific national or tribal community. Even if we may say that mythical structures *founded* political institutions, they always go beyond the territorial limitations imposed by politics. Nothing travels more extensively and effectively than myth. Therefore we must conclude that while mythic symbols are rooted in a particular culture, they also have the capacity to emigrate and develop within new cultural frameworks.

RK: Is there not a sense in which perhaps the source and not only the historical transmission of symbols may be responsible for their universal dimension?

PR: It is quite possible that the supranational quality of myth or symbol may be ultimately traced back to a prehistorical layer from which all particular 'mythical nuclei' might be said to emerge. But it is difficult to determine the nature of this prehistory, for all myths as we know them come down to us through history. Each particular myth has its own history of reinterpretation and emigration. But another possible explanation of the universally common dimension of myth might be that because the myth-making powers of the human imagination are finite, they ensure the frequent recurrence of similar archetypes and motifs.

RK: Certainly the myth of the Fall as you analyse it in *The Symbolism of Evil* would seem to be common to many different cultures.

PR: Yes. We could say that genuine myth goes beyond its claim to found a particular community and speaks to man as such. Several exegetes of Jewish literature, for example, have made a distinction between different layers of myth: those which are foundational for the Jewish culture – the 'chronicle dimension' – and those which make up a body of truths valid for all mankind – the 'wisdom dimension'. This seems to me an important distinction and one applicable to other cultures.

RK: In Irish literature over the last fifty years or so one finds a similar distinction between these dimensions. In the Fenian literature of the nineteenth century or the Celtic Twilight literature of Yeats, Lady Gregory and others, myth seems to have been approached as a 'chronicle' of the spiritual origins of the race. For this reason it often strikes one as suffering from a certain hazy occultism and introversion. Joyce, on the other hand, used myth, and particularly the myth of Finn, in its 'wisdom dimension', that is, as an Irish archetype open to, and capable of assimilating, the rich resources of entirely different cultures. *Finnegans Wake* or *Ulysses* seem to represent an exemplary synthesis of the particular and universal claims of myth.

PR: The important point here is that the original potential of any genuine myth will always transcend the confines of a particular community or nation. The *mythos* of any community is the bearer of something which exceeds its own frontiers; it is the bearer of other *possible* worlds. And I think it is in this horizon of the 'possible' that we discover the *universal* dimensions of symbolic and poetic language.

RK: You have stated that what animates your philosophical research on symbolism and myth is not 'regret for some sunken Atlantis' but 'hope for a re-creation of language' (*The Symbolism of Evil*). What precisely do you mean by this?

PR: Language has lost is original unity. Today it is fragmented not only geographically into different communities but functionally into different disciplines – mathematical, historical, scientific, legal, psychoanalytic and so on. It is the function of a philosophy of language to recognize the specific nature of these disciplines and thereby assign each 'language-game' its due (as Wittgenstein would have it), limiting and correcting their mutual claims. Thus one of the main purposes of hermeneutics is to refer the different uses of language to different regions of being – natural, scientific, fictional and so on. But this is not all. Hermeneutics is also concerned with the permanent spirit of language. By the spirit of language we mean not just some decorative excess or effusion of subjectivity, but *the capacity of language to open up new worlds*. Poetry and myth are not just nostalgia for some forgotten world. They constitute a disclosure of unprecedented worlds, an opening on to other *possible* worlds which transcend the established limits of our *actual* world.

RK: How then would you situate your philosophy of language in relation to analytic philosophy?

PR: I certainly share at least one common concern of analytic philosophy: the concern with ordinary language in contradistinction to the scientific language of documentation and verification. Scientific language has no real function of communication or interpersonal dialogue. It is important therefore that we preserve the rights of ordinary language where the communication of experience is of primary significance. But my criticism of ordinary-language philosophy is that it does not take into account the fact that language itself is a place of prejudice and bias. Therefore, we need a third dimension of language, a critical and creative dimension, which is directed towards neither scientific verification nor ordinary communication but towards the disclosure of possible worlds. This third dimension of language I call the poetic. The adequate self-understanding of man is dependent on this third dimension of language as a disclosure of *possibility*.

RK: Is not this philosophy of language profoundly phenomenological in character?

PR: Yes it is, because phenomenology as it emerged in the philosophies of Husserl and Heidegger raised the central question of 'meaning'. And it is here that we find the main dividing line between the structuralist analysis and phenomenological hermeneutics. Whereas the former is concerned with the immanent arrangement of texts and textual codes, hermeneutics looks to the 'meaning' produced by these codes. It is my conviction that the decisive feature of hermeneutics is the capacity of world-disclosure yielded by texts. Hermeneutics is not confined to the *objective* structural analysis of texts nor to the *subjective* existential analysis of the authors of texts; its primary concern is with the worlds which these authors and texts open up. It is by an understanding of the worlds, actual and possible, opened by language that we may arrive at a better understanding of ourselves.

The Creativity of Language (1981)*

RK: How do your later works on metaphor (*La Métaphore vive*, 1975) and narrativity (*Temps et récit*, vol. 1, 1983) fit into your overall programme of philosophical hermeneutics?

PR: In *La Métaphore vive* (*The Rule of the Metaphor*) I tried to show how language could extend itself to its very limits forever discovering new resonances within itself. The term *vive* (living) in the title of this work is all-important, for it was my purpose to demonstrate that there is not just an epistemological and political imagination, but also, and perhaps more fundamentally, a *linguistic* imagination which generates and regenerates meaning through the living power of metaphoricity. *La Métaphore vive* investigated the resources of rhetoric to show how language undergoes creative mutations and transformations. My work on narrativity, *Temps et récit*, develops this inquiry into the inventive power of language. Here, the analysis of narrative operations in a literary text, for instance, can teach us how we formulate a new structure of 'time' by creating new modes of plot and characterization. My chief concern in this analysis is to discover how the act of *raconter*, of telling a story, can transmute *natural* time into a specifically *human* time, irreducible to mathematical, chronological 'clock' time. How is narrativity, as the construction or deconstruction of paradigms of story-telling, a perpetual search for new ways of expressing human time, a production or creation of meaning? That is my question.

RK: How would you relate this hermeneutics of narrativity to your former phenomenology of existence?

PR: I would say, borrowing Wittgenstein's term, that the 'language-game' of narration ultimately reveals that the meaning of human existence is itself narrative. The implications of narration as a retelling of history are considerable. For history is not only the story (*histoire*) of triumphant kings and heroes, of the powerful; it is also the story of the powerless and dispossessed. The history of the vanquished dead crying out for justice demands to be told. As Hannah Arendt points out, the meaning of human existence is not just the power to change or master the world, but also the ability to be remembered and recollected in narrative discourse, to be *memorable*. These existential and historical

---

* Recorded in Paris in 1981 and first published in *Dialogues with Contemporary Continental Thinkers* (Manchester: Manchester University Press, 1984).

implications of narrativity are very far-reaching, for they determine what is to be 'preserved' and rendered 'permanent' in a culture's sense of its past, of its own 'identity'.

RK: Could you outline some such implications for a political rereading of the past? How, for example, would it relate to a Marxist interpretation?

PR: Just as novelists choose a certain plot (*intrigue*) to order the material of their fiction into a narrative sequence, so too historians order the events of the past according to certain choices of narrative structure or plot. While history has traditionally concerned itself with the plot of kings, battles, treaties and the rise and fall of empires, one finds alternative readings emerging from the nineteenth century onwards whose narrative selection focuses on the story of the victims – the plot of suffering rather than that of power and glory. Michelet's romantic historiography of the 'people' was a case in point. And a more obvious and influential example is the Marxist rereading of history according to the model of the class struggle which champions the cause of the oppressed workers. In such ways, the normal narrative ordering of history is reversed and the hero is now the 'slave' rather than the 'master' as before; a new set of events and facts are deemed to be relevant and claim our attention; the relations of labour and production take precedence over the relations between kings and queens. But here again one must remain critical lest the new heroes of history become abstractions in their turn, thus reducing an alternative 'liberating' plot to another reified version of events which might only deepen the illusion that history somehow unfolds of its own accord independently of the creative powers of the labouring human subject. In such a manner, Marxism as an ideology of liberation, of the powerless, can easily become – as happened with the German Social Democrats or with Stalin – an ideology which imposes a new kind of oppressive power: the proletariat thus ceases to be a living human community of subjects and becomes instead an impersonal, abstracted concept in a new system of scientific determinism.

RK: Is narrative language primarily an intentionality of subjective consciousness, as phenomenology argued; or is it an objective and impersonal structure which predetermines the subjective operations of consciousness, as structuralism maintained?

PR: It is both at once. The invaluable contribution made by structuralism was to offer an exact scientific description of the codes and paradigms of language. But I do not believe that this excludes the creative expression of consciousness. The creation of meaning in language comes from the specifically *human* production of new ways of expressing the objective paradigms and codes made available by language. With the same grammar, for example, we can utter many novel and different sentences. Creativity is always governed by objective linguistic codes which it continually brings to their limit in order to invent something new. Whereas I drew on the objective codes of rhetoric in my analysis of the creative power of metaphor, in my study of narrativity I refer to the linguistic structures disclosed by the Russian Formalists, the Prague school and more recently by the structuralism of Lévi-Strauss and Genette. My philosophical project is to show how human language is *inventive* despite the objective limits and codes which govern it, to reveal the diversity and potentiality of language which the erosion of the everyday, conditioned by technocratic and political interests, never ceases to obscure. To become aware of the metaphorical and narrative resources of language is to recognize that its flattened or diminished powers can always be rejuvenated for the benefit of all forms of language usage.

RK: Can your research on narrativity also be considered as a search for a shared meaning beyond the multiplicity of discourses? In other words, does the act of narrating history render it universal and common to all?

PR: This problem of unity and diversity is central to narrativity and can be summarized in terms of the two following, conflicting interpretations. In the *Confessions* Augustine tells us that the 'human body is undone', that human existence is in discord in so far as it is a temporal rupturing and exploding of the present in contrast to the eternal presence of God. To this Augustinian reading of human existence as *dispersion*, I would oppose Aristotle's theory of tragedy in *The Poetics* as a way of *unifying* existence by retelling it. Narrativity can be seen in terms of this opposition: the discordance of time (*temps*) and the concordance of the tale (*récit*). This is a problem which faces all historians, for example. Is history a narrative tale which orders and constructs the fragmentary, empirical facts offered by sociology? Can history divorce itself from the narrative structure of the tale, in its *rapprochement* to sociology, without ceasing to be history? It is interesting that even Fernand Braudel, who champions the sociological approach to history in his preface to *The Mediterranean in the Time of Philippe II*, still retains the notion of history as temporal duration; he stops short of espousing a temporal paradigm, *à la* Lévi-Strauss, for that would spell the demise of history. Lévi-Strauss's social anthropology can afford to dispense with history since it is only concerned with 'cold societies': societies without historical or diachronic development, whose customs and norms – the incest taboo, for example – are largely unaffected by temporal change. History begins and ends with the reciting of a tale (*récit*); and its intelligibility and coherence rest upon this recital. My task is to show how the narrative structures of history and of the story (that is, of the novel or fiction) operate in a parallel fashion to create new forms of human time, and therefore new forms of human community, for creativity is also a social and cultural act; it is not confined to the individual.

RK: What exactly do you mean by 'human' time?

PR: I mean the formulation of two opposing forms of time: public time and private time. Private time is mortal time, for, as Heidegger says, to exist is to be a being-towards-death (*Sein-zum-Tode*), a being whose future is closed off by death. As soon as we understand our existence as this mortal time, we are already involved in a form of private narrativity or history; as soon as the individual comes up against the finite limits of its own existence, it is obliged to recollect itself and to make time its *own*. On the other hand, there is public time. Now I do not mean public in the sense of physical or natural time (clock time), but the time of language itself, which continues on after the individual's death. To live in human time is to live between the private time of our mortality and the public time of language. Even Chénu, who tends towards a quantitative assessment of history, acknowledges that the kernel of history is demography, that is, the regeneration of generations, the story (*histoire*) of the living and the dead. Precisely as this recollection of the living and the dead, history – as public narrativity – produces human time. To summarize, I would say that my analysis of narrativity is concerned with three interrelated problems: (i) narration as history; (ii) narration as fiction; and (iii) narration as human time.

RK: What can this analysis contribute to your study of the biblical patterns of narration in *La Symbolique du mal* (*The Symbolism of Evil*)?

PR: The hermeneutics of narration is crucial to our understanding of the Bible. Why is it, for example, that Judaeo-Christianity is founded on narrative episodes or stories? And how is it that these succeed in becoming *exemplary*, coordinated into laws, prophecies and psalms and the like? I think that the biblical coordination of narratives can perhaps best be understood in terms of Kristeva's notion of *intertextuality*: the idea that every text functions in terms of another. Biblical narratives operate in terms of other prescriptive texts. The kernel of biblical hermeneutics is this conjunction of narrativity and prescription.

RK: What is the rapport between your earlier analysis of the 'creative imagination' as an 'eschatological hope' for the 'not yet' of history, and your more recent analysis of narrativity as the production of human time and history?

PR: Whereas the analysis of creative imagination dealt with creativity in its prospective or futural aspect, the analysis of narrativity deals with it in a retrospective fashion. Fiction has a strong relation to the past. Camus's *L'Etranger*, like most other novels, is written in the past tense. The narrative voice of a novel generally retells something that has taken place in a fictional past. One could almost say that fictional narration tends to suspend the eschatological in order to inscribe us in a meaningful past. And I believe that we must have a sense of the meaningfulness of the past if our projections into the future are to be more than empty utopias. Heidegger argues in *Being and Time* that it is because we are turned towards the future that we can possess and repossess a past, both our personal past and our cultural heritage. The structure of narrativity demonstrates that it is by trying to put order on our past, by retelling and recounting what has been, that we acquire an identity. These two orientations – towards the future and towards the past – are not, however, incompatible. As Heidegger himself points out, the notion of 'repeating' (*Wiederholung*) the past is inseparable from the existential projection of ourselves towards our possibilities. To 'repeat' our story, to retell our history, is to recollect our horizon of possibilities in a resolute and responsible manner. In this respect, one can see how the retrospective character of narration is closely linked to the prospective horizon of the future. To say that narration is a recital which orders the past is not to imply that it is a conservative closure to what is new. On the contrary, narration preserves the meaning that is behind us so that we can have meaning before us. There is always *more* order in what we narrate than in what we have actually already lived; and this narrative excess (*surcroît*) of order, coherence and unity, is a prime example of the creative power of narration.

RK: What about the modernist texts of Joyce and Beckett and so on, where the narrative seems to disperse and dislocate meaning?

PR: These texts break up the habitual paradigms of narrative in order to leave the ordering task of creation to the reader himself. And ultimately it is true that the reader composes the text. All narrative, however, even Joyce's, is a certain call to order. Joyce does not invite us to embrace chaos but an infinitely more complex order – what he calls 'chaosmos'. Narrative carries us beyond the oppressive order of our existence to a more liberating and refined one. The question of narrativity, no matter how modernist or avant-garde, cannot be separated from the problem of order.

RK: What compelled you to abandon the Husserlian phenomenology of
        consciousness, with its claim to a direct and immediate apprehension of
        meaning, and to adopt a hermeneutic phenomenology where the
        meaning of existence is approached indirectly through myth, metaphor
        or narrativity, that is, through the detour of mediation?

PR: I think that it is always through the mediation of structuring operations
        that one apprehends the fundamental meaning of existence, what
        Merleau-Ponty called *l'être sauvage*. Merleau-Ponty sought this *être
        sauvage* throughout his philosophical career and consistently criticized
        its deformation and obfuscation in science. I for my part have always
        attempted to identify those mediations of language which are not
        reducible to the dissimulations of scientific objectivity, but which
        continue to bear witness to creative linguistic potentialities. Language
        possesses deep resources which are not immediately reducible to
        knowledge (particularly the intellectualist and behaviourist forms of
        knowledge which Merleau-Ponty rejected). And my interest in
        hermeneutics, and its interpretation of language which extends to the
        limits of logic and the mathematical sciences, has always been an
        attempt to detect and describe these resources. I am convinced that all
        figurative language is potentially conceptualizable and that the
        conceptual order can possess a form of creativity. This is why I insisted,
        at the end of La *Métaphore vive*, upon the essential connection or
        intersection between speculative and poetic discourse – evidenced, for
        example, in the whole question of analogy. It is simplistic to suggest
        that conceptualization is *per se* antagonistic to the meaning of life and
        experience; concepts can also be open, creative and living, though they
        can never constitute a knowledge which would be immediately
        accessible to some self-transparent *cogito*. Conceptualization cannot
        reach meaning directly or create meaning out of itself *ex nihilo*; it
        cannot dispense with the detour of mediation through figurative
        structures. This detour is intrinsic to the very working of concepts.

RK: In study 8 of *La Métaphore vive* you raised the complex philosophical
        problem of 'reference' in language. How does narrativity relate to this
        problem of reference?

PR: This question brings us to the intersection between history, which
        claims to deal with what actually happens, and the novel, which is of
        the order of fiction. Reference entails a conjunction of history and
        fiction. And I reckon that my chances of demonstrating the validity of
        reference are better in an analysis of narrativity than in one of
        metaphoricity. Whereas it is always difficult to identify the referent of
        poetic or metaphorical discourse, the referent of narrative discourse is

obvious – the order of human action. Now of course human action itself is charged with fictional entities such as stories, symbols, rites and so on. As Marx pointed out in *The German Ideology*, when men produce their existence in the form of *praxis* they represent it to themselves in terms of fiction, even at the limit in terms of religion (which for Marx is the model of ideology). There can be no *praxis* which is not already symbolically structured in some way. Human action is always figured in signs, interpreted in terms of cultural traditions and norms. Our narrative fictions are then added to this primary interpretation or figuration of human action; so that narrative is a redefining of what is already defined, a reinterpretation of what is already interpreted. The referent of narration, namely human action, is never raw or immediate reality but an action which has been symbolized and resymbolized over and over again. Thus narration serves to displace anterior symbolizations on to a new plane, integrating or exploding them as the case may be. If this were not so, if literary narrative, for example, were closed off from the world of human action, it would be entirely harmless and inoffensive. But literature never ceases to challenge our way of reading human history and *praxis*. In this respect, literary narrative involves a creative use of language often ignored by science or by our everyday existence. Literary language has the capacity to put our quotidian existence into question; it is *dangerous* in the best sense of the word.

RK: But is not the hermeneutic search for mediated and symbolized meaning a way of escaping from the harsh, empirical reality of things? Is it not always working at one remove from life?

PR: Proust said that if play were cloistered off in books, it would cease to be formidable. Play is formidable precisely because it is loose in the world, planting its mediations everywhere, shattering the illusion of the immediacy of the real. The problem for a hermeneutics of language is not to rediscover some pristine immediacy but to mediate again and again in a new and more creative fashion. The mediating role of imagination is forever at work in lived reality (*le vécu*). There is no lived reality, no human or social reality, which is not already *represented* in some sense. This imaginative and creative dimension of the social, this *imaginaire social,* has been brilliantly analyzed by Castoriadis in his book, *L'Institution imaginaire de la société.* Literature supplements this primary representation of the social with its own narrative representation, a process which Dagonet calls 'iconographic augmentation'. But literature is not the only way in which fiction can iconographically mediate human reality. There is also the mediating role of models in science or of utopias in political ideologies. These three modes of fictional mediation – literary, scientific and political – effectuate a metaphorization of the real, a creation of new meaning.

RK: Which returns us to your original question: what is the meaning of creativity in language and how does it relate to the codes, structures or laws imposed by language?

PR: Linguistic creativity constantly strains and stretches the laws and codes of language that regulate it. Roland Barthes described these regulating laws as 'fascist' and urged the writer and critic to work at the limits of language, subverting its constraining laws in order to make way for the free movement of *desire*, to make language festive. But if the narrative order of language is replete with codes, it is also capable of creatively violating them. Human creativity is always in some sense a response to a regulating order. The imagination is always working on the basis of already established laws and it is its task to make them function creatively, either by applying them in an original way or by subverting them; or indeed both – what Malraux calls 'regulated deformation'. There is no function of imagination, no *imaginaire*, that is not structuring or structured, that is not said or about-to-be-said in language. The task of hermeneutics is to charter the unexplored resources of the to-be-said on the basis of the already-said. Imagination never resides in the unsaid.

RK: How would you respond to Lévi-Strauss's conclusion, in *L'Homme nu*, that the structures and symbols of society originate in 'nothing' (*rien*)?

PR: I am not very interested in Lévi-Strauss's metaphysics of nothingness. The great contribution made by Lévi-Strauss was to identify the existence of enduring symbolic structures in what he called 'cold societies', that is, societies (mainly South American Indian) resistant to historical change. The Greek and Hebraic societies which combined to make up our Western culture are, by contrast, 'hot societies'; they are societies whose symbolic systems change and evolve over time, carrying within themselves different layers of interpretation and reinterpretation. In other words, in 'hot' societies the work of interpretation is not – as in 'cold' societies – something which is introduced from without, but an internal component of the symbolic system itself. It is precisely this diachronic process of reinterpretation that we call 'tradition'. In the Greek *Iliad*, for example, we discover a myth that is already reinterpreted, a piece of history that is already reworked into a narrative order. Neither Homer nor Aeschylus invented their stories; what they did invent were new narrative meanings, new forms of retelling the same story. The author of the *Iliad* has the entire story of the Trojan War at his disposal, but chooses to isolate the exemplary story of Achilles' wrath. He develops this exemplary narrative to the point where the wrath expires in the cathartic reconciliation – occasioned by Hector's death – with King Priam. The story produces and exemplifies a particular meaning: how the vain and meaningless wrath of one hero (Achilles) can be overcome when this hero becomes reconciled with his victim's father (Priam) at the funeral banquet. Here we have a powerful example of what it means to create meaning from a common mythic heritage, to receive a tradition and recreate it poetically to signify something new.

RK: And of course Chaucer and Shakespeare produced different 'exemplary' reinterpretations of the *Iliad* myth in their respective versions of Troilus and Cressida; as did Joyce once again in *Ulysses*. Such reinterpretation would seem to typify the cultural history of our Hellenic heritage. Is this kind of historical reinterpretation also to be found in the biblical or Hebraic tradition?

PR: Yes, the biblical narratives of the Hebraic tradition also operate in this exemplary or exemplifying fashion. This is evident in the fact that the biblical stories or episodes are not simply added to each other, or juxtaposed with each other, but constitute a cumulative and organic development. For example, the promise made to Abraham that his people would have a salvific relation with God is an inexhaustible promise (unlike certain legal promises which can be immediately realized); as such it opens up a history in which this promise can be repeated and reinterpreted over and over again – with Moses, then with David, and so on, so that the biblical narrative of this 'not-yet-realized' promise creates a cumulative history of repetition. The Christian message of crucifixion and resurrection then inserts itself into this biblical history, as a double rapport of reinterpretation and rupture. Christianity plays both a subversive and preservative role *vis-à-vis* the Judaic tradition. Saint Paul talks about the overcoming of the Law; and yet we find the synoptic authors continually affirming that the Christian event is a response to the prophetic promise, 'according to the Scriptures'. The Judaic and Christian reinterpretations of biblical history are in 'loving combat', to borrow Jaspers' phrase. The important point is that the biblical experience of faith is founded on stories and narratives – the story of the exodus, the crucifixion and resurrection and so on – *before* it expresses itself in abstract theologies which interpret these foundational narratives and provide religious tradition with its sense of enduring identity. The *future* projects of every religion are intimately related to the ways in which it remembers itself.

RK: Your work in hermeneutics always displays a particular sensitivity to this 'conflict of interpretations' – even to the point of providing one of the titles of your books. Your hermeneutics has consistently refused the idea of an 'absolute knowledge' which might reductively totalize the multiplicity of interpretations – phenomenological, theological, psychoanalytic, structuralist, scientific, literary and so on. Is there any sense in which this open-ended intellectual itinerary can be construed as a sort of odyssey which might ultimately return to a unifying centre where the conflicting interpretations of human discourse could be gathered together and reconciled?

PR: When Odysseus completes the circle and returns to his island of Ithaca there is slaughter and destruction. For me the philosophical task is not to close the circle, to centralize or totalize knowledge, but to keep open the irreducible plurality of discourse. It is essential to show how the different discourses may interrelate or intersect, but one must resist the temptation to make them identical, the same. My departure from Husserlian phenomenology was largely due to my disagreement with its theory of a controlling transcendental *cogito*. I advanced the notion of a wounded or split *cogito*, in opposition to the idealist claims for an inviolate absolute subjectivity. It was in fact Karl Barth who first taught me that the subject is not a centralizing master but rather a disciple or auditor of a language larger than itself. At a broader cultural level, we must also be wary of attending exclusively to Western traditions of thought, or becoming Eurocentric. In emphasizing the important of the Greek or Judaeo-Christian traditions, we often overlook the radically heterogeneous discourses of the Far East for example. One of my American colleagues recently suggested to me that Derrida's deconstruction of logocentrism bears striking resemblances to the Buddhist notion of nothingness. I think that there is a certain 'degree zero' or emptiness which we may have to traverse in order to abandon our pretension to be the centre, our tendency to reduce all other discourses to our own totalizing schemata of thought. If there is an ultimate unity, it resides elsewhere, in a sort of eschatological hope. But this is my 'secret', if you wish, my personal wager, and not something that can be translated into a centralizing philosophical discourse.

RK: It appears that our modern secularized society has abandoned the symbolic representations or *imaginaire* of tradition. Can the creative process of reinterpretation operate if the narrative continuity with the past is broken?

PR: A society where narrative is dead is one where men are no longer capable of exchanging their experiences, of sharing a common experience. The contemporary search for some narrative continuity with the past is not just nostalgic escapism but a contestation of the legislative and planificatory discourse which tends to predominate in bureaucratic societies. To give people back a *memory* is also to give them back a *future*, to put them back in time and thus release them from the 'instantaneous mind' (*mens instans*), to borrow a term from Leibniz. The past is not *passé*, for our future is guaranteed precisely by our ability to possess a narrative identity, to recollect the past in historical or fictive form. This problem of narrative identity is particularly acute, for instance, in a country like France, where the Revolution represented a rupture with the patrimony of legend and folklore and so on. (I have always been struck, for example, by the fact that most of the so-called 'traditional' songs the French still possess are drinking songs.) Today the French are largely bereft of a shared *imaginaire*, a common symbolic heritage. Our task, then, is to reappropriate those resources of language which have resisted contamination and destruction. To rework language is to rediscover what we are. What is lost in experience is often salvaged in language, sedimented as a deposit of traces, as a thesaurus. There can be no pure or perfectly transparent model of language, as Wittgenstein reminds us in his *Philosophical Investigations*; and if there were it would be no more than a universalized *vide*. To rediscover meaning we must return to the multilayered sedimentations of language, to the complex plurality of its instances, which can preserve what is said from the destruction of oblivion.

RK: In *History and Truth* you praise Emmanuel Mounier as someone who refused to separate the search for philosophical truth from a political pedagogy. What are the political implications, if any, of your own philosophical thinking?

PR: My work to date has been a hermeneutic reflection upon the mediation of meaning in language, and particularly in poetic or narrative language. What, you ask, can such hermeneutics contribute to our understanding of the rapport between the mediations of such symbolic discourses and the immediacy of political *praxis*? The fact is that language is disclosed by hermeneutics (and also by the analytic philosophy of Wittgenstein) as a non-totalizable plurality of interpretations or 'language-games' and so cannot claim to the status of a universal science. Some recent exchanges I had with Czech philosophers and students in the Tomin seminar in Prague taught me that the problem of totalitarianism resides in the lie that there can be a universally true and scientific discourse of politics (in this instance, the communist discourse). Once one recognizes that political language is basically a rhetoric of persuasion and opinion, one can tolerate free discussion. An 'open society', to use Popper's term, is one which acknowledges that political debate is infinitely open and is thus prepared to take the critical step back in order to continually interrogate and reconstitute the conditions of an authentic language.

RK: Can there be a positive rapport between language, as a political ideology, and utopia?

PR: Every society, as I mentioned earlier, possesses, or is part of, a socio-political *imaginaire*, that is, an ensemble of symbolic discourses. This *imaginaire* can function as a rupture or a reaffirmation. As reaffirmation, the *imaginaire* operates as an 'ideology' which can positively repeat and represent the founding discourse of a society, what I call its 'foundational symbols', thus preserving its sense of identity. After all, cultures create themselves by telling stories of their own past. The danger is of course that this reaffirmation can be perverted, usually by monopolistic élites, into a mystificatory discourse which serves to uncritically vindicate or glorify the established political powers. In such instances, the symbols of a community become fixed and fetishized; they serve as lies. Over against this, there exists the *imaginaire* of rupture, a discourse of utopia which remains critical of the powers that be out of fidelity to an 'elsewhere', to a society that is 'not yet'. But this utopian discourse is not always positive either. For beside the authentic utopia of critical rupture there can also exist a dangerously schizophrenic utopian discourse which projects a static future without ever producing the conditions of its realization. This can happen with the Marxist–Leninist notion of utopia if one projects the final 'withering away of the State' without undertaking genuine measures to ever achieve such a goal. Here utopia becomes a future cut off from the present and the past, a mere alibi for the consolidation of the repressive powers that be. The utopian discourse functions as a mystifactory ideology as soon as it justifies the oppression of today in the name of the liberation of tomorrow. In short, *ideology* as a symbolic confirmation of the past and *utopia* as a symbolic opening towards the future are complementary; if cut off from each other they can lead to a form of political pathology.

RK: Would you consider the Liberation Theology of Latin America to be an example of a positive utopian discourse in so far as it combines a Marxist utopianism with the political transformation of *present* reality?

PR: It also combines it with the *past*, with the memory of the archetypes of exodus and resurrection. This memorial dimension of Liberation Theology is essential, for it gives direction and continuity to the utopian projection of the future, thus functioning as a *garde-fou* [safeguard] against irresponsible or uncritical futurism. Here the political project of the future is inseparable from a continuous horizon of liberation, reaching back to the biblical notions of exile and promise. The promise remains unfulfilled until the utopia is historically realized; and it is precisely the not-yet-realized horizon of this promise which binds men together as a community, which prevents utopia detaching itself as an empty dream.

RK: How exactly does utopia relate to history?

PR: In his *History of the Concept of History*, Reinhart Koselleck argues that until the eighteenth century, the concept of history, in the West at any rate, was a plural one; one referred to 'histories', not History with a capital H. Our current notion of a single or unique history only emerged with the modern idea of progress. As soon as history is thus constituted as a single concept, the gap between our 'horizon of expectancy' and our 'field of experience' never ceases to widen. The unity of history is founded on the constitution of a common horizon of expectancy; but the projection of such a horizon into a distantly abstract future means that our present 'field of experience' can become pathologically deprived of meaning and articulation. The universal ceases to be concrete. This dissociation of *expectancy* from *experience* enters a crisis as soon as we lack the intermediaries to pass from the one to the other. Up to the sixteenth century, the utopian horizon of expectancy was the eschatological notion of the Last Judgement, which had as mediating or intermediating factors the whole experience of the millennium of the Holy Roman and Germanic Empires. There was always some sort of articulated path leading from what one had to what one expected to have. The liberal ideology of Kant and Locke produced a certain discourse of democracy which served as a path for the citizen towards a better humanity; and Marxism also promoted mediating stages leading from capitalism through socialism to communism. But we don't seem to believe in these intermediaries any more. The problem today is the apparent impossibility of unifying world politics, of mediating between the polycentricity of our everyday political practices and the utopian horizon of a universally liberated humanity. It is not that we are without utopia, but that we are without *paths* to utopia. And without a path towards it, without concrete and practical mediation in our field of experience, utopia becomes a sickness. Perhaps the deflation of utopian expectancies is not entirely a bad thing. Politics can so easily be injected with too much utopia; perhaps it should become more modest and realistic in its claims, more committed to our practical and immediate needs.

RK: Is there any place in contemporary politics for a genuine utopian discourse?

PR: Maybe not in politics itself but rather at the junction between politics and other cultural discourses. Our present disillusionment with the political stems from the fact that we invested it with the totality of our expectancies – until it became a bloated imposture of utopia. We have tended to forget that beside the public realm of politics, there also exists a more private cultural realm (which includes literature, philosophy and religion, and so on) where the utopian horizon can express itself. Modern society seems hostile to this domain of private experience, but the suppression of the private entails the destruction of the public. The vanquishing of the private by the public is a pyrrhic victory.

RK: Are you advocating a return to the bourgeois romantic notion of private subjectivity removed from all political responsibility?

PR: Not at all. In my recent discussions with the Prague philosophers I spoke about the crisis of the subject in contemporary continental philosophy, particularly structuralism. I pointed out that if one does away with the idea of a subject who is responsible for his or her words, we are no longer in a position to talk of the freedom or the rights of man. To dispense with the classical notion of the subject as a transparent *cogito* does not mean that we have to dispense with all forms of subjectivity. My hermeneutical philosophy has attempted to demonstrate the existence of an opaque subjectivity which expresses itself through the detour of countless mediations – signs, symbols, texts and human *praxis* itself. This hermeneutical idea of subjectivity as a dialectic between the self and mediated social meanings has deep moral and political implications. It shows that there is an *ethic of the word*, that language is not just the abstract concern of logic or semiotics, but entails the fundamental moral duty that people be responsible for what they say. A society which no longer possesses subjects ethically responsible for their words is a society which no longer possesses citizens. For the dissident philosophers in Prague the primary philosophical question is the integrity and truthfulness of language. And this question becomes a moral and political act of resistance in a system based on lies and perversion. The Marxism of Eastern Europe has degenerated from dialectics to positivism. It has abandoned the Hegelian inspiration which preserved Marxism as a realization of the universal subject in history, and has become instead a positivistic technology of mass manipulation.

RK: So the hermeneutical interrogation of the creation of meaning in language can have a political content?

PR: Perhaps the most promising example of a political hermeneutics is to be found in the Frankfurt School synthesis between Marxist dialectics and Heideggerean hermeneutics – best expressed in Habermas's critique of ideologies. But here again one must be careful to resist the temptation to engage in an unmediated politics. It is necessary for hermeneutics to keep a certain distance so as to critically disclose the underlying mediating structures at work in political discourse. This hermeneutic distance is particularly important today with the post-1968 disillusionment, the demise of Maoist ideology and the exposure of Soviet totalitarianism by Solzhenitsyn and others.

RK: Is this disillusionment a worldwide phenomenon?

PR: It exists in varying degrees, but is most conspicuous in countries like France where the essential distinction between state and society has been largely occluded. The French Revolution apportioned political sovereignty to all levels of the community, from the government at the top to the individuals at the bottom. But in this process, the state became omnipresent, the citizen being reduced to a mere fragment of the state. What was so striking in the Solidarity movement in Poland was their use of the term 'society' in opposition to the term 'state'. Even in the Anglo-Saxon countries one finds certain national institutions – such as the media or universities – which are relatively independent of state politics. (It is difficult to find examples of this in France.) The weak ideologization of politics in America, for instance, means that it can at least serve as a sprawling laboratory where a multiplicity of discourses can be tried and tested. This phenomenon of the 'melting-pot' is an example of what Montesquieu called the 'separation of powers'. It is interesting to remember that the state was originally conceived by the liberal thinkers as an agency of toleration, a way of protecting the plurality of beliefs and practices. The liberal state was to be a safeguard against religious and other forms of fanaticism. The fundamental perversion of the liberal state is that it came to function as a totalizing rather than a detotalizing agency. That is why it is urgent for us today to discover a political discourse which would not be governed by states, a new form of society guaranteeing universal rights yet dispensing with totalizing constraints. This is the enormous task of reconstituting a form of sociality not determined by the state.

RK: How does one go about discovering this new discourse of society?

PR: One of the first steps would be to analyse what exactly happened in the eighteenth century when the Judaeo-Christian horizon of eschatology was replaced by the Enlightenment horizon of humanism with its liberal notions of autonomy, freedom and human rights. We must see how this Enlightenment humanism developed through the Kantian notion of the autonomous will, the Hegelian notion of the universal class (of civil servants) to the Marxist universal class of workers and so on, until we reached a secularized version of utopia which frequently degenerated into scientific positivism. We must ask: can there be any sort of continuity between the religious eschatological projection of utopia and the modern humanist projection of a secularized utopia? The challenge today is to find alternative forms of social rationality beyond the positivistic extremes of both state socialism and utilitarian–liberal capitalism. Habermas's distinction between three forms of rationality is essential here: (i) *calculative rationality*, which operates as positivistic control and manipulation; (ii) *interpretative rationality*, which tries to represent the cultural codes and norms in a creative way; (iii) *critical rationality*, which opens up the utopian horizon of liberation. For a genuine social rationality to exist we must refuse to allow the critical and interpretative functions to be reduced to the calculative. Habermas is here developing Adorno's and Horkheimer's critique of *positivist rationality*, which exists in both state communism and in the argument of liberal capitalism that once the society of abundance has been achieved all can be distributed equally (the problem being, of course, that liberalism employs the means of a hierarchical and unequal society to achieve such an end of abundance – an end which never seems to be realized). So our task remains that of preserving a utopian horizon of liberty and equality – by means of interpretative and critical rationality – without resorting to a positivistic ideology of bad faith. I agree here with Raymond Aron's contention that we have not yet succeeded in developing a political model which could accommodate the simultaneous advancement of liberty and equality. Societies which have advocated liberty have generally suppressed equality and vice versa.

RK: Do you think that the critique of political power carried out by left-wing political philosophers in France, such as Castoriadis and Lefort, contributes to the hermeneutic search for a new discourse of sociality?

PR: Their contribution has been absolutely decisive. This critique has attempted to show that the error of Marxism resides not so much in its lack of a political horizon as in its reduction of the critique of power to the economic transfer of work to capital (that is, the critique of surplus value). Thus the Marxist critique tends to ignore that there can be more pernicious forms of power than capital – for example, the totalization of all the resources of a society (the resources of the workforce, of the means of discussion and information, education, research and so on) by the central committee of the party or state. In this manner the handing over of the private ownership of the means of production to the state can often mean a replacement of the alienation of society by the alienation of the state. The power of the totalitarian party is perhaps more nefarious than the dehumanizing power of capital in so far as it controls not only the economic means of production but also the political means of communication. Maybe the economic analysis of class struggle is but one of the many plots that make up the complex of history. Hence the need for a hermeneutics of sociality that could unravel the plurality of power plots which enmesh to form our history.

RK: In 'Non-violent Man and his Presence in History' (*History and Truth*) you asked: 'Can the prophet or non-violent man have a historical task which would obviate both the extreme inefficacity of the Yogi and the extreme efficacity of the Commissar?' In other words, can one commit oneself to the efficacious transformation of political reality and still preserve the critical distance of transcendence?

PR: This idea of transcendence is essential for any sort of non-violent discourse. The pacifist ideal resists violence by attesting to values which transcend the arena of political efficacity, without becoming irrelevant dreams. Non-violence is a form of genuine utopian vigil or hope, a way of refuting the system of violence and oppression in which we live.

RK: Is it possible to reconcile the exigency of an authentic social rationality with the eschatological hope of religion?

PR: This has never struck me as an insoluble problem for the basic cultural reason that our Western religiosity of Judaeo-Christianity has always functioned in the philosophical climate of Greek and Latin rationality. I have always objected to the simplistic opposition of Jerusalem and Athens, to those thinkers who declare that true spirituality can only be found in monotheism; or try to drive a wedge between Greek and Hebraic culture, defining the former as a thought of the cosmos and the latter as a thought of transcendence and so on. From the eleventh century onwards we find models for reconciling reason and religion – in Anselm, for example – and the Renaissance confirms this primary synthesis of rationality and spirituality. If it is true that the rationality of scientific positivism has divorced itself from spirituality, there are many signs today that we are searching for new forms of connection.

Universality and the Power of Difference (1991)*

RK: Do you believe in the idea of a European identity?

PR: Europe has produced a series of cultural identities, which brought with them their own self-criticism, and I think that this is unique. Even Christianity encompassed its own critique.

RK: And how would you see this ability to criticize ourselves operating? In terms of Reformations and Renaissances?

PR: Yes. Plurality is within Europe itself. Europe has had different kinds of Renaissance, Carolingian, twelfth-century, Italian and French, fifteenth-century, and so on. The Enlightenment was another expression of this; and it is important that in the dialogue with other cultures we keep this element of self-criticism, which I think is the only specificity of Europe (along with, of course, the enhancement of science). Europe is unique in that it had to interweave several heritages – Jewish–Christian, Greek–Roman, then the Barbarian cultures which were encompassed within the Roman Empire, the heritage within Christianity of the Reformation, Renaissance Enlightenment, and also the three nineteenth-century components of this heritage, *nationalism*, *socialism*, and *romanticism*...

RK: How does this pluralist legacy fit with the European claim to universality?

PR: The kind of universality that Europe represents contains within itself a plurality of cultures, which have been merged and intertwined, and which provide a certain fragility, an ability to disclaim and interrogate itself.

RK: This of course opens the question, doesn't it, of how we in Europe relate not just to the differences within our borders, but also how we relate to the differences of other non-European continents and countries; and how the universalist project of Europe can engage in dialogue with their differences, their nationalisms, their fundamentalisms? I mean, can we preach to others if we haven't sorted out our own problems of national identity?

---

* Recorded in Paris in 1991 and first published in *Visions of Europe* by Richard Kearney (Dublin: Wolfhound Press, 1992).

PR: I think we must be very cautious here in Europe when we speak of fundamentalism, because it is immediately a pejorative word, and this prevents good analysis. We have to look at the phenomenon because there are several kinds of fundamentalism. We put one word above a multiplicity of events. But there is, for instance, a difference between a return to a culture close to the practice of the people and a fundamentalism imposed from above.

RK: Well, if we take the example of the Baltic states, do you have a sympathy with what their nationalist claims for sovereignty and autonomy are trying to achieve?

PR: I must say that I am surprised by the extent of the phenomenon, but also the extremist dimension, because in my own philosophical culture, I had underestimated the capacity of language to reorganize a culture and to unify it. And second, I had also underestimated the fragility of each identity which feels threatened by another. People must be very unsure to feel threatened by the otherness of the other. I did not realize that people are so unsure when they claim so emphatically to be what they are.

RK: Wouldn't you agree that there are very good historical reasons for this insecurity, not only in the Baltic states, but also in Yugoslavia, in Czechoslovakia, or in Northern Ireland – hence the need to attach themselves to a separatist national identity?

PR: But there is also the fact that there is no political distribution of borders which is adequate to the distribution of languages and cultures, so there is no political solution at the level of the nation-state. This is the real irritator of the nineteenth century, this dream of a perfect equation between state and nation.

RK: That clearly has failed.

PR: Yes, that has failed. So, we have to look for something else.

RK: There is much talk now in Europe about the necessity to go beyond the limitations of the nation-state (while preserving it as an intermediary model) to a transnational federation of states on the one hand, and a devolution of power from the nation-state to regions on the other hand – to regions that would be more self-governing, that would encourage the practice of local democracy, of participatory democracy. Do you think that might work?

PR: Yes, but there is a political problem here. Is the project of European federalism to be a confederation of regions, or of nations? I don't know the solution because it is something without a precedent. Modern history has been made by nation-states. But there are problems of size. We have five or six nation-states in Europe of major size, but we have micro-nations which cannot become micro-states in the same way as nation-states have done.

RK: One could argue that it's not unprecedented in what some call the 'other Europe' of Canada and the United States, where they did develop a model of federation, and indeed a certain amount of local autonomy in government at the level of the town halls, particularly at the beginning of the American Revolution.

PR: In a sense, the United States is a different case because it is a melting-pot of immigrants.

RK: But surely we've also got an opportunity here in Europe to accommodate the immigrants from those countries we colonized for two or three centuries.

PR: The United States has solved the problem due to its unit of language, English, to a certain extent. We have an opposite problem, with our multiplicity of languages and national dialects.

RK: I'd like to bring in the question of sovereignty here. At the moment we're pooling sovereignty in Europe. The notion of sovereignty, if I'm not mistaken, actually goes back to the idea, first of all, that God is the universal sovereign, later replaced by the king as sovereign, as the centre of one indivisible power. Then, with the replacement of monarchy by republics, with the French Revolution, for example, the nation-state becomes sovereign.

PR: In modern republics, the origin of sovereignty is in the people, but now we recognize that we have *many* peoples. And many peoples means many centres of sovereignty – we have to deal with that.

RK: Wasn't one of the problems of the French Revolution the definition of sovereignty as one and indivisible? That creates problems when you export the Revolution to other countries or continents.

PR: Take the Corsican people, who are also members of the French people. Here we have two meanings of the word *people*. On the one hand, 'people' means to be a citizen in a state, so it's not an ethnic concept. But, on the other hand, Corsica is a people in an ethnic sense – within the French people, which is not an ethnic concept. So, we are struggling with two concepts of people, and I think it's an example of what is happening throughout Europe now.

RK: Does this mean two different kinds of membership – ethnic membership and civic membership?

PR: Yes, because the notion of 'people' according to the French
        Constitution is not ethnic. Its citizenship is defined by the fact that
        somebody is born in the territory of France. For example, the son or
        daughter of an immigrant is French because he or she was born in this
        territory. So, the rule of membership has nothing to do with ethnic
        origin. This is why it was impossible to define Corsican people,
        because we had to rely on criteria other than citizenship, on ethnic
        criteria, and to whom are we to apply these criteria?

RK: Does this not raise the problem of ethnic nationalism and racism?

PR: The criterion of citizenship is there to moderate the excess of the ethnic
        criterion.

RK: To enlarge the discussion somewhat, could one not say that there are in
        fact several Europes?

PR: The German thinker Karl Jaspers used to say that Europe extends from
        San Francisco to Vladivostok. This raises the issue of the cultural
        expansion of Europe.

RK: Perhaps the solution, if there is one, is not to be found within the limits of
        Europe. Maybe we need to extend those limits and go further to what
        some people have called a world republic, a cosmopolitan society which
        can harbour differences yet bind all peoples and continents together?

PR: Even in political terms, it may be impossible to solve the problem of the
        unification of Europe without solving the problem of some inter-
        national institution which would provide the proper framework.

RK: This utopian vision of a cosmopolitan republic is one that goes back to
        the Enlightenment, to Kant and Montesquieu . . .

PR: We need now a plurality of utopias, utopias of different kinds. Surely, a
        basic utopia is a world economy which is not ruled by efficiency, by
        productivity, but based on needs. Maybe this will be the problem for the
        next century – how to move from an economy ruled by the laws of the
        market to a universal economy based on the real needs of people. We
        are now at the stage where the market is winning and provides the only
        source of productivity, but this productivity is not shared, because the
        success of productivity increases inequality. We'll have to address that.
        And then there's the political problem of resolving the hierarchy of
        sovereignties – global, continental (European, American, African and
        so on), national and regional.

RK: Maybe we can take a step back from the immediate political
        implications of this problem and say a little about the cultural and
        philosophical presuppositions of this discussion.

PR: I would like to focus on the role of *memory* in this context. On the one hand, memory is a burden; if we keep repeating the story of wars won or lost, we keep reinforcing the old hostilities. Take the different states of Europe. In fact, we cannot find a pair who weren't at war at one time or another. The French and the British, the Poles and Germans, and so on. So, there is memory which is a prison, which is regressive. But, on the other hand, we cannot do without the cultivation of the memory of our cultural achievements, and also of our sufferings. This brings me to the second element. We need a memory of the second order which is based on forgiving. And we cannot forgive if we have forgotten. So, in fact we have to *cross* our memories, to *exchange* our memories with each other to the point that, for example, the crimes of the Germans become part of our own memory. Sharing the memory of cruelty of my neighbour is a part of this political dimension of forgiving. We have some examples. When the German chancellor went to Warsaw and knelt down and asked for pardon, I think that was very important for Europe. Because, while we have to get rid of the memory of wars, of victory, and so on, we must keep the memory of the scars. Then we can proceed to this exchange of memories, to this mutual forgiveness.

RK: It's an unusual idea.

PR: I don't see how we can solve Europe's problems only in terms of a common market or a political institution. We need these, of course. We need the extension of a market which would be the basis of unification for Europe and also a relationship between Europe and the rest of the world, the invention of new institutions to solve the problem of the multiplicity of nation-states. But there is a *spiritual* problem underlying both the economic problem of a common market and the political problem of new institutions.

RK: What would be the role of narrative – one of the key concepts in your philosophy – in relation to this cultural crisis we are facing in Europe today? I mean narrative as story-telling, as remembrance or as projection.

PR: I would say three things concerning the role of narrative. First you have the narration of founding events, because most cultures have some original happening or act which gives some basis of unity to the diversity within the culture. Hence the need to commemorate founding events.

RK: Such as the French Revolution, the Soviet Revolution, 1916 in Ireland?

PR: Yes. We have to keep that because we have to retain some claims, some convictions that are rooted in these founding events. Second, I would say that one of the resources of the theory of narrativity is that now we may tell *different* stories about ourselves. So, we have to learn how to vary the stories that we are telling about ourselves. And third, we have to enter this process of exchange, which the German philosophers called *Auseinandersetzung*. We are caught in the stories of others, so we are protagonists in the stories we are told by others, and we have to assume for ourselves the stories that the others tell about us, which have their own founding events, their own strategies, their own plots.

RK: So the crossing of memories involves the crossing of stories. But is there any sense in which in Europe today we can tell each other the same story, a common universal story? Is there anything to bind us together?

PR: I would say that this concept of universality may be used in different contexts. On the one hand, you may speak of universal rules of discourse – what Habermas says about rules of discussion, let us say the logic and ethics of argumentation. This is one level of universality, but it is too formal to be operative. Second, you have a universalist claim within our own culture. For example, we may claim that some rights to free speech are universal, in spite of the fact that for the time being they cannot be included within other cultures. But it's a claim, and remains only a claim as long as it is not recognized by the others. So we bring to the discussion not only procedures of universality but *claims* of universality. The project of universality is central to the whole debate about human rights. Take the example of the mutilation of women. I am sure that we are right to say that there is something universal in our assertion that women have a right to pleasure, to physical integrity and so on, even if it is not recognized. But we have to bring that into the discussion. It's only discussion with the other which may finally convince the other that it's universal. And third, I would say that you have a kind of eschatological universalism – the universal as an ultimate project or goal as in Kant's *Essay on Perpetual Peace*.

RK: The project of some kind of universal republic.

Imagination, Testimony and Trust (1998)*

Q: I am sure that Professor Ricoeur realizes that in a country like Ireland we have a particular interest in the idea of obsessive memorization, and of repetition and ritual in political terms, so that if we could retell stories, if we could recreate a narrative and liberate ourselves from this, we would be looking to a better future. But the problem of retelling the narrative is that it is told and retold, so that you get not one agreed narrative but two narratives, and the competing narratives simply duplicate the conflicting ideologies from which they come. How, in this country, can you get to a shared narrative about identity?

PR: This problem of a common narrative calls for an ethics of discussion. In so-called discourse ethics, developed by people like Habermas and Apel, we argue one against the other, but we understand the argument of the other without assuming it. This is what John Rawls calls 'reasonable disagreements'. I take the example of the relationship between Europe and the Islamic world, where we distinguish between those Islamic speakers with whom we can discuss and others with whom we cannot. We make the difference between reasonable disagreement and intractable disagreement. A common or identical history cannot be reached – and should not be attempted – because it is a part of life that there are conflicts. The challenge is to bring conflicts to the level of discourse and not let them degenerate into violence; to accept that they tell history in their own words as we tell our history in our own words, and that these histories compete against each other in a kind of competition of discourse, what Karl Jaspers called a loving conflict. But sometimes consensus is a dangerous game, and if we miss consensus we think that we have failed. To assume and live conflicts is a kind of practical wisdom.

Q: You speak, in relation to Freud, of repetition as an obstruction to memory. But might it not also be, in certain instances, a way of constructing a memory one could be comfortable with?

* Our thanks to the following for contributing to this dialogue held at University College Dublin in 1998 and first published in *Question Ethics*, ed. Richard Kearney and Mark Dooley (London and New York: Routledge, 1999): Brian Cosgrave, Gayle Freyne, David Scott, Imelda McCarthy, Redmond O'Hanlon, Brian Garvey, John Cleary, Margaret Kelleher, Dermot Moran and Maeve Cooke, in addition to the editors.

PR: This is why Freud speaks of patience. The work of memory is a slow transformation of compulsive repetition into a talking cure, a liberation from pathological obsession into words as free association. Freud provides some historical examples where repressed feelings and memories were allowed to be brought to the surface; and it is quite possible that the positive side of commemoration has, in a sense, to do with this 'acting out' which is a form of substitution allowing for healthy memory. This sort of patience is very important: to let time do its own work, which is not destruction but a diluting resistance.

Q: I'd like to raise the question of historical retrieval.

PR: Let me cite a situation where there are several different interpretations of the same past event. I take the case of the French Revolution since, over nearly two centuries, it has been a bone of contention among French historians. We have many stories of the French Revolution, and it is the competition between these stories that makes for historical education. There are two extreme approaches. That of claiming the event as the beginning of everything, a new creation of a new human being; some of the revolutionary leaders even tried to invent a new calendar with a new way of dividing times and years and months and weeks (a week of ten days and so on). So it claimed to be the master of time and history. The opposite interpretation claims the French Revolution to have been only an acceleration of the centralizing trend of the monarchy, or a mere prefiguration of the Bolshevik Revolution. Here the French Revolution is not seen as a unique event but a mere variation on a larger historical movement. By acknowledging that the history of an event involves a conflict of several interpretations and memories, we in turn open up the future. And this retrieval-projection of history has ethical and political implications. Different political projects concerning the future invariably presuppose different interpretations of the past. Utopian projects, for instance, are about unkept promises of the historical past being reprojected, reanimated in terms of a better future which might realize such lost opportunities or unfulfilled, betrayed, possibilities. So here we have to connect past and future in an exchange between memory and expectation. The German historian Reinhart Koselleck put this past–future relation well in saying that there is a permanent tension between what he calls the space of experience (*Erfahrungsfeld*) and the horizon of expectation. This critical exchange between memory and expectation is, I believe, fundamental.

Q: You say utopias are places where we reactivate unkept promises of the past. Does that mean there are no new dreams to dream? That the future is just a recollection of past historical movements, fulfilled or unfulfilled?

PR: The epistemic status of utopia is very complex. I tried to explore this issue in my book *Lectures on Ideology and Utopia.* There I argued that ideology usually reasserts the historical field of past experience in a gesture of reassurance; utopia, by contrast, attempts a kind of excursion out of time, a radical break into the future. There is a moment of madness in utopia which is irreducible to mere repetition. Utopia claims to be imagination of the new, of a pure beginning. But the opposition is not so simple. No historical period ever exhausted its own dreams. What happened in the past is only a partial realization of what had been projected. We may say this of the Greek city which failed, of the Roman Empire which was rescued by the Catholic Church as the Holy Roman Empire, before it collapsed again. The promise of a historical event is always more than what was actually realized. There is more in the past than what happened. And so we have to find the *future of the past,* the unfulfilled potential of the past. That is why Raymond Aron argues that one of the tasks of the historian is to return to the moment of time when the actors did not know what would happen later, and therefore to assume the state of uncertainty in which these actors were positioned, exploring the multiplicity of their expectations, few of which were ever fulfilled. Even Habermas approaches the Enlightenment in this way, as a still unfulfilled project. There is something still unfulfilled in the Greek heritage, in the Christian heritage, in the Enlightenment heritage, in the Romantic heritage. There is never pure rupture. There is always reactualization to some degree or another.

Q: In Ireland we have a saying: if you want to know what happened ask your father, and if you want to know what people say happened, ask your mother. There is this double attitude to the history of the past – what actually happened (history) and the way in which people interpreted what happened (story). Do we not always select and edit memories? Is it not true that to remember everything, as the Irish playwright Brian Friel says, is a form of madness?

Q: Following on from the previous question, if you allow many different interpretations of your own memory and of the memories of the nation, and if you claim that the healthy thing is a conflict of interpretations which disallows any final consensus – since there is no one who has the perspective from which to say what *really* happened – how can you talk of the *abuse* of memory, either on a personal level or on the level of the nation? If there are only competing interpretations, each with a claim on truth, how can we speak of truth or untruth in history? To speak of abuse assumes you have some perspective from which you can judge that someone is making a proper use of memory, and that someone is making an improper use of memory.

PR: In relation to both questions, allow me to refer to my essay 'Memory and Forgetting', in which I spoke of the truth-claim of memory. This should not be forgotten. There could be no *good* use of memory if there were no aspect of truth. So in a sense what 'really happened' must keep concerning us. And here I am faithful to the German school of historians of the nineteenth century in saying that we have to tell things as they really happened (*wie es eigentlich gewesen*). This is a very difficult problem because we have two ways of speaking of the past. The past is something that is no longer there but which has been there, which once was there. So the grammar of the past is a twofold grammar. It is no longer and yet it *has been*. In a sense we are summoned by what was beyond the loss of what is no longer to be faithful to what happened. Here we confront problems of historical representation and reference to the past, but we must never eliminate the truth-claim of what has been. This is so for ethical as well as epistemological reasons.

Q: You are not saying that history is a matter of a pure relativism of interpretations where anything goes?

PR: No. This crucial issue brings us to the borderline between imagination and memory. In his book on imagination – *The Psychology of Imagination* – Sartre said that imagination is about the unreal and memory is about the (past) real. So there is a positing act in memory whereas there is an unrealizing of history in imagination. It is very difficult to maintain the distinction; but it must be kept at least as a basic recognition of two opposite claims about the past, as *unreal* and *real*. In that sense, memory is on the side of perception whereas imagination is on the side of fiction. But they often intersect. What we call 'Revisionist' historians, those who like Faurrison deny the existence of extermination camps, ignore this problem of 'factual' truth. This is why historical memory needs to be supplemented by documentary and archival evidence. The Popperian criterion of falsifiability must be observed. This is not to ignore the fact that sometimes fictions come closer to what really happened than do mere historical narratives, where fictions go directly to the *meaning* beyond or beneath the facts. It is puzzling. But, finally, we have to return to a body count. You have to accurately *count* the corpses in the death camps as well as offering vivid narrative *accounts* that people will remember.

Q: Is it possible to get a balance between the two approaches, between a narrative retelling (which evokes in us the feeling of the horror of what happened) and a critical, scientific, objective distance (which informs us of the 'facts' of what happened)? Is this not a paradox?

PR: I would say that the paradox is not on the side of memory but of imagination. This is the case because imagination has two functions: one is to bring us outside of the real world – into unreal or possible worlds – but it has a second function which is to put memories *before our eyes*. Bergson touches on this in the second chapter of *Matter and Memory*. He says that pure memory is virtual and has to be brought back into the field of consciousness *as* an image. This is why writing history as memory is so difficult. We are dealing with memory-images where imagination serves as a kind of *mise-en-scène* of the past. The reality of history is made 'visible' again through images; and this makes memory a reproduction, a sort of second production. Yet, at the same time, the difference *remains* between the unreal and the real. So the paradox of imagination–memory is very puzzling indeed. Many philosophers, such as Spinoza, have treated memory as a province of imagination. And we also have the view, expressed by Pascal and Montaigne, that memory is a form of imagination which is to be guarded against. This is why I stress so strongly the reality claims of memory to remain faithful to our *debt* to the past, to the pastness of the past. Which brings me finally to the indispensable issue of *testimony*. Testimony is the ultimate link *between* imagination and memory, because the witness says 'I was part of the story. I was there.' At the same time, the witness tells a story that is a living presentation, and therefore deploys the capacity of imagination to place the events before our eyes, as if we were there. Testimony would be a way of bringing memory and imagination together. It is very difficult of course. I am struggling with this difficulty at present. Maybe it has to do with the two meanings of pastness, no longer there and still there, absent and present (or quasi-present). How do we make the past visible, as if it were present, while acknowledging our debt to the past as it actually happened? That is my main ethical question of memory.

Q: Is it not the case that testimonies can be manipulated and distorted to serve certain interests? If so, what critical tools must we avail ourselves of to unmask such manipulation?

PR: In order to answer this we must refer to the epistemological structure of historical knowledge. The fundamental objective of the *good* historian is to enlarge the sphere of archives; that is, the conscientious historian must open up the archive by retrieving traces which the dominant ideological forces attempted to suppress. In admitting what was originally excluded from the archive the historian initiates a critique of power. He gives expression to the voices of those who have been abused, the victims of intentional exclusion. The historian opposes the manipulation of narratives by telling the story differently and by providing a space for the confrontation between opposing testimonies. We must remember, however, that the historian is also embedded in history, he belongs to his own field of research. The historian is an actor in the plot. Our condition dictates that we can never be in a state of pure indifference. The historian's testimony is therefore not completely neutral; it is a selective activity. It is, however, far less selective than the testimony of the dominant class. Here we should invoke what John Rawls calls 'reflective equilibrium'. He speaks of the need for reflective equilibrium between predominantly held beliefs and the findings of critical minds represented by professional people such as historians. Such a mechanism helps us to distinguish good from bad history. In the final analysis, however, we must emphasize the role of 'trust'. When I testify to something I am asking the other to trust that what I am saying is true. To share a testimony is an exchange of trust. Beyond this we cannot go. Most institutions rely fundamentally on the trust they place in the word of the other.

Q: How do you reconcile the emphasis which you place on the role of 'trust' with what you call 'the hermeneutics of suspicion'?

PR: The hermeneutics of suspicion functions against systems of power which seek to prevent a confrontation between competing arguments at the level of genuine discourse. In such discourse we bring together diverse and opposing *interests* with the hope that they will engage at the level of rigorous argumentation. Habermas sees in such a strategy an 'ethics of discussion'. Such an ethics of discourse obliges me to give my best argument to my enemy, in the hope that he will in turn articulate his resentment and aggression in the form of an equally plausible argument. It is through discussion of this sort that suspicion between opposing interests gives way to trust and a certain level of consensus.

Q: How can an 'ethics of discussion' help us to forgive and forget?

PR: It is always better to give expression to anger or hatred than to repress it. It is good that the wounds of history remain open to thought. There is indeed something healthy in the expression of anger. To repress *grievances* is certainly bad. Expression and discussion are ways of healing. Psychoanalysis relies precisely on this expressive function of language. To hear the anger of other people forces us to confront our wrongdoings, which is the first step towards forgiveness. We must have trust in language as a weapon against violence, indeed the best weapon there is against violence.

On Life Stories (2003)*

Followed by a Discussion on the Crisis of Authority and the Power of the Possible

Q: You have written much about the power of narrative to provide people with a sense of identity and cohesion. You have also written much about the fact that human existence is always in quest of narrative by way of providing us with a historical memory or future. Do you believe that narrative has a positive therapeutic potential?

PR: Well, Hannah Arendt claims that 'all sorrows may be borne if you may put them into a story or tell a story about them'. She uses Isak Dinesen's beautiful proverb as the epigraph to her great chapter 'Action' in *The Human Condition*. Now this chapter is based on the remarkable theme of the 'disclosure of the agent in speech and action' (§ 24), followed by its corollary, that it is in narrative that the disclosure of the 'who' is fulfilled, thanks to its weaving of 'the web of relationships' between agents and the circumstances of action. What is lost, at least for a moment (it is explored a little later in 'the frailty of human affairs' §26), is the burden of these 'sorrows' in the epigraph. Whence my question: what resources does the 'story' have to make sorrows *bearable*?

It is in examining this question that I would like to enrich and reinforce the conclusions of your *On Stories*. I will do this by adding to the adjective 'acting' that of 'suffering', referring to the acting and suffering person. This topic is not absent in *On Stories*. Its three 'case histories' – Joyce's Daedalus, Freud's Dora, and Spielberg's representation of Schindler compared with Lanzmann's *Shoah* – are about sorrows, whether they be the torments of hysteria or the unspeakable horror of the death camps. In this way sorrow is in each case the answer to the question which opens the book: 'Where do stories come from?' However, in none of these cases does the 'story' make sorrow bearable: Molly's final soliloquy in *Ulysses* does not achieve this effect; similarly, Dora is not cured (perhaps because her 'case' was used to verify a theory which would take a more definite shape in Freud's biography); and the sufferings of extermination exceed the resources of narrative, cinematic as much as literary. If

---

* Paul Ricoeur in conversation with Richard and Anne Bernhard Kearney and Fabrizio Turoldo. Recorded and written in Paris, 2001–2003.

sorrow is neither absent nor resolved in your journey through personal narratives, it is no different in the 'national narratives', those founding Roman myths, those humiliating representations of the Irish by the British until recently, those relating to the distorted relationships of the Americans with their Others, the 'border crossings' that prove to be the source of an alienation that makes neighbours into 'strangers'.

What then can I add to this ensemble of stories generated in some way or other by the innumerable figures of sorrow? I propose a reflection on the capacity 'to bear' – to *endure* – that is generated by narrative. A void indeed remains to be filled in the vigorous concluding chapter of *On Stories* entitled 'Narrative Matters'. This chapter remains centered, like Arendt's chapter on 'Action', on the relationship between the narrative and the acting person. You show yourself to be concerned by the postmodern criticism of traditional narratives, be they fiction or history (coinciding, paradoxically, though for opposite reasons, with the negationist criticism of the *Shoah*). At stake in the quarrel is the persistence of the very capacity to narrate in a time of fragmentation and the dispersion of human experience in its totality. In response, you find support from that which seems to validate the persistence of the capacity to narrate, exemplified in the perennial nature of the categories of narrative theory drawn from Aristotle's *Poetics*; it is the link between narrative and action that is at the centre of the theory, which is a matter of *mythos*, *mimesis*, or *catharsis*. The basic argument is that life itself is in search of narrative 'because it strives to discover a pattern to cope with the experience of chaos and confusion.' Cast in these terms, the argument leaves me enough leeway to join suffering to action. However, following Aristotle, what is said of life is recentred on action in order to introduce the topic of mimesis, which is the mimesis of action, by virtue of the thesis taken from the anthropological part of the *Nichomachean Ethics*, according to which action 'is always conducted in view of some end'. We may thus affirm that 'each human life is always already an implicit story'.

But does not sorrow come to cast its shadow on the finalist version of human action that secures the primacy of action in the theory of narrative? Does it not place in doubt the assertion according to which it would be the life of each person that would 'always already' be an implicit story? My suggestion here is that the arguments that follow the definition of narrative as 'mimesis of action' or 'acting persons' would emerge reinforced by the addition of suffering to action, whether it be a matter of redefining *mimesis* as 're-creation', *catharsis* as 'release', *phronesis* as 'wisdom', and finally *ethos* as an 'ethics' concerned with a persisting 'self-identity', which perdures through a life of our memories, projects and presence in the world.

How would this widening of the referential base of narrative be carried out? It would need, I suggest, to recapture the theme of mourning by revealing its narrative component.

To this end I will rely on the rapprochement, suggested in *La Mémoire, l'histoire, l'oubli*, between (a) what Freud says in 'Mourning and Melancholia' about the distinctive features of mourning compared to melancholia, and (b) his comments in 'Recollection, Repetition, and Working Through' on the distinctive features of recollection when 'working through' frees it from repetition. But, as you have done in *On Stories*, I will not make psychoanalysis the only resource for a reflection on the narrative component of mourning. Psychoanalysis operates under the restrictive conditions that comprise the rule of 'telling all', the abandon of free association, the role of transference and counter-transference. I want to hold up the experience of analysis as a model and guide concerning the ways of facing tragedy and sorrow in the normal circumstances of life, let us say those of ordinary neurosis. It was these circumstances of tragedy which I took as my reference point in my essay 'Evil, a Challenge to Philosophy and Theology' (1986), included in *Lectures 3* (and in *Figuring the Sacred*).

I return to my attempt to learn a lesson from the rapprochement between 'Mourning and Melancholia' and 'Recollection, Repetition, and Working Through'. The title of the first essay does not evoke narrative at all, but introduces the idea of the 'work of mourning', onto which I will graft my theme of the work of narrative as applied to sorrow. The situations to which mourning reacts are indeed situations of sorrow: the loss of a loved one or of an abstraction set up in place of this person. As for the work of mourning, it consists of this: 'the test of reality showed that the loved object ceased existing and the entire *libido* is commanded to give up the bond which attached it to this object. It is against this that there is an understandable revolt.' There follows Freud's description of the 'large cost of time and cathectic energy' that this obedience of the libido to the orders of reality requires, in spite of the continued existence of the lost object in psychic intimacy. 'The detailed realization of each order laid down by reality is the work of mourning.' Is it not to a work of memory that the work of mourning can in its turn cathect? Is the feeling of mourning not based on complaints that melancholy has transformed into accusations (*Ihre Klagen sind Anklagen*)? Is it not these complaints and accusations that narrative struggles to *tell differently*?

This suggestion finds support precisely in Freud's second essay. Here it is the tendency to act out (*passer à l'acte*), which Freud sees as a 'substitute for memory', that occasions a transition towards narrative. The patient, says Freud, 'does not reproduce the forgotten fact in the form of remembering but in the form of action; he *repeats* it, obviously without knowing that he repeats it'. Freud explains the phenomenon in terms of the link between the compulsion to repeat and resistances. This is where the obstacle to remembering resides. It is then the 'translaboration' or 'working out' which makes recollection a work, the work of memory. Is this not, once again, a contact point for a narrative that should be called a labour of narrative? Does this work of narrative not lie in the transition between what I call in *Time and Narrative* the 'configuration' constitutive of emplotment and the 'refiguration' of life by the practice of narrative? The work of narrative would thus be the narrative form of 'working through'.

It is in widening this breach in the direction of the work of mourning with which all acting and suffering beings are someday or other confronted that I return to your closing statement in *On Stories* in order to amplify it and reinforce it. Yes, 'all sorrows can be borne if you put them into a story or tell a story about them'. But these narratives that are able to make sorrows *bearable* and to make us able to endure them constitute but one element of the work of mourning. Peter Homans, in *The Ability to Mourn*, shows that this work, which all of psychoanalysis seeks to explore, extends to the whole of our archaic and infantile beliefs, to our disappointments and disillusions, and in general to everything in our existence that bears the mark of *loss*. Loss is the overarching pattern into which sorrow fits. It is this that was implied in my 1986 essay on evil. It spoke initially about mourning to address speculative explanations in the form of theodicy and evoked a *broken dialectic*, perhaps close to what you are developing elsewhere, on your 'God who may be'. The essay continued by referring to work carried out in the field of action (evil is that which *must* be fought), and completed in the transformation of *feeling*: at this point I evoked the work of mourning put at the service of appeasing the complaint.

It is here that the work of narrative constitutes an essential element of the work of mourning understood as the acceptance of the irreparable.

My conviction is that the final chapter of *On Stories*, 'Narrative Matters', emerges reinforced by the addition of suffering to acting, of sorrow to *praxis*. It works better than ever thanks to this expanding of the ways 'of *making* our lives into life-stories'.

(Translated by Boyd Blundell)

The Crisis of Authority

Q: One of my main arguments in both *On Stories* and *Strangers, Gods and Monsters* was that we live in a time of crisis – crisis of identity, crisis of legitimation, crisis of authority. In recent years in American and Western society we have witnessed the collapse of a number of major national and international institutions – from the Catholic Church (due to abuse scandals) and corporate capitalism (Enron and Wall Street post 9/11) to the basic practice of the United Nations around the Iraq débâcle. How do you think philosophy might best respond to this climate of crisis?

PR: A key problem today is authority. Authority is disappearing from our world. When Hannah Arendt asks 'What *is* authority?' she immediately adds 'What *was* authority?' But what has vanished? I would say it is the right to be ordered or obeyed without having to be legitimated, because the great problem of authority is legitimation. Especially after the 1970s, there was suspicion of anyone having authority. This crisis laid bare the very structure of authority which is the role of hierarchical relationship amongst equalitarian relations – or to put it in a spatial metaphor, a vertical relationship crossing a horizontal one – living together as equals on the one hand and obeying orders on the other. Authority has to be legitimated. It is the capacity to give reasons in a situation which is now in crisis. Before, too, of course, one had to give reasons, but in a sense authority worked by a kind of social inertia because it was learned. The antiquity of authority was considered enough because it had a long past in itself. Authority relied on memory.

Nowadays people need explanations for authority. In his book, *On Justification*, the French sociologist Luc Boltanski argues that today everyone must be able to justify what she or he does, and that this necessity to be justified in each situation is new. In the past, the very fact that there was 'authorized' authority meant that 'it was so'. But today authority is always in question. As we say in French: '*Qui t'a fait roi*?' We always look for another authority behind authority. So it is regressive. We ask where is the end point? Is there something indefinite in authority? Or a kind of ultimate point where something will authorise itself? It is the lack of this ultimate point of reference that defines our modern situation. To go beyond these generalities, I should distinguish between some typical situations, because authority does not work the same way according to different circles of allegiance. Following Luc Boltanski, we may distinguish between five or six different 'worlds' or 'cities'. Concerning the grammar of *grandeur* – we could say that in a traditional society the model would be the king. But in a modern democratic society, what is the paradigm of *grandeur*? We are not 'great' in every respect. We are 'great' according to certain rules of estimation. In a city of creativity or inspiration, for example, among artists and writers, the paradigm of greatness is the recognition of creativity, and we have many criteria for this. It must be something which has to do with the capacity to produce something new. But if you speak of the city of fame, if you speak of sports, a great cyclist, for example, you are 'great' according to quite different rules – for example recognized performance, because fame here is to be recognized in the opinion of others. You are not necessarily 'great' in domestic relationships, because fame is something larger than the family. Still now, in our modern society, the model of the couple involves what the Greeks would have called the *oikos*, the home; the relationship between father, mother and child is one part of it, the relationship between the sexes another part. In medieval society, for the traditional aristocracy, for example, we could say that the model of the home was prevalent. The French or British Court was both a *house* and the central *power*. The model of the home absorbed the political relationship. Then in the merchant bourgeois relationship, the capacity to exchange, and to invent new modes of exchange, became the prevalent model of the city. Today the Internet is the typical model of a world expansion of the relationship of merchants. Everything is merchandise.

So where does authority now reside? Today political relationships are part of our system, but they are only partial relationships in that we are not always concerned with voting, giving our opinion in opinion polls or taking part in political meetings. But we remain citizens, the authority of the state still obtains. It concerns only part of our activity but at the same time it is the condition of all the other relationships of the modern nation-state – this is especially so in Europe. Here the problem of authority is brought to its extreme. Why? Because there is no end to the problem of legitimacy. What makes the authority of the governing power from Hobbes and Machiavelli to Hegel, for instance, is the recurring question: who or what possesses the right to corrupt others? Because the problem of authority becomes that of *sovereignty* – what is so supreme that there is nothing higher? Then we come back to the core problem: what makes the legitimacy of hierarchical relationship in our democratic tradition of equality? This was the problem of de Tocqueville, especially in his famous book, *Democracy in America*, because coming from Europe where there was the presupposition of aristocratic superiority, he encountered a society in America where there was no theoretical supremacy, no superiority.

Where, therefore, was the recognition of superiority to come from? That was de Tocqueville's question. And then we have Rousseau, of course, speaking of the 'labyrinth of politics'.

Now today we have the additional question of international authority. We know how the nation-state works, but the state is afraid of political authority; it has limits of its own, its space is closed. There are two central features of the nation-state. On the one hand, we have the fact that the state has appropriated and absorbed the evils of revenge, as Hegel and Max Weber say: it has the monopoly of violence; but it has the power of implementing its decisions, whereas international society today doesn't have this power. It relies only on good will, especially of the great powers. But there already we have a silent progression of the international lobby, particularly after the great criminal trials of the middle of the twentieth century – Nuremberg, Tokyo, Buenos Aires – where the tyrants were judged by the victors. The winners of the Great War were able to establish a tribunal which had a certain authority. I think this is a new phenomenon – the idea that criminal law could cover the entire globe. As in the Pinochet case, we see how for the first time all the other states have a right to say something about what happens within the boundaries of the Chilean state. Why? Because we recognize that nation-state sovereignty is not absolute, it has rules of its own. The first rule of the sovereign state is to provide security for all its members. In tyrannies, the state has failed to provide this security, so therefore this failure gives a right to all the other states to intervene. You have now an international right of intervention in the affairs of particular nations. This involves a certain *external* limitation of sovereignty.

There was a time when after a certain period a crime was forgotten, but now even decades later you can be judged. This was only made possible after the victory of the democratic states over the Nazis on the one hand and the communist tyranny on the other. This is new and positive. We can judge people who were guilty many years ago because there is a world public opinion.

So how is world opinion linked to the question of authority? How does it work? We could say that there is a trial going on at the level of authority beyond the tribunals. The sentences of tribunals have to be recognized by public opinion. And it is in this process of recognition that something new happens. Before we did not have this global judgement, this support of international opinion. Maybe it existed within certain quarters in the eighteenth century, under the French intellectual domination of Europe – to a certain extent at the time of the Enlightenment, for instance – but today we are witnessing a new world enlightenment.

If we turn, on the other hand, to the whole question of regionalism in the emerging federal project for a Europe of regions, we encounter the problem of the *internal* limitations of the nation-state. Here we witness the growth of intermediary powers at subnational levels, so we witness two systems of limitation: the international limitation of the absoluteness of sovereignty and the regional limits to state sovereignty from within. We now have a very complex system and many options, going from a real plurality of subsystems as in federal states like Germany or the USA, to the very subtle conjunction between regional governments and national governments in a country like Spain for example, between the Catalans and the Spanish state, or in Italy between several regional authorities. France is arguably the most resistant to this plurality of substates. Sorting out the various relations between international, national and subnational power is a good example of practical wisdom in the political field.

Or take, finally, the quarrels between one province and another in Canada: this cannot be decided *from outside*. It is a negotiation between powers and the peoples concerned. The big problem is whether they are consulted in a free and fair way.

Authority involves the crucial question of *legislation* – and this arises at critical moments in the life of a state, usually after a civil war or constitutional crisis. In France we had seven or eight procedures of amnesty, after the Commune in 1871, after the First World War, after the Algerian War. Sometimes this can involve a big lie – 'nothing happened'. But it can also be a way of saying we are not at war, a way of preserving peace. I would say it is a matter of official forgetfulness, institutional forgetfulness, '*un oubli institutionnel*'. The American use the word 'pardon'. When Ford gave a pardon to Nixon, it was a remnant of a regal right, the right of grace, but in Europe it has disappeared. In France only the President of the Republic is allowed to give such a 'pardon'; we call it '*grâce*'. It's a remnant of the right of the king. But it had already been criticized by Kant in his theory of rights, where he says that '*le droit de grâce*' is a privilege of the king, but if he uses it for the benefit of culprits it would be a great injustice. Why? Because then victims would be deprived of the right to be recognized and the law would be despised.

A purely utilitarian practice of amnesty would be a way of saying the war did not appear, that the war between citizens did not occur, it would be a way of effacing '*le tort*', the harm done. Such amnesty would be a denial of harms. We are not allowed to speak about it. The first model of this is to be found in the Greek city in 403 BC. There was a decree in Athens: you will not speak about the evils – *ta kaka*. There was an oath that you took not to speak, notice or even remember. It was a censorship of memory. It was a 'big lie', because the harm done and the suffering were not recognized; there was an injustice, because there was a lack of recognition. It was a harm done to truth. It is interesting to see in a Greek tragedy how it is the poetry which preserves the memory of suffering. In all the great tragedies, we have the problem of the harm of the powerful and the memories of great families and so on. We could say that politics starts with the prose of peace pitted against the poetry of war. There is a kind of truthfulness in the preservation by poetry of the memory of harm and suffering, which is often denied in the prose of political life.

At one level, then, this forgetfulness, this amnesty of crimes of the past is not a good thing. It seems better to remember. There is the work of mourning. Amnesty and forgetfulness may prevent mourning. They can prevent a second suffering of harm done, but also the suffering of mourning which is a working through, a creative process. I refer again here to the important essay by Freud, 'Mourning and Melancholia', where he speaks of the necessity of preserving mourning from being swallowed up by melancholia. When we prevent mourning we succumb to melancholia. As we see in Europe, after the French Revolution, when there was a law of forgetfulness with the end of the Napoleonic Wars, we had the spleen of the Romantic generation.

So it is not harmless to implement amnesty. What I am saying is at best '*un moindre mal*', the lesser of two evils. Two great sufferings are prevented, hate and revenge, at the expense of the suffering of memory, and the liberating power of this suffering. But we should not underestimate *mourning*. It is a way of giving people the right to start anew, by remembering in such a way that we may overcome obsessive or compulsive repetition. It is a matter of the right balance between memory and forgetting.

Narrative has a crucial role here. I speak, especially now, of narrative at the public level, because collective memory and collective identity are based on stories concerning the founding events; and because founding events have civil dates whereby memory is both created and preserved by telling stories. As a result, history has the function of adjudicating commemorations in a kind of public ritual. Does this found authority? All kinds of authority are ways of telling the story and repeating and therefore preserving what I call the social inertia of the past by providing a kind of effectiveness of the past. In spite of all the changes in one's society, this is a matter of preserving the invisible roots of community by telling stories.

The Power of the Possible

Q: A central theme explored in *The God Who May Be* is that of
        'possibility'. While I was dealing there primarily with eschatological
        and ontological notions of the possible, ranging from Cusanus to
        Heidegger and Derrida, I am aware that you have dealt with this theme
        in a number of your writings and that you expressed to me recently the
        wish to write a last book – if you have the time and energy – entitled
        L'homme capable. What sorts of things would you probably explore in
        such a book?

PR: As I get older I have been increasingly interested in exploring certain
        metaphysics of potency and act. In *Oneself as Another*, I broach this
        in my analysis of the *capacity* to speak, narrate and act. This
        phenomenology of the 'I can', in turn, brings me to Aristotle's attempt
        in the *Metaphysics* E 2 to outline meta-categories of potentiality and
        actuality in line with his commitment to a plurality of meanings of
        being. So in this respect I no longer subscribe to the typically anti-
        metaphyiscal Protestant lineage of Karl Barth (though it is true that in
        early works like *The Symbolism of Evil* I was still somewhat under this
        influence). But if I am on the side of metaphysics here, it is, admittedly,
        in the somewhat minority camp of those who prefer the categories of
        possibility and actuality to that of 'substance'. If the mainstream and
        official tradition of Western metaphysics has been substantialist, this
        does not preclude other metaphysical paths, such as those leading from
        Aristotle's *dunamis* to Spinoza's *conatus* and Schelling's and Leibniz's
        notions of potentiality (*puissance*). Here we find a dynamic notion of
        being as potency and action (Spinoza reformulates substance as a
        substantia actuosa) which contrasts sharply with the old substantialist
        models of scholasticism or the mechanistic models of Descartes. This is
        a matter of dynamism versus mechanism – the idea of a dynamic in
        being that grows towards consciousness, reflection, community. Here I
        think it is important to think of ontology in close rapport with ethics.
        And that is why in *Thinking Biblically*, I endeavour to unravel some of
        the ontological and eschatological implications of the 'I am who am'
        episode in Exodus 3:14. We encounter in this passage a notion of being
        which is alien to the Greek usage; and so its translation into Greek
        language and thought signals an alteration of the existing meaning of
        being to include new notions of being-with, being-faithful, being-in-
        accompaniment with one's community or people (which is precisely
        what Yahweh promises Moses when he says 'I am he who will be with
        you'). Now Aristotle had never considered this signification of being
        when he wrote the *Metaphysics*. But that didn't and doesn't prevent the
        enlargement of Greek ontology to accommodate and respond to such

'other' meanings: a better solution it seems to me than setting up an unbridgeable antagonism between Hellenic and Hebraic meanings of being and then having to choose one or the other. What I am exploring in *Thinking Biblically* is a sort of philosophical theology or theological philosophy – not an easy task in a contemporary intellectual culture which still wants people to say whether they are 'philosophers' *or* 'theologians' and is uncomfortable with overlaps. This recent return to religious thinking is intimately linked with my growing interest in the whole field of action and *praxis* which increasingly drew me away from the abstract universalism of Kant towards a more Aristotelian ethics of the 'good life' (*bien vivre*). And of course I would not deny for a moment here the important Heideggerian analysis of 'care' and the whole post-Heideggerian retrieval of Greek thinking. Not that I have ever found my ontological feet in any final or absolute sense. It is no accident that the title of the last chapter of *Oneself as Another* is in the form of an interrogation rather than an assertion – 'Towards which Ontology?' Here I try to explore possibilities of an ethical ontology beyond the Heideggerian model of *ontology without ethics* and the Levinasian model of *ethics without ontology*. By trying to think ethics in terms of action (*praxis/pragma*) and action in terms of being as potency and act I am seeking ways beyond the either/or of Heidegger/ Levinas. The ultimate purpose of hermeneutic reflection and attestation, as I see it, is to try to retrace the line of intentional capacity and action behind mere objects (which we tend to focus on exclusively in our natural attitude) so that we may recover the hidden truth of our operative acts, of *being capable*, of being *un homme capable.* So if hermeneutics is right, in the wake of Kant and Gadamer, to stress the finitude and limits of consciousness, it is also wise to remind ourselves of the tacit potencies and acts of our lived existence. My bottom line is a *phenomenology of being able.*

Q: It is remarkable that you should begin your philosophical career by reflecting on the nature of *l'homme faillible* (*fallible man*) and conclude by shifting the focus to *l'homme capable*. One might have expected it the other way around! But could you tease out a little more what you mean by this idea of a phenomenology of 'I am able' (*une phenomenology du je peux*)? As you know in my own work on the possible, from *Poétique du Possible* (1984) to *The God who May Be* (2001), I have been trying to develop a post-Heideggerean hermeneutics of possibility inspired, in part, by Heidegger's reversal of the old metaphysical priority of act (*energeia*) over potency (*dunamis*). I wonder if our respective paths are not converging more and more on this question.

PR: I believe that the ontology and analogy of action which I am trying to think through plays itself out on the basis of a differentiated phenomenology of 'I can speak', 'I can act', 'I can narrate' and 'I can designate myself as imputable' (*imputabilite*). What all these instances of 'I am able to...' articulate is the basic capacity of a human being to act and suffer. I am interested here in an anthropology of potency and impotency (*puissance et impuissance*). And in one sense what I find intriguing about Spinoza's notion of *conatus* is that it refuses the alternative between act and potency, between *energeia* and *dunamis*. For Spinoza each concrete thing or event is always a mélange of act and possibility. And I would be closer here to Spinoza or Heidegger than to Aristotle, for what is the meaning of an 'architect in potency', to take Aristotle's example, if it is not already an architect who is thinking architecturally, making plans, preparing to realize a building project and so on? I would hold to the idea of a profound continuity between *dunamis* and *energeia*, since *energeia* is the *ergon* and this, as we know from the *Ethics*, can be translated as the *task*. Whether being an architect, doctor, musician and so on is exercised or not, it remains an *ergon*. So that possibility as 'capacity' to realize a task is by no means the same thing as possibility as an abstract or logical 'virtuality'. Think of the sprinter poised on the starting block. There are different modalities of the possible – the possible that is not yet possible, the possible that is on the way to being realized, the possible that is already a certitude and so on.

Q: Unlike Aristotle, then, who argues that we can only know possibility through actuality, you would say that 'attestation' is already a way of knowing possibility (*puissance*).

PR: Yes, I would say that and I think this has important ethical consequences. I would insist, for example, that certain people who are deprived of their rights or means to exercise their capacities – for example the imprisoned or the mentally ill – none the less are worthy of respect because they still possess these capacities as possibilities. Likewise, if I say that I can speak a certain foreign language I do not have to be actually speaking it to have this capacity or skill. Or indeed when it comes to language generally; it is true that I *can* speak and use all sorts of different words and constructions, even if I am not actually doing so and will arguably never be in a position to speak *all* of language. And here it might be useful to rethink the Aristotelian notion of *dunamis* and Spinoza's notion of *conatus* in rapport with Leibniz's notion of *appetites* – possibility as a dynamic tendency or inclination. These philosophers, and Heidegger and yourself too, of course, offer great resources for a new thinking about the possible. But my own interest in these questions is ultimately inseparable from the *moral* question – how do we relate a phenomenology of 'being able' to the ethical events of 'imputability' and 'attestation'? And I might even concede here a point made recently by my young colleagues, Dominico Jervolino and Fabrizio Turoldo, that my thought is not so removed from certain religious and biblical issues as my standard policy of 'conceptual ascetism' might have been prepared to admit in the past. I am not sure about the absolute irreconcilability between the God of the Bible and the God of Being (understood with Jean Nabert as 'primary affirmation' or with Spinoza as '*substantia actuosa*'). The tendency of modern French thought to eclipse the Middle Ages has prevented us from acknowledging certain very rich attempts to think God and being in terms of each other. I no longer consider such conceptual asceticism tenable.

Q: Would you say that there is difference between your early and late thinking?

PR: Is there a difference between the beginning and the end? It's true that I have changed in the last fifty years. I have read lots of new books and the whole philosophical climate has altered in all kinds of important ways. I began in an era of existentialism, I traversed structuralism and now I find myself before a 'post-I-know-not-what', deconstruction and so on. A long life like mine has meant passing through a great variety of philosophical landscapes and negotiating with my contemporaries – sometimes friends, sometime adversaries – each time different according to the specific nature and singularity of the encounter. And yet perhaps history will link these different situations in some way.

Conclusion

We have endeavoured in this volume to revisit some of the key moments of Ricoeur's hermeneutic philosophy. Foremost among these, we have suggested, is Ricoeur's exploration of the dialectic between poetics and ethics. By way of conclusion we will briefly review this critical relationship between narrative *poiesis* and ethical *phronesis* under three basic headings – vision, initiative and empathy.

As we have seen in our studies and dialogues above, narrative plays a pivotal role in providing us with ethical *vision* in that it enables us to see essential connections between our actions and their ends *qua* good and evil. If it is true, as Ricoeur emphasizes in his chapters on 'narrative identity' in *Oneself as Another*, that fiction serves as an 'immense laboratory' for experimenting with an 'endless number of imaginative variations', then these experiments are also 'explorations in the realm of good and evil'.[1] Ethical judgement is not abolished in fiction. On the contrary, it is opened up to increasingly extended horizons of vision. Or to put it another way, narrative invites ethical judgement to submit itself to the imaginative variations proper to fiction. And this amplification of ethical vision clearly exceeds the conventional moralities of rule and duty. Thus we might say with Ricoeur that if narrative fiction is free from morality, it is committed to ethics.

Second, we have seen how narrative serves our capacity for *initiative*. To see our being-in-the-world in terms of larger possibilities of vision often empowers us to undertake action, that is, to better identify our goals and so inaugurate a new beginning. Given Ricoeur's deep concern for an ontology of action, this question of initiative is indispensable. 'With the help of narrative beginnings which our reading has made familiar to us ... we stabilize the real beginnings formed by the initiatives we take ... Literature helps us in a sense to fix the outline of these provisional ends.'[2] In other words, the more we learn about narrative emplotment in fiction, the more we learn how to plot our own lives (that is, how to combine and configure the heterogeneous elements of our temporality and identity). Because fiction enables us to better perceive the connection between agent, action and goal in concentrated form, it prepares us to become 'better readers and authors of our own lives'.[3] This involves a certain schematization of the network of aims and means whereby we are free

---

[1] Ricoeur, *Oneself as Another* (University of Chicago Press, 1992), p. 164.

[2] Ibid., p. 162.

[3] Ibid., p. 159.

to try out various courses of action and play with practical possibilities. Moreover, Ricoeur establishes that this projective function of narrative actually generates action by furnishing us with a clearing in which 'motives may be compared and measured, even if they are as heterogeneous as desires and ethical commands'.[4] It is, then, ultimately in narrative imagination that we are most at liberty to test our ethical capabilities.

As we have had occasion to note in several of our studies, Ricoeur applies the emancipating energy of inauguration not only to individual life but to history in the larger sense. Ethical intervention in history occurs in that moment of initiative 'when the weight of history that has already been made is deposited, suspended and interrupted and when the dream of history yet to be made is transposed into a responsible decision'.[5] In this manner, the power of initiative proposed by narrative imagination may be said to synthesize our dual fidelities to past and future, tradition and expectation, ideology and utopia.

---

[4] Ricoeur, 'Imagination in Discourse and Action', in *Du texte à l'action*, pp. 213–36, in particular pp. 224–7.

[5] Ricoeur, *Time and Narrative*, Vol. 3, pp. 208ff, 258, 370. Ricoeur acknowledges an ethical and political task for narrative imagination in ensuring that 'the tension between the horizon of expectation (future/utopia) and the space of experience be preserved without giving way to schism' (*Time and Narrative*, Vol. 3, p. 258). Here the narrative imagination takes on the role of a 'social imagination' in both its ideological function of legitimation and its utopian function of subversion. Both these sociopolitical axes presuppose a certain ethical vision of the good life, that is, the configuration of communal life by narrative imagination. See Peter Kemp's excellent analysis of this question in 'Ethique et narrativité', where he argues that the acceptance or rejection of ideologies and utopias is only possible on the basis of this imaginative vision of the good life in society. If ethics is a vision rather than a rule, it consists of intuitive models for action and not of purely abstract maxims. By imagining and narrating wise forms of action and communication, it expresses the practical truth of human life. Kemp writes:

> This imagination is not possible without narrative, because without emplotment there would be no sense in unfolding some models for action. Thus ethics must necessarily be the narrative configuration of the good life. Had this not from the start been configured by stories, it would not have been capable of being integrated either into the author's works or into those of the historian as that vision which would never affect the reader in an ethically neutral manner. It would have the same affect as a foreign body in the eye.

This raises the vexed question of criteria for judging and adjudicating between rival narratives. The narrative configuration of ethics which is invoked to evaluate between stories is, Kemp concludes, to be found on a different level than that of the stories themselves. Nevertheless, he does not appeal to some 'Archimedean point' or meta-narrative, admitting that the ethical evaluation of narratives can only be based on other narratives. But Kemp refuses to see this as a vicious (rather than a healthy hermeneutic) circle:

> This does not necessarily mean that ethical criticism is arbitrary. The stories on which an ethics well rooted in life are founded are those whose guiding power remains throughout history, and which, in times of crisis, have demonstrated their ability to encourage people to stop thinking in terms of fixed ideas.

Finally, Ricoeur powerfully demonstrates how narrative serves ethical *phronesis* in its power to *empathize*. In addition to its capacity to envision a new project, evaluate its motivations, and initiate a viable course of action, narrative enables us to identify with others. And it does this by furnishing us with an 'intersubjectivity of freedom' without which we would not be inclined to commit ourselves to other persons. There is neither love nor hate, care nor concern, without an 'imaginary transfer of my "here" into your "there"'.[6] It could be said that this last point challenges a certain postmodern assumption that poetics has no truck with ethics.[7] What Ricoeur claims is that narrative understanding provides us with *both* a poetics *and* an ethics of responsibility in that it propels us beyond self-reference to relation with others (via analogy/empathy/apperception). This extension of the circle of selfhood involves an 'enlarged mentality' capable of imagining the self in the place of the other.[8] Ricoeur's argument here finds support in Proust's famous suggestion that art is

---

Though Kemp does not, unfortunately, cite any examples of these 'guiding' narratives, I take him to be referring to the abiding ethical stories of resistance, heroism, charity and courage that inform the great traditions of ethical humanism and spirituality – the classical stories of Socrates and Seneca, the biblical stories of Moses, Jesus, St Francis, the mythical stories of Antigone, Achilles, Iphigenia and so on. Each ethical culture, Western and non-Western, contains a series of recurring and paradigmatic narratives that each historical generation hermeneutically retrieves and retells in order to preserve and cultivate its sense of ethical memory, identity and responsibility. For a development of these ideas see Kemp, 'Toward a Narrative Ethics: A Bridge between Ethics and the Narrative Reflection of Ricoeur', in *The Narrative Path: The Later Works of Paul Ricoeur*, ed. Kemp and Rasmussen, pp. 45–65.

[6] Ricoeur, 'Imagination and Discourse in Action', in *Du texte à l'action*, p. 227. This empathic power of what we might, with T. S. Eliot, call 'auditory imagination' is also adverted to by Gadamer when he speaks of a 'learning through suffering' with the other when we recognize our own life limits and begin to listen to the other: 'Anyone who listens is fundamentally open. Without such openness to one another there is no genuine human bond ... Openness to the other involves recognizing that I myself must accept some things that are against *me*, even though no one else forces me to do so' (*Truth and Method*, New York: Crossroad, 1991, p. 361). For Gadamer the properly hermeneutic understanding is one that allows the other to really say something to us, to listen and to respond.

[7] See James Miller, *The Passion of Michel Foucault* (New York: Simon and Schuster, 1993), p. 5, and our dialogue with Derrida entitled 'Deconstruction and the Other' in my *Debates in Continental Philosophy* (New York: Fordham University Press, 2004).

[8] Hannah Arendt considers this mentality to be essential to genuine ethical judgement:

> The power of judgment rests on a potential agreement with others, and the thinking process which is active in judging something is not, like the thought process of pure reasoning, a dialogue between me and myself, but finds itself always in an anticipated communication with others with whom I know I must finally come to some agreement. From this potential agreement judgment derives its specific validity ... It needs the special presence of others 'in whose place' it must think, whose perspectives it must take into consideration, and without whom it never has the opportunity to operate at all. (Arendt, 'The Crisis in Culture', in *Between Past and Future*, pp. 220–21)

the form of human relation nearest to genuine altruism. But the point, as Ricoeur makes clear, is not to conflate art and life, imagination and reality, text and action. It is rather to see how, guarding their distinctive characters, they can interweave with each other. In other words, Ricoeur is not saying that poetics and ethics are exactly the same, only that they can, at propitious moments, prove mutually supplementary. Poetic imagining has the capacity to make us better human beings, while ethical action has the task of soliciting imaginative sympathy with others.

In short, Ricoeur praises narrative understanding – where one represents oneself as another – to the extent that it serves to liberate us from narcissistic interests without liquidating our identity. In so doing, it generates a basic act of empathy whereby the self flows from itself toward the other in a free variation of imagination. *Qua* dialogue which opens us to foreign worlds, enabling us to tell and listen to other stories, narrative imagination functions as precondition for the 'representative' subject. It transfigures the self-regarding self into a self-for-another, the *moi* into a *soi*.

It would appear that our contemporary society of spectacle and simulation has much need of the powers of narrative imagination identified by Ricoeur. Without them, we would be deprived of the ability to refigure historical memory and to transform self-identity into an ethical mode of selfhood. Narrative is not, to be sure, always on the side of the angels. But Ricoeur convincingly shows that it does possess a singular capacity to commit us to a dimension of otherness beyond ourselves – a commitment that, in the moment of decision, invites the self to imagine itself as another and to imagine the other as another self. Were we devoid of such narrative capacity, we would

---

A similar claim is made by Martha Nussbaum in *Love's Knowledge* when she argues for an ethic of imaginative perception inspired by art:

> When we examine our own lives, we have so many obstacles to correct vision, so many motives to blindness and stupidity. The 'vulgar heat' of jealousy and personal interest comes between us and the living perception of each particular. A novel, just because it is not our life, places us in a moral position that is favourable for perception and it shows us what it would be like to take up that position in life. We find here love without possessiveness, attention without bias, involvement without panic (*Love's Knowledge*, p. 162).

In his essay, 'Life in Quest of Narrative', Ricoeur confirms Arendt's and Nussbaum's neo-Aristotelian celebration of the powers of narrative when he writes: 'If it is true that fiction is only completed in life and that life can be understood only through the stories that we tell about it, then an *examined* life, in the sense of the word as we have borrowed it from Socrates, is a life *recounted*' (p. 31). This recounted good life entails both poetics and ethics, both the free play of fiction and the responsibility of ethics – or to put it in Yeatsian terms, both 'perfection of the life and of the work'. But this complementarity of narrative poetics and ethics is not a matter of inidistinction; it is by guarding over each other's difference that poetics and ethics mutually serve each other's interests and aims.

be bereft of poetic freedom and also, in the long run, of ethical sensitivity and vision.

Thinking poetically, acting poetically, dwelling poetically are all modalities of imagining poetically. They are ways of realizing the fundamental *possibilities* of what we are. For as the poet Emily Dickinson wrote, 'possibility is the fuse lit by the spark of imagination'.

Select Bibliography of Works by Ricoeur in English

Fallible Man (Regnery/Chicago, 1965).

History and Truth (Evanston, IL: Northwestern University Press, 1965).

Freedom and Nature: The Voluntary and the Involuntary (Evanston, IL: Northwestern University Press,1966).

Husserl: An Analysis of his Phenomenology (Evanston, IL: Northwestern University Press, 1967).

The Symbolism of Evil (New York: Harper and Row, 1967).

Freud and Philosophy: An Essay on Interpretation (New Haven, CT: Yale University Press, 1970).

Tragic Wisdom and Beyond [with Gabriel Marcel] (Evanston, IL: Northwestern University Press, 1973).

The Conflict of Interpretations: Essays in Hermeneutics (Evanston, IL: Northwestern University Press, 1974).

Political and Social Essays, ed. D. Stewart and J. Bien (Athens, OH: Ohio University Press, 1974).

Interpretation Theory: Discourse and the Surplus of Meaning (Fort Worth, TX: Texas Christian University Press, 1976).

The Philosophy of Paul Ricoeur: An Anthology of his Work, ed. C. Reagan and D. Stewart (Boston, MA: Beacon Press, 1978).

The Rule of Metaphor: Multi-disciplinary Studies in the Creation of Meaning in Language (London: Routledge and Kegan Paul, 1978).

Main Trends in Philosophy (New York: Holmes and Meier, 1979).

The Contribution of French Historiography to the Theory of History (Oxford: Clarendon Press, 1980).

Essays on Biblical Interpretation, ed. L. S. Mudge Philadelphia, PA: Fortress Press, 1980).

Hermeneutics and the Human Sciences, ed. J. B. Thompson (Cambridge: Cambridge University Press, 1981).

Time and Narrative, 3 vols (Chicago IL: University of Chicago Press, 1984, 1985, 1988).

Lectures on Ideology and Utopia (New York: Columbia University Press, 1986).

A Ricoeur Reader: Reflection and Imagination, ed. M. J. Valdés (New York and London: Harvester Wheatsheaf, 1991).

From Text to Action: Essays in Hermeneutics II (London and New York: The Athlone Press, 1991).

'Life in Quest of Narrative' in: *On Paul Ricoeur: Narrative and Interpretation*, ed. David Wood (London: Routledge, 1991).

Oneself as Another (Chicago, IL: University of Chicago Press, 1992).

Figuring the Sacred: Religion, Narrative and Imagination (Minneapolis, MN: Fortress Press, 1995).

'Towards a New Ethos for Europe' and 'Love and Justice' in: *Paul Ricoeur: The Hermeneutics of Action*, ed. Richard Kearney (London: Sage Publications, 1996).

Thinking Biblically: *Exegetical and Hermeneutical Studies*, P. Ricoeur and André LaCocque (Chicago, IL: University of Chicago Press, 1998).

'Memory and Forgetting' in: *Questioning Ethics*, ed. Mark Dooley and Richard Kearney (London and New York: Routledge, 1999).

The Just (Chicago, IL: University of Chicago Press, 2001).

Memory, History, Forgetting (Chicago, IL: University of Chicago Press, 2004).

Recognition (Cambridge, MA: Harvard University Press, forthcoming.

Philosophy of Paul Ricoeur, ed. Louis E. Hahn, The Library of Living Philosophers (La Salle, IL: Open Court, 1995). This text includes Ricoeur's autobiography, 25 critical essays with replies by P. Ricoeur, and a complete Ricoeur bibliography of primary and secondary sources compiled by Frans D. Vansina and P. Ricoeur, pp. 605–815.

Index